maid

maid

hard work, low pay, and a mother's
will to survive

Stephanie Land

Foreword by Barbara Ehrenreich

hachette
BOOKS

New York Boston

Author's Note: This memoir has been pieced together with the help of journals, photographs, blogs, and Facebook posts. Most names and identifying characteristics have been changed to protect them from recognition. Time has been compressed. Dialogue has been approximated and in some cases compositely arranged. Great care has been taken to tell my truths. This is my story and how I remember it.

Hachette Books
Hachette Book Group
1290 Avenue of the Americas, New York, NY 10104
hachettebooks.com
twitter.com/hachettebooks

First Edition: January 2019

Hachette Books is a division of Hachette Book Group, Inc. The Hachette Books name and logo are trademarks of Hachette Book Group, Inc.

The publisher is not responsible for websites (or their content) that are not owned by the publisher.

The Hachette Speakers Bureau provides a wide range of authors for speaking events. To find out more, go to www.hachettespeakersbureau.com or call (866) 376-6591.

LCCN 2018954908

ISBNs: 978-0-316-50511-6 (hardcover), 978-0-316-50510-9 (ebook), 978-0-316-45450-6 (Canadian trade paperback)

Book design by Marie Mundaca

Printed in the United States of America

LSC-C

10   9   8   7   6   5   4   3   2   1

For Mia:
Goodnight
I love you
See you in the morning.
—Mom

Contents

PART THREE

I've learned that making a living is not the same thing as making a life.

—Maya Angelou

Foreword

Welcome to Stephanie Land's World

The price of admission requires that you abandon any stereotypes of domestic workers, single parents, and media-derived images of poverty you may be harboring. Stephanie is hardworking and "articulate," to use the condescending praise word bestowed by elites on unexpectedly intelligent people who lack higher education. *Maid* is about her journey as a mother, trying to provide a safe life and home for her daughter Mia while surviving on pieced-together bits of public assistance and the pathetically low income she earned as a maid.

"Maid" is a dainty word, redolent of tea trays, starched uniforms, Downton Abbey. But in reality, the maid's world is encrusted with grime and shit stains. These workers unclog our drains of pubic hairs, they witness our dirty laundry literally and metaphorically. Yet, they remain invisible—overlooked in our nation's politics and policies, looked down upon at our front doors. I know because I briefly inhabited this life as a reporter working in low-wage jobs for my book *Nickel and Dimed*. Unlike Stephanie, I could always go back to my far-more-comfortable life as a writer. And unlike her, I was not trying to support a child on my income. My children were grown and had no interest in living with me in trailer parks as part of some crazy journalistic endeavor. So I know about the work of cleaning houses—the exhaustion and the contempt I faced when I wore my company vest, emblazoned with "The Maids International," in public. But I could only guess at the anxiety and despair of so many of my coworkers. Like Stephanie, many of these women were single mothers who cleaned houses as a means of survival, who agonized throughout the day about the children they sometimes had to leave in dodgy situations in order to go to work.

With luck, you have never had to live in Stephanie's world. In *Maid*, you will see that it's ruled by scarcity. There is never enough money and sometimes not enough food; peanut butter and ramen noodles loom large; McDonald's is a rare treat. Nothing is reliable in this world—not cars, not men, not housing. Food stamps are an important pillar of her survival, and the recent legislation that people be required to work for their food stamps will only make you clench your fists. Without these government resources, these workers, single parents, and beyond would not be able to survive. These are not handouts. Like the rest of us, they want stable footing in our society.

Perhaps the most hurtful feature of Stephanie's world is the antagonism beamed out toward her by the more fortunate. This is class prejudice, and it is inflicted especially on manual laborers, who are often judged to be morally and intellectually inferior to those who wear suits or sit at desks. At the supermarket, other customers eye Stephanie's shopping cart judgmentally while she pays with food stamps. One older man says, loudly, "You're welcome!" as if he had personally paid for her groceries. This mentality reaches far beyond this one encounter Stephanie had and represents the views of much of our society.

The story of Stephanie's world has an arc that seems headed for a disastrous breakdown. First, there is the physical wear and tear that goes along with lifting, vacuuming, and scrubbing six-to-eight hours a day. At the housecleaning company that I worked for, every one of my coworkers, from the age of nineteen on, seemed to suffer from some sort of neuromuscular damage—back pain, rotator cuff injuries, knee and ankle problems. Stephanie copes with the alarming number of ibuprofen she consumes per day. At one point, she looks wistfully at the opioids stored in a customer's bathroom, but prescription drugs are not an option for her, nor are massages or physical therapy or visits to a pain management specialist.

On top of, or intertwined with the physical exhaustion of her lifestyle, is the emotional challenge Stephanie faces. She is the very model of the "resilience" psychologists recommend for the poor. When confronted with an obstacle, she figures out how to move forward. But the onslaught of obstacles sometimes reaches levels of overload. All that keeps her together is her bottomless love for her daughter, which is the clear bright light that illuminates the entire book.

It's hardly a spoiler to say that this book has a happy ending. Throughout the years of struggle and toil reported here, Stephanie nourished a desire to become a writer. I met Stephanie years ago, when she was in the early stages of her writing career. In addition to being an author, I am the founder of the Economic Hardship Reporting Project, an organization that promotes high-quality journalism on economic inequality, especially by people who are themselves struggling to get by. Stephanie sent us a query, and we snatched her up, working with her to develop pitches, polish drafts, and place them in the best outlets we could find, including the *New York Times* and the *New York Review of Books*. She is exactly the kind of person we exist for—an unknown working-class writer who needed just a nudge to launch her career.

If this book inspires you, which it may, remember how close it came to never being written. Stephanie might have given in to despair or exhaustion; she might have suffered a disabling injury at work. Think too of all the women who, for reasons like that, never manage to get their stories told. Stephanie reminds us that they are out there in the millions, each heroic in her own way, waiting for us to listen.

—*Barbara Ehrenreich*

maid

PART ONE

1

The Cabin

My daughter learned to walk in a homeless shelter.

It was an afternoon in June, the day before her first birthday. I perched on the shelter's threadbare love seat, holding up an old digital camera to capture her first steps. Mia's tangled hair and thinly striped onesie contrasted with the determination in her brown eyes as she flexed and curled her toes for balance. From behind the camera, I took in the folds of her ankles, the rolls of her thighs, and the roundness of her belly. She babbled as she made her way toward me, barefoot across the tiled floor. Years of dirt were etched into that floor. As hard as I scrubbed, I could never get it clean.

It was the final week of our ninety-day stay in a cabin unit on the north side of town, allotted by the housing authority for those without a home. Next, we'd move into transitional housing—an old, run-down apartment complex with cement floors that doubled as a halfway house. However temporary, I had done my best to make the cabin a home for my daughter. I'd placed a yellow sheet over the love seat not only to warm the looming white walls and gray floors, but to offer something bright and cheerful during a dark time.

By the front door, I'd hung a small calendar on the wall. It was filled with appointments with caseworkers at organizations where I could get us help. I had looked under every stone, peered through the window of every government assistance building, and joined the long lines of people who carried haphazard folders of paperwork to prove they didn't have money. I was overwhelmed by how much work it took to prove I was poor.

We weren't allowed to have visitors, or to have very much at all. We had one bag of belongings. Mia had a single basket of toys. I had a small stack of books that I'd placed on the little shelves separating the living area from the kitchen. There was a round table that I clipped Mia's high chair to, and a chair where I sat and watched her eat, often drinking coffee to quell my hunger.

As I watched Mia take those first few steps, I tried to keep my eyes from the green box behind her where I kept the court documents detailing my fight with her father for custody. I fought to keep my focus on her, smiling at her, as if everything was fine. Had I turned the camera around, I wouldn't have recognized myself. The few photos of me showed almost a different person, possibly the skinniest I had been in my whole life. I worked part-time as a landscaper, where I spent several hours a week trimming shrubs, fighting back overgrown blackberries, and picking tiny blades of grass from places they weren't supposed to be. Sometimes I cleaned the floors and toilets of homes whose owners I knew, friends who had heard I was desperate for money. They weren't rich, but these friends had financial cushions beneath them, something I didn't. A lost paycheck would be a hardship, not a start of events that would end with living in a homeless shelter. They had parents or other family members who could swoop in with money and save them from all of that. No one was swooping in for us. It was just Mia and me.

On the intake papers for the housing authority, when asked about my personal goals for the next few months, I wrote about trying to make it work with Mia's dad, Jamie. I thought if I tried hard enough, we could figure it out.

Sometimes I would imagine moments when we were a real family—a mother, a father, a beautiful baby girl. I'd grasp onto those daydreams, like they were a string tied to a huge balloon. The balloon would carry me over Jamie's abuse and the hardship of being left as a single parent. If I kept hold of that string, I'd float above it all. If I focused on the portrait of the family I wanted to be, I could pretend the bad parts weren't real; like this life was a temporary state of being, not a new existence.

Mia got new shoes for her birthday. I'd saved up for a month. They were brown with little pink-and-blue birds embroidered on them. I sent out party invitations like a normal mom and invited Jamie like we were a normal co-parenting couple. We celebrated at a picnic table overlooking the ocean on a grassy hillside at Chetzemoka Park in Port Townsend, the city in Washington State where we lived. People sat smiling on blankets they'd brought. I'd bought lemonade and muffins with my remaining food stamp money for that month. My dad and my grandfather had traveled for almost two hours from opposite directions to attend. My brother and a few friends came. One brought a guitar. I asked a friend to take pictures of Mia, Jamie, and me, because it was so rare, the three of us sitting together like that. I wanted Mia to have a good memory to look back on. But Jamie's face in the photos showed disinterest, anger.

My mom had flown in with her husband, William, all the way from London, or France, or wherever they were living at the time. The day after Mia's party, they came over—violating the homeless shelter's "no visitors" rule—to help me move to the transitional apartment. I shook my head a little at their outfits—William in his skinny black jeans, black sweater, and black boots; Mom in a black-and-white-striped dress that hugged her round hips too tight, black leggings, and low-top Converse shoes. They looked ready for sipping espresso, not moving. I hadn't let anyone see where we'd been living, so the intrusion of their British accents and Euro outfits made the cabin, our home, feel even dirtier.

William seemed surprised to see that there was only one duffel bag to move us out. He picked it up to bring it outside, and Mom followed him. I turned back to take a final look at that floor, at the ghosts of myself reading books on the love seat, of Mia rummaging through her basket of toys, of her sitting in the built-in drawer under the twin bed. I was happy to be gone. But it was a brief moment to take in what I had survived, a bittersweet goodbye to the fragile place of our beginning.

Half the residents in our new apartment building, the Northwest Passage Transitional Family Housing Program, were like me, moving out of homeless shelters, but the other half were people who had just gotten out of jail. It was supposed to be a step up from the shelter, but I already missed the seclusion of the cabin. Here, in this building, my reality felt exposed for all to see, even me.

Mom and William waited behind me as I approached the door to our new home. I struggled with the key, setting the box down to fumble harder with the lock, until finally we were in. "Well, at least that's secure," William joked.

We walked into a narrow entryway; the front door sat opposite the bathroom. Right away I noticed the tub, where Mia and I could take a bath together. We hadn't had the luxury of a tub in a long time. Our two bedrooms were on the right. Each had a window that faced the road. In the tiny kitchen, the refrigerator door grazed the cupboards on the opposite side. I walked across the large white tiles, which resembled the floor at the shelter, and opened the door to a small outdoor deck. It was just wide enough where I could sit with my legs stretched out.

Julie, my caseworker, had briefly shown me the place in a walk-through two weeks earlier. The last family who'd lived in the apartment had stayed for twenty-four months, the maximum amount of time possible. "You're lucky this one opened up," she said. "Especially since your days were up at the shelter."

When I first met with Julie, I sat across from her, stammering in my attempts to answer questions about what my plans were, how I planned to provide shelter for my child. What my path to financial stability looked like. What jobs I could do. Julie seemed to understand my bewilderment, offering some suggestions on how to proceed. Moving into low-income housing seemed to be my only option. The trouble was finding an empty slot. There were advocates at the Domestic Violence and Sexual Assault Services Center who kept a protected shelter available for victims who had nowhere to turn, but I had gotten lucky when the housing authority offered me my own space and a path to stability.

Julie and I went over a four-page list of terse rules during that first meeting, rules I'd have to agree to in order to stay at their shelter.

Guest understands that this is an emergency shelter;
it is NOT your home.
RANDOM URINALYSIS may be requested
at any time.
Visitors are NOT allowed at the shelter.
NO EXCEPTIONS.

Julie made clear they'd still do random checks to make sure the daily household chore minimums were met, like cleaning the dishes, not leaving food out on the counter, and keeping the floor tidy. I again agreed to random urine analysis tests, random unit inspections, and a ten p.m. curfew. Overnight visitors were not allowed without permission, and for no more than three days. All changes in income had to be reported immediately. Monthly statements had to be submitted with details about what money came in and how and why it went out.

Julie was always nice and kept smiling as she spoke. I appreciated that she didn't have that worn, drawn-out look that other caseworkers in government offices seemed to have. She treated me like a person, tucking her short, copper-red hair behind her ear as she spoke. But my thoughts were stuck on when she called me "lucky." I didn't feel lucky. Grateful, yes. Definitely. But having luck, no. Not when I was moving into a place with rules that suggested that I was an addict, dirty, or just so messed up in life that I needed an enforced curfew and pee tests.

Being poor, living in poverty, seemed a lot like probation—the crime being a lack of means to survive.

William, Mom, and I moved things at a reasonable pace from the pickup truck I'd borrowed to the stairs leading up to my door on the second floor. We'd taken my stuff out of a storage unit my dad got me before I moved into the cabin. Mom and William were so overdressed I offered them t-shirts, but they declined. Mom had been overweight my whole life, except during the period when she divorced my dad. She had attributed her weight loss to the Atkins Diet. Dad later discovered that her sudden gym motivation was not fitness but an affair, along with a new desire to escape the constraints of being a wife and mother. Mom's metamorphosis was a coming out or an awakening to the life she had always wanted but sacrificed for her family. For me, it felt like she was suddenly a stranger.

The spring my brother, Tyler, graduated from high school, my parents divorced, and Mom moved to an apartment. By Thanksgiving, she had shrunk down to half her previous dress size and grown her hair long. We walked down to a bar, and I watched her kiss men my age, then pass out in a diner booth. I was embarrassed, but later that feeling transformed into a loss that I did not know how to grieve. I wanted my mom back.

Dad had dissolved himself into a new family for a while, too. The woman he dated right after the divorce was jealous and had three boys. She didn't like me coming around. "Take care of yourself," he said to me once after breakfast at a Denny's near their house.

My parents had moved on, leaving me emotionally orphaned. I vowed to never put the same amount of physical and emotional space between Mia and me.

Now, staring at Mom, married to a British man who was only seven years older than me, I saw she had ballooned several sizes larger than she'd ever been, so much that she seemed uncomfortable in her body. I couldn't help but stare at her while she stood next to me speaking in a fake British accent. It had been maybe seven years since she'd moved to Europe, but I'd seen her only a handful of times.

Halfway through moving my many boxes of books, she started talking about how good a burger sounded. "And a beer," she added the next time we passed each other on the stairs. It was barely noon, but she was in vacation mode, which meant drinking began early. She suggested we go to Sirens, a bar downtown with outdoor seating. My mouth watered. I hadn't been out to eat in months.

"I have to work after this, but I can go," I said. I had a job cleaning my friend's preschool once a week for $45. I also needed to return the truck and pick up Mia from Jamie's.

That day Mom cleared out several huge bins of her own—old photos and knickknacks she had stored in a friend's garage. She brought it all over to my new place as a gift. I took it willfully, with nostalgia, and as evidence of our former life together. She'd kept every school portrait, every Halloween photo. Me holding my first fish. Cradling flowers after my school musical. Mom had been in the audience, supporting me, smiling and holding up a camera. Now, in the apartment, she looked at me only as another adult in the room, an equal, while I stood there feeling more lost than I'd ever been. I needed my family. I needed to see them nodding, smiling, reassuring me that I was going to be okay.

When William got up to use the bathroom, I sat next to Mom on the floor. "Hey," I said.

"Yes?" she answered, like I was about to ask her for something. I always got the feeling she worried I'd ask her for money, but I never did. She and William lived a frugal life in Europe, renting out William's flat in London while they lived in a cottage in France, not far from Bordeaux, which they would turn into a bed-and-breakfast.

"I wondered if maybe you and I could spend some time together?" I asked. "Just the two of us?"

"Steph, I just don't think that would be appropriate."

"Why?" I asked, straightening.

"I mean, if you want to spend time with me, then you'll have to accept that William will be there, too," she said.

At that moment, William walked toward us, loudly blowing his nose into his handkerchief. She grabbed for his hand and looked at me with her eyebrows raised, like she was proud of herself for setting that boundary.

It was no secret that I didn't like William. When I'd gone to visit them in France a couple of years earlier, William and I had had a fierce argument that upset my mother so much she went out to the car to cry. This visit, I wished to gain back the lost relationship with my mother, but not just as someone who could help me care for Mia. I craved a mom, someone I could trust, who would accept me unconditionally despite my living in a homeless shelter. If I had a mom to talk to, maybe she could explain what was happening to me, or make it easier, and help me not see myself as a failure. It was hard, admitting that level of desperation, vying for the attention of your own mother. So I laughed whenever William made jokes. I smiled when he poked fun at American grammar. I didn't comment on my mother's new accent or the fact that she now acted uppity, as if Grandma didn't make salad from cans of fruit and containers of Cool Whip.

Mom and Dad grew up in different parts of Skagit County, an area known for its fields of tulips, located about an hour north of Seattle. Both their families had lived in poverty for generations. Dad's family was rooted deep in the wooded hillsides above Clear Lake. His distant relatives were rumored to still make moonshine. Mom lived down in the valley, where farmers grew fields of peas and spinach.

Grandma and Grandpa had been married for close to forty years. My earliest memories are of them in their trailer home in the woods that sat next to a creek. I stayed with them during the day while my parents worked. Grandpa would make us mayonnaise and butter sandwiches on Wonder bread for lunch. They didn't have much money, but my memories of my maternal grandparents were filled with love and warmth: Grandma stirring Campbell's tomato soup on the stove, she'd have a soda in one hand and stand on one foot with the other tucked into her thigh like a flamingo, and there was always a cigarette burning in an ashtray nearby.

They'd moved to the city to an old house next to downtown Anacortes that became so run-down over the years it was nearly inhospitable. Grandpa was a real estate agent and would pop in between showing houses and burst through the door with little toys he'd found for me or won from the claw machine at the bowling alley.

As a child, when I wasn't at their house, I'd call Grandma on the telephone. I spent so much time talking to her that in the bin of photos were several of me at four and five years old standing in the kitchen with a large yellow phone pressed to my ear.

Grandma had paranoid schizophrenia, and over time it became nearly impossible to have a conversation with her. She had grown delusional. The last time Mia and I visited, I'd brought her a Papa Murphy's pizza that I purchased with my food stamps. Grandma, with thick black eyeliner and hot pink lipstick, stood outside smoking most of the visit. We had to wait for Grandpa to get home so we could eat. When he did, Grandma then said she wasn't hungry anymore and accused Grandpa of having an affair, even of flirting with me.

But Anacortes was the keeper of my childhood memories. Though I had fewer and fewer ties to my family, I always told Mia about Bowman Bay, an area of Deception Pass—a crevasse in the ocean dividing Fidalgo and Whidbey islands, where my dad took me hiking as a little girl. That small pocket of Washington State, with its towering evergreens and madronas, was the only place that felt like home to me. I'd explored every nook of it, knew its trails and the nuances of the ocean currents, and had carved my initials into the twisted reddish-orange trunk of a madrona tree and could point out exactly where it was. Whenever I returned to Anacortes to visit my family, I found myself walking the beaches below Deception Pass Bridge, taking the long way home through Rosario Road, past the large houses on bluffs.

I missed my family but took solace that Mom and Grandma still talked every Sunday. Mom called her from wherever she was in Europe. It consoled me, like I hadn't lost Mom entirely, that she still had some remembrance inside of the people she'd left behind.

Mom ordered another beer when the bill came for our lunch at Sirens. I checked the time. I needed to give myself two hours to clean the preschool before I picked up Mia. After watching Mom and William amuse themselves with out-landish anecdotes about their neighbors in France for fifteen more minutes, I admitted that I had to leave.

"Oh," William said, his eyebrows rising. "Do you want me to get the waitress's attention so you can pay for lunch?"

I stared at him. "I don't," I said. We looked at each other, in some kind of standoff. "I don't have money to pay."

It would have been appropriate for me to buy them lunch, since they were visiting and had helped me move, but they were supposed to be my parents. I wanted to remind him that he just moved me out of a homeless shelter, but I didn't and turned to my mom with pleading eyes. "I can put the beer on my credit card," she offered.

"I only have ten bucks in my account," I said. The knots in my throat were growing in size.

"That barely pays for your burger," William blurted out.

He was right. My burger was $10.59. I had ordered an item exactly twenty-eight cents less than what I had in my bank account. Shame pounded inside my chest. Any triumph I felt that day about my move out of the shelter was shattered. I could not afford a damn burger.

I looked from my mom to William and then excused myself to use the bathroom. I didn't have to pee. I needed to cry.

My reflection in the mirror showed a rail-thin figure, wearing a kid-sized t-shirt and tight-fitting jeans that I'd rolled up at the bottom to hide that they were too short. In the mirror, there was that woman—overworked but without any money to show for it, someone who couldn't afford a fucking burger. I was often too stressed to eat, and many mealtimes with Mia were just me watching her spoon food into her mouth, thankful for each bite she took. My body looked sinewy and sunken, and all I had left in me was to cry it out in that bathroom.

Years ago, when I thought about my future, poverty seemed inconceivable, so far away from my reality. I never thought I would end up here. But now, after one kid and a breakup, I was smack in the middle of a reality that I didn't know how to get out of.

When I returned, William still sat with his nostrils flared, like some kind of miniature dragon. Mom leaned toward him, whispering something, and he shook his head in disapproval.

"I can pay ten dollars," I said, sitting down.

"Okay," Mom said.

I hadn't expected her to accept my offer. It'd be days before I'd get a paycheck. I fumbled in my bag for my wallet and then handed my card to include with hers. After signing the check, I stood and stuffed my card into my back pocket and barely gave her a hug goodbye as I walked out. I was only a few steps from the table when William said, "Well, I've never seen someone act more entitled!"

2

The Camper

For Christmas in 1983, I got a Cabbage Patch Kid from my parents. Mom had waited for hours in lines at JCPenney before the doors opened. The department store managers held baseball bats over the shoppers' heads to keep the mobs from rushing the counter. Mom elbowed shoppers from left to right like a fighter and grabbed the last box from the shelf right before a woman tried to snatch it. Or that was how she told the story. I listened with wide eyes, relishing the fact that she had fought for me. My mom, the hero. The champion. Bringer of sought-after dolls.

On Christmas morning, I held my new Cabbage Patch Kid on my small hip. She had short, looped blond hair and green eyes. I stood in front of Mom, raised my right hand, and pledged, "After meeting this Cabbage Patch Kid, and learning of her needs, I want to make the major commitment of becoming a good parent to Angelica Marie." Then I signed the adoption papers, which was the key part of the Cabbage Patch Kid phenomenon. It expressed family values and encouraged responsibility. When I received the doll's birth certificate with my name printed on it, Mom wrapped both me and Angelica, who was carefully cleaned and dressed for the occasion, in a proud embrace.

For as long as I can remember, I have wanted to be a writer. Growing up, I wrote stories and disappeared with books like they were old friends. Some of my favorite days off were the rainy ones, when I'd start a new book in the morning at a coffee shop, finishing it late that evening in a bar. It was during that first summer in my late twenties with Jamie that the University of Montana in Missoula began wooing me with postcards for their creative writing program. I imagined myself inside the photos, walking through the pastoral landscapes of Montana, somewhere beneath the quotes from Steinbeck's *Travels with Charley* scrawled above in scripted fonts: "...but with Montana it is love," he'd written simply. They were words that brought me to the "Big Sky Country" of Montana, in my search for a home in the next phase of my life.

I met Jamie walking home from a bar, where my coworkers and I went after our closing shift. It was close to midnight, and the midsummer crickets hummed from the grass. My hooded sweatshirt had been tied around my waist while I sweated and danced all night. Now I grabbed for it in anticipation of a long bike ride home. The front of my Carhartt pants still had little drips of espresso from the café where I worked, and I could still taste that last sip of whiskey in my mouth.

Outside into the refreshing breeze, I heard the wafted sound of a guitar coming from a park bench and the unmistakable voice of John Prine. I paused long enough to recognize the song and noticed a guy holding an MP3 player and portable speakers in his lap. He wore a red flannel coat and a brown fedora and sat hunched over, gently nodding his head, taking in the music.

Without thinking, I sat down next to him. The warmth of the whiskey stirred in my chest. "Hi," I said.

"Hi," he said, and smiled at me.

We sat like that for a while, listening to his favorite songs, breathing in the night air on the banks of Port Townsend's downtown strip. Brick Victorian buildings towered above the waves lapping against the docks.

When I stood up to leave, in the excitement of meeting a new boy, I scrawled my phone number across a page of my journal and then ripped it out.

"You wanna go out sometime?" I asked, handing him the page. He looked up at me, then glanced toward the sound of laughter as people stumbled out of Sirens. He took the slip of paper from my hand, looked at me, and nodded.

The next evening, while I was driving into town, my phone rang.

"Where you headed?" he asked.

"Downtown." I swerved my car, failing to downshift, steer, and hold the phone at the same time.

"Meet me outside the Penny Saver Market," he said, and hung up.

About five minutes later, I pulled into the parking lot. Jamie leaned against the back of a red, pieced-together Volkswagen Bug, wearing the same clothes from the night before, waiting for me. He smiled at me coolly, showing crooked teeth that I hadn't noticed in the darkness.

"Let's get some beer," he said, throwing the butt of a rolled cigarette onto the pavement.

He paid for two bottles of Samuel Smith stout, and then we climbed into his Volkswagen and drove to a bluff to watch the sunset. While he talked, I thumbed through a *New York Times Book Review* that I found on the passenger seat. He told me about a bike trip he had planned—down the Pacific Coast on Highway 101 all the way to San Francisco.

"I already got the time off work," he said, glancing at me. His eyes were a darker brown than mine.

"Where do you work?" I asked, realizing that I knew nothing about him other than his music preferences.

"The Fountain Café." He took a drag of his cigarette. "I used to be a sous chef. But now I just make the desserts there." He exhaled, and a plume of smoke disappeared over the bluff.

"You make the tiramisu?" I asked, pausing in my feeble attempt to roll a cigarette of my own.

He nodded, and I knew I'd go to bed with him. The tiramisu was that good.

Later that week, Jamie brought me to his camper trailer for the first time. I stood in the tiny space, taking in the wood paneling, the orange beanbag, and the shelves lined with books.

Jamie apologized when he noticed me looking around and fumbled to explain that the trailer was just to save money for his bike trip. But I'd seen Bukowski and Jean-Paul Sartre in a line of books above the table and couldn't care less about the trailer's appearance. I turned immediately to kiss him.

He pushed me slowly to the white down of his bed. We kissed for hours, as though nothing else in the world existed. He encased me.

Eventually, Jamie and I planned to go our separate ways—me to Missoula, and him to Portland, Oregon. When he suggested that I move into his trailer to save money, I did so immediately. We lived in a twenty-foot camper trailer, but the rent was only $150 apiece. Our relationship was one with a definitive end, each of us helping the other toward the goal of getting out of town.

Port Townsend's work force was mainly that of the service industry, catering to tourists and those with disposable incomes who arrived in droves during the warmer months. The ferries were packed with them, crawling over the waters between the mainland and the peninsula, the gateway to the rain forests and hot springs on the coast. The Victorian mansions, shops, and cafés on the waterfront brought the city money and in turn provided livelihoods for many residents. Still, it wasn't a ton of money pouring in. Unless a Port Townsend resident started a business, there wasn't much more the average worker could do to build a future.

Many of the core residents already had their futures firmly set in place. In the late sixties or early seventies, a band of hippies had moved into Port Townsend, then a near ghost town barely surviving, thanks to a paper mill that employed most of its residents. The town had been built on the promise of being one of the biggest western seaports and failed when lack of funding from the Depression rerouted railroads to Seattle and Tacoma. The hippies, some of whom were now my employers and loyal customers, bought the Victorian mansions, which loomed with decay from a near century of abandonment. They spent years working on the buildings, preserving them as historical landmarks, improving the town, building bakeries, cafés, breweries, bars, restaurants, grocery stores, and hotels. Port Townsend became known for harboring wooden boats, with interest evolving into a formal school and yearly festival. Now that core group who'd worked to revive the town kicked back, slowed their pace, and settled into being the bourgeoisie. All of us service workers catered to them, worked for them in our various ways, living in tiny cabins, yurts, or studio apartments. We were there for the weather—the rain shadow the Olympic Mountains provided—and for the hidden artsy community that was only a ferry ride from Seattle. We were there for the calm ocean water in the bay and the sweaty work and lifestyle bustling kitchens provided.

Jamie and I both worked at cafés, relishing the youth and freedom to do so. We both knew we were on to bigger and better things. He helped out with his friend's catering business and did whatever side work he could find that paid under the table. In addition to the café, I worked at a doggy day care and sold bread at farmers' markets. Neither of us had college degrees—Jamie admitted that he hadn't even graduated from high school—and we did whatever work we could to make money.

Jamie had typical restaurant shifts, from the late afternoon well into the night, so most of the time I was already asleep by the time he came home, a little drunk after hanging out at the bar. Sometimes I'd go down and meet him, spending my tips on a few beers.

Then I found out I was pregnant. Through a wall of morning sickness, my stomach dropped, and the world suddenly started shrinking until it seemed to stop. I stood in front of the bathroom mirror for a long time with my sweatshirt lifted to examine my stomach. We'd conceived on my twenty-eighth birthday, the day before Jamie left for his bike trip.

In choosing to keep the baby, I would be choosing to stay in Port Townsend. I wanted to keep the pregnancy a secret and continue with my plan to move to Missoula, but that didn't seem possible. I needed to give Jamie a chance to be a father—it felt wrong to deny him that opportunity. But staying would mean delaying my dreams of becoming a writer. Delaying the person I expected myself to be. The person who would move on, become someone great. I wasn't sure I wanted to give that up. I had been on birth control, and I didn't believe it was wrong to get an abortion, but I couldn't stop thinking about my mother, who'd possibly stared at her belly, debating her options for my life in the same way.

In spite of all my hopes for a different path, I softened in the days that followed and began to fall in love with motherhood, with the idea of me as a mother. When I told Jamie about the baby, he'd just finished his bike trip. His initial tenderness in coaxing me to terminate the pregnancy abruptly changed when I told him I would not be doing that. I had known Jamie only four months, and his rage, his hatred toward me, was frightening.

One afternoon, Jamie barged into the trailer where I sat

on the built-in couch by the television, trying to stomach chicken soup while I watched Maury Povich reveal the results of paternity tests. Jamie paced while he stared at me, mirroring the men on the show, yelling about not wanting his name on the birth certificate. "I don't want you to come after me to pay for that fucking kid," he kept saying, pointing to my stomach. I stayed quiet like I usually did when he went on these tirades, hoping he didn't start throwing things. But this time, the more he yelled, the more he fought and told me what a mistake I was making, the more it pushed me closer to the baby, to protect it. After he left, I called my dad, my voice shaking.

"Am I making the right decision?" I asked after telling him what Jamie had said. "Because I really don't know. But I feel like I should be sure. I don't know anything anymore."

"Damn," he said, then paused. "I'd really hoped Jamie would step up to the plate on this one." He paused again, maybe waiting for me to respond, but there was nothing to say. "You know your mom and I were in the same position when we found out about you, except we were in our teens. And, you know, it wasn't perfect. I don't know if it was ever even close. We didn't know what we were doing, or if we were doing the right thing. But you, your brother, me, and your mom—we're all okay. We turned out okay. And I know you, Jamie, and this baby will be okay, too, even if it's not what you think it's going to be."

After that call, I sat and looked out the window. I tried not to let my current surroundings—the camper sitting next to a large shop in the woods—distract me from envisioning my future. I started speaking differently to myself, quelling my doubts. Maybe Jamie would come around. Maybe it would just take some time. If he didn't, I decided I could deal with that, even though I had no idea how. I couldn't base my decisions on him, to have a baby with him, but I knew I had to at least give him the opportunity to be a dad. My kid deserved that. Though it wasn't an ideal situation, I would do what parents do, what parents had done for generations—I'd make it work. There was no questioning. No other option. I was a mother now. I would honor that responsibility for the rest of my life. I got up, and on my way out, I ripped up my college application and went to work.

3

Transitional Housing

My parents moved us out of Washington when I was seven, away from all of our relatives. We lived in a home tucked into the foothills of the Chugach mountain range in Anchorage, Alaska. The church we went to then had several outreach programs for homeless and low-income communities. As a child, my favorite was giving to families in need during the holidays. After Sunday service, Mom would let my brother and me select a paper angel off a Christmas tree in the church lobby. We'd go to the mall after brunch to select the listed items for a nameless girl or boy close to our age whom we'd give new toys, pajamas, socks, and shoes.

One year, I went with my mom to deliver dinner to a family. I waited until it was my turn to give my delicately wrapped presents to the man who opened the door of a damp apartment. He had thick, dark hair and leather-tanned skin under a white t-shirt. After I gave him my bag of presents, my mom handed him a box with a turkey, potatoes, and canned vegetables. He nodded and then quietly closed his door. I walked away disappointed. I thought he'd invite us in so I could help his little girl open the presents I had handpicked, wanting to see how happy my presents made her. "The new shiny shoes were the prettiest in the store," I would tell her. I wondered why her father wasn't happier to give them to her.

As a teenager, I spent some afternoons in downtown Anchorage handing out bagged lunches to homeless people. We were there to "witness" and share the gospel with them. In exchange for their listening ears, we fed them apples and sandwiches. I'd say Jesus loves you, though one man smiled at me and said, "He seems to love you a little more." I washed cars to fund-raise for our travel to orphanages in Baja Mexico or to do Bible camps for children in Chicago. Looking back on those efforts and the place I was now, scrambling to find work and safe housing, those efforts, though noble, were charity and Band-Aid work that made poor people into caricatures—anonymous paper angels on a tree. I thought back to the man who'd answered the door, the one I had given a small bag of gifts. Now I'd be opening the door, accepting charity. Accepting that I couldn't provide for my family. Accepting their small token—a new pair of gloves, a toy—in their impulse to feel good. But there wasn't any way to put "health care" or "childcare" on a list.

Since my parents raised my brother and me thousands of miles away from our roots in Northwest Washington where my grandparents lived, my upbringing became what most think of as middle-class American. We didn't lack for any basic needs, but my parents couldn't afford a lot of expenses like dance or karate lessons, and there was no account for our college education. I learned the importance of money pretty quickly. I started babysitting at eleven and almost always had a job or two after that. It was in my blood to work. My brother and I were protected through the shroud of our religion and my parents' financial security.

Safety was instilled in me. I was safe, and never questioned that, until I wasn't.

Jamie's eyes narrowed when I told him I wanted to take Mia to go live with my dad and stepmother, Charlotte. Mia was barely seven months old but had witnessed too many of his angry outbursts; the lashing out and destruction had traumatized me.

"I looked online," I said, reaching for a piece of paper in my pocket while holding Mia on my hip. "They have a child support calculator, and the amount seems more than fair."

He snatched the paper out of my hand, crumpled it, and threw it at my face, his intense glare not leaving my eyes. "I'm not gonna pay you child support," he said evenly. "You should be the one paying me!" His voice grew louder as he spoke and paced back and forth. "You're not going anywhere." He pointed to Mia. "I'll take her so fast it'll make your head spin." With that, he turned to leave, releasing a yell of rage as he punched a hole through the Plexiglas window on the door. Mia jumped and let out a high-pitched scream that I had never heard before.

My hand trembled while I dialed the domestic violence hotline. I was barely able to explain what was happening before Jamie started calling repeatedly. They advised me to hang up and call the police. Minutes later, the headlights of a patrol car lit up the entire side of the single-wide trailer. An officer knocked gently at the broken door. He stood so tall, his head nearly grazed the ceiling. While I told him what had happened, he took a few notes, examining the door, nodding, asking if we were okay. If we felt safe. After a year of abuse, threats, and screaming insults thrown at me, that question came with much relief. Most of Jamie's rage had been invisible. It didn't leave bruises or red marks. But this—this I could point to. I could ask someone to look at it. I could say, "He did this. He did this to us." And they could look at it, nod, and tell me, "I see that. I see that he did this to you." The police report the officer left was a validation that I wasn't crazy. I carried it in my purse for months like a certificate.

Those first nights we spent in the transitional housing apartment building off a main street filled me with uncertainty. Every noise that echoed through the walls and floors of the complex made me jump. I constantly checked to make sure the door was locked when we were home, something I'd never done before. But it was just my daughter and me, and I was our only protection.

When we lived in the homeless shelter, the driveway led straight to my cabin's door, so my car was parked right outside if we ever needed to get away. I never saw or heard my neighbors, who all lived in separate cabins, and we were surrounded by nature—trees and fields that triggered a sense of peace, not trouble. That little space was my own, and I didn't fear invasion. But in the apartment, the walls and floors seemed so thin, and there were so many unfamiliar voices. In the stairwell, strangers filed up and down, yelling at each other. I'd stare at my front door, the only thing between us and the rest of the world, knowing that someone could break through it at any moment.

Apartments surrounded us in that gray rectangle, but the only evidence of occupants was the voices from behind the walls, the trash piled high in the dumpster, the cars pulled into the parking lot. Maybe I would have felt safer had I met my neighbors, had I seen what they looked like. Their night sounds, heels that clicked across the floor, an unexpected deep voice, then the laughter of a child, paddled my sleep. I'd get up several times throughout the night to check on Mia. She slept in the next room in a portable crib.

Most nights, I'd lay awake for hours replaying the moments in court with Jamie.

I'd stood in front of a judge, next to Jamie and his lawyer. I was homeless and fighting for custody of Mia. It was no secret that months of Jamie's angry words against me had caused my depression, and now he used this as the basis of his claim that I was unfit to parent our daughter. My failure seemed to shroud me. It was like Jamie's lawyer and the judge thought I preferred it this way, like I thought raising a child without a stable home was okay. Like I didn't think every single second about how I needed to improve our situation, if I had the ability to. Somehow, it reflected badly on me that I'd removed Mia from a place where I was punished and brutalized until I was curled up on the floor, sobbing like a toddler. No one saw that I was trying to give my daughter a better life—they only saw that I'd taken her out of what they considered a financially stable home.

Somewhere, I found an almost primal strength, and I won the custody case. I got my own space, a place for Mia to be with me. Still, most nights I wrapped myself in guilt for what we lacked. Some days, the guilt was so heavy that I couldn't be totally present with Mia. I'd muster reading her books before bed, rocking her gently in the same chair where my mom had read me stories. I'd tell myself that tomorrow would be better; I'd be a better mother.

I'd sit and watch Mia eat, or I'd pace around the kitchen, drinking my coffee and staring at our budget and my work schedule, which I hung on the walls. If we went out and got groceries, I'd spend the morning scrolling my bank account balance and my EBT (electronic benefit transfer) card, a debit card for food paid by the government, to see how much money we had left. EBT cards were still relatively new and had been used only since 2002. I'd applied for food stamps when I was pregnant, and Jamie still remembered his mom paying for groceries with paper stamps and always sneered at the memory. I was grateful for programs that fed my family, but I'd also carry back home a bag of shame, each time mentally wrestling with what the cashier thought of me, a woman with an infant in a sling, purchasing food on public assistance. All they saw were the food stamps, the large WIC paper coupons that bought us eggs, cheese, milk, and peanut butter. What they didn't see was the balance, which hovered around $200 depending on my income, and that it was all the money I had for food. I had to stretch it to the end of each month until the balance was re-upped after the beginning of the month. They didn't see me eating peanut butter sandwiches and hard-boiled eggs, rationing my morning cup of coffee to make it stretch. Though I didn't know it then, the government had worked that year to change the stigma surrounding the twenty-nine million people who used food stamps by giving it a new name: the Supplemental Nutrition Assistance Program (SNAP). But whether you called it SNAP or food stamps, the assumption that the poor stole hardworking Americans' tax money to buy junk food was unchanged.

Despite getting lost in my head, I obsessed over whether or not I was a good mother. I was failing; I was more in tune with how we'd survive the week than with my child. When I was with Jamie, his job had provided me the ability to stay home with Mia. I missed having whole days to ourselves, stopping to look and learn and wonder. Now it felt like we barely got by. Always late for something. Always in the car. Always in a rush to finish meals and clean up. Always moving, barely pausing to take a breath. In fear that I'd fall behind on something, forget something, screw up our lives even more— I just didn't have time for Mia to watch a caterpillar inch its way across the sidewalk.

Though I heard almost every ghostlike toilet flush and chair moving across the floor of my neighbors' apartments, the lady who lived below me would make herself known, hitting her ceiling with a broom or mop handle and yelling whenever Mia ran across the floor. When we first moved in, I swept the leaves and spider webs off the deck to the ground below. She yelled, "What the fuck?" out from under me. Besides the broom-handle banging, that was the first time she'd spoken even semi-directly to me. "What's all this shit?" she went on.

"You're fuckin' shitting on me!" I slinked inside, shut the door softly, and sat stiffly on the couch, hoping she wouldn't run up and knock on my door.

My upstairs neighbors—a mom and her three children—were hardly ever home. For the first few weeks I only heard them. I'd go to bed around ten p.m., and they'd come walking up the stairs around that time. After twenty minutes or so, they'd quiet again.

One morning as the sun came up I heard them leaving and ran to the window to see them, curious about who the other people in my same situation were.

The woman was tall and wore a purple-and-red wind-breaker jacket and white sneakers. She limped from side to side when she walked. Two school-age boys and a girl walked behind her. I couldn't imagine what she was going through. I only had one to care for. I saw her from time to time after that. The little girl's hair was always neat, in cornrow braids decorated with bright ribbons. I wondered where they went all day, how she kept her kids so quiet and well behaved. She seemed like a good mother—respected by her children, which I envied. My kid had just learned how to walk upright and seemed to run from or fight me every second she was awake.

"You learn to love your coffee," my neighbor Brooke had told me when we saw each other after a house check, refer-ring to us being prohibited alcohol. We had sort of awkwardly shuffled past each other, and this was the first time we spoke. I'd known Brooke in what felt like a former life now, back when she poured the beers I'd ordered from her at the bar. I wondered what brought her to this place. But I never asked. Just like I didn't want her to ask me.

I never talked to any of the men who lived in the halfway house on the far side of the complex. I'd see them standing on the path that went to their apartments, smoking cigarettes in sweatpants and slippers. One older man had family who picked him up every so often, but the others didn't seem to go anywhere. Maybe they were just doing their time in that place. I kind of felt the same way.

I missed going out to bars. I missed having a beer if I wanted to, not necessarily the beer itself, but not having to worry about the housing authority popping up, having that freedom. I missed having so many freedoms: to go, to stay, to work, to eat or not eat, to sleep in on days off, to have a day off.

Mia and I had what looked like a normal life, one with places we needed to be during the day. I qualified for a child-care grant, but only for half days. My friend's husband, John, had a small landscaping business, and he paid me $10 an hour to pull weeds, prune shrubs, and clear rhododendron bushes of dead flowers. I'd drive all around the northeast section of the Olympic Peninsula, to little gated communities, with a large garbage can in the back of my car, which contained a white paint bucket with tools and a few pairs of gloves. Some clients had a designated area for me to dump weeds and clippings, or I had to bag them up and set them by the curb, or even wrestle them into the back of my car. John had just a few regular clients with big enough jobs that required my help, so I filled the majority of my time with jobs I found on my own and worked my way up to charging $20 to $25 an hour, but with travel time I could work only two to three hours a day.

Landscaping meant crawling. Most people hired me to clear weeds from whole hillsides covered in wood chips. I'd spend hours on my gloved hands and double-kneed Carhartts, filling buckets, trash cans, and garbage bags with weeds that people paid me to organically kill by pulling out of the ground. It was good work. But, being seasonal, it would end in a matter of weeks, and I didn't know what I'd do for work after that. Port Townsend's job market was seasonal, too, dependent on tourists with full pockets and empty bellies. There weren't a lot of "normal" jobs with "mom hours," or ones I had any experience in, anyway. I'd always worked in coffee shops or at odd gigs that I couldn't really list on a résumé. Even cleaning the preschool every Sunday wasn't enough. But I had work, for the time being, and I tried to focus on doing the best I could with that.

I'd drop Mia off for day care by noon, and three days a week her dad picked her up and kept her until seven. Some evenings while Mia was with Jamie, I sat out on the deck, my back against the wall. One of my neighbors always seemed to be outside with her daughter, on the small strip of grass between the building and the trees. Her daughter was a little younger than Mia. They both had very fair, almost transparent skin. I'd listen to the young mother gently ask, "Are you gonna go down the slide?" as her daughter crawled up the steps of the faded red-and-blue plastic slide. It had probably been left there a few tenants ago. "Wheee!" the mother would say as the baby slid down. *That's a better mom than me*, I'd think, listening to her narrate her daughter's trips up and down the slide, knowing I could never muster the same excitement.

But on one of those late afternoons, paramedics and firemen walked past the little slide in the grass, moving it out of the way. They all went into the fair-skinned mom's apartment. I didn't hear the baby. I leaned forward on the rail of my porch to see what was going on. Several of my neighbors did the same. One of the firemen looked up at all of us, and I instinctively ducked back a step to hide. He shook his head from side to side. I wondered what we all looked like, women and men in transitional housing, peeking over the rails. I wondered how the police and firemen talked about the building, us; what other reasons they had been called here. I went inside before they wheeled the mother away on a stretcher. I didn't want her to see me watching, even if her eyes were closed; I wanted to give her the dignity she deserved. I'd want the same.

An hour later, when I left my apartment to get Mia, Brooke came out, her eyes wide, cheeks red, ready to spill the gossip. "You know what happened, right?" she said, rushing toward me.

I shook my head. She said that someone had come to return the baby when they found her mother passed out on the bed. They couldn't wake her up. She'd taken sleeping pills and chugged an entire bottle of vodka. "They found her in time, though. She's alive," Brooke reassured me. Then she sighed and shrugged. "So much for no alcohol."

My first thoughts weren't whether the lady was okay or about the little girl. I just hoped Jamie wouldn't hear about it. I lived in fear that anything bad happening around Mia, including at the Early Head Start day care she attended, would reflect badly on my fragile permission to mother her full-time.

I'd immersed Mia in a world of poverty, surrounded her with some who tried to cope with it in sometimes tragic ways; some who had gone to prison or rehab long enough to lose their homes, some so angry from never getting a break, some who suffered symptoms of mental illness. A mother had chosen to give up completely. A choice so tantalizing, for a flash of a moment, I felt a twinge of envy.

4

The Fairgrounds Apartment

Is Julie around?" I asked, waiting for the woman behind the glass to write the receipt for my rent check. Each month's rent amount was different, depending on what my reported income was, and remained around $200.

The woman squinted at the whiteboard on the back wall of her front office. "No," she said with a sigh. "She's out with a client. Do you want to leave a message?"

I did.

"I'm having trouble settling into the apartment," I said to Julie the next day in the conference room.

Julie, much to my relief, didn't ask why.

It was all overwhelming: wondering if there'd be a knock on my door by the housing authority or tiptoeing around the apartment afraid of the woman yelling at us from downstairs, pounding on the floor with her broom handle. I had even asked Jamie over for dinner once because my loneliness had started to consume me. I hadn't been out, seen my friends, or invited any over. I felt isolated. This was no place for me.

"Wait here," Julie said, then returned a couple minutes later with some packets. "We can sign you up for TBRA." She pronounced it *tee-bra*, which stood for Tenant-Based Rental Assistance. "It's a lot like Section Eight. You're on the waitlist for Section Eight, right?"

I nodded. Section 8 felt like the unicorn of government assistance—you always heard about it but never knew anyone who had it. It's a rent voucher that pays for any housing costs beyond 30 to 40 percent of the tenant's income. So, someone working minimum wage, who brings home $1,000 a month, with a voucher would pay only $300 rent, and the government would pay for the rest as long as it followed what the tenant qualified for—usually two or three bedrooms. The building had to meet Section 8 standards, which are pretty basic—like no lead paint, working plumbing, and things like that. Once someone has it, it's honored—as long as you can find a landlord who'll accept it—anywhere in the state, and it never expires.

I was on waitlists in three different counties. Jefferson County, where Port Townsend was, had the shortest at only a year, but most places I called had a waiting period of five years or more. Some weren't even accepting new applicants, the need was so high.

Julie introduced me to a new caseworker who worked specifically with the Section 8 and TBRA programs. This woman sat behind a large desk, her short, dark, wavy hair framing her unsmiling face. She had me fill out several applications with questions about my plans for the next year and beyond. With detailed proof and calculations of my income, plus the $275 monthly child support, the amount of rent I'd expect to pay for a two-bedroom, $700-per-month apartment would currently be $199.

"That amount will go up or down depending on what your reported income is," Julie added, who I was thankful had sat with me through the appointment.

TBRA also required me to go to a class or seminar, where I'd learn about the program, but mainly how to approach potential landlords about using TBRA (and eventually Section 8) to pay my rent. "Most landlords have some experience with Section Eight," Julie said on our way out. "Or they at least know about the program. But some of them aren't aware that it can be a really good thing." I wasn't sure what she meant and wondered why it would be a bad thing, but I didn't ask.

We stopped in the parking lot, where she wrote down the time and directions to the class on housing assistance. "You're lucky, there's one tomorrow," she said optimistically. "You should be able to get into a new place pretty fast!"

I gave her a smile and nodded, but I was not holding onto hope that any of these programs would be able to help. The trauma from the last six months since we'd been homeless, and dealing with Jamie always fighting me, had paralyzed my whole system. My brain, stomach, nerves, everything was on constant high alert. Nothing was safe. Nothing was permanent. Every day I walked on a rug that could be yanked out from under me at any moment. I watched people smile at me, nodding their heads, again telling me how lucky I was to have this program or place available to us, but I didn't feel fortunate at all. My whole life had become unrecognizable.

Caseworkers told me where to go, where to apply, what form to fill out. They'd ask me what I needed, and I'd say, "A place to live," or "To eat," or "Childcare so I can work," and they'd help, or find someone who could, or not help at all. But that was all they could do. Recovering from the trauma was also vital, maybe the most critical, but not only could no one help me with that, I didn't know yet that I needed it. The months of poverty, instability, and insecurity created a panic response that would take years to undo.

"You'd think landlords would appreciate it," the man standing at the front of the room said to about twenty people sitting around two tables in a narrow room. He was Mark, the same guy who'd taught the class for LIHEAP (the Low-Income Home Energy Assistance Program). It'd been a year since I'd attended a three-hour seminar on how to use electricity most efficiently. The information was so redundant and common-sense, I tried to find humor in it, separating myself from my situation, that learning how to turn off the lights was required in order to receive a grant for $400 of heating fuel. More and more, I got the feeling that people who needed government assistance were assumed to be a very uneducated bunch and were treated accordingly. How degrading, to learn that since I needed money, I must not know how to keep my utility costs low.

Now I had to sit through several hours of learning how a rent assistance program paid landlords so I could *assure* them they'd get paid. To the government and everyone else, it was inherent they shouldn't trust me. All of it seemed so counterproductive. I'd taken time off work to be there and had to arrange for childcare. I sat there, glaring at Mark, who stood at the front of the room. He wore the same long-sleeved flannel shirt and high-waisted blue jeans pulled up to his abdomen he'd worn when he taught the LIHEAP class. His thin ponytail had gotten a little longer over the year since I'd seen him. I smiled at the memory of his suggestion to save money on the electric bill by not preheating the oven and by letting it cool with the door open. He'd said, after a bath or shower, to never immediately drain the hot water because the heat from the water could go into the house and heat it.

"Section Eight is great for landlords because it's guaranteed rent payments. They just don't like to rent to the *people* on Section Eight," Mark said. "It's your job to show them how it's worth it."

I thought of how many times the police, firemen, and paramedics had come to our building in the last couple of months; of the random checks to make sure living spaces were kept clean or to make sure broken-down cars in the parking lot had been repaired; to patrol us so that we weren't doing the awful things they expected poor people to do, like allowing the laundry or garbage to pile up, when really, we lacked physical energy and resources from working jobs no one else wanted to do. We were expected to live off minimum wage, to work several jobs at varying hours, to afford basic needs while fighting for safe places to leave our children. Somehow nobody saw the work; they saw only the results of living a life that constantly crushed you with its impossibility. It seemed like no matter how much I tried to prove otherwise, "poor" was always associated with dirty. How was I supposed to present myself to landlords as a responsible tenant when I was faced with a wall of stigmas stacked so high?

"Those of you with TBRA will have to explain how that program transitions into Section Eight, but make sure you highlight the benefits of both equally!" Mark insisted. "What these wonderful programs do is break down rent into two payments—yours and the portion paid by the program." He looked thrilled by this statement. You would have thought he was auctioning items, not talking to Section 8 applicants. "Landlords don't like that the Section Eight payment comes on a set day; they want it to come at the first of the month, but you can convince them!" He picked up another pile of papers to hand out. "Section Eight is guaranteed money," he repeated.

There were more hurdles to jump over after you broke through the walls of judgment and convinced a landlord to take you on as a tenant. Though it was supposed to be the landlord's responsibility to get approved for funds from the program, the house or apartment had to meet several safety standards, including working smoke detectors and other safe living conditions, and most of the time that meant if a house or apartment didn't meet the standards, it wouldn't be available for a family with a voucher to rent. Which set us up for a conundrum, since landlords in the nicer neighborhoods didn't want to rent to "Section 8 people." We had to look for housing in places that were run-down and where we risked not passing the move-in inspection.

"Landlords are required to meet Section Eight standards, but a lot of them just don't want to do it," Mark pointed out. "It's their choice. It's not illegal or anything like discrimination—"

"It's totally discrimination," the girl next to me shouted.

I knew her from Waterfront Pizza. We'd smiled at each other. I thought I remembered her name was Amy, but I wasn't sure.

"My boyfriend and I found a great little house," she said, "but my friend ended up getting the place. The landlord said he didn't want to rent to Section Eight people because they'd end up trashing it." She rubbed the base of her pregnant belly. "He said he didn't want to be a slumlord."

Everyone's heads turned to Mark, who just stuffed his hands into his pockets.

Somehow, it took only a week for me to find a place. Not only that, it was available right away and passed the safety inspection. We could move out of transitional housing immediately. The apartment was in a building that faced the fairgrounds, just a few blocks from North Beach. Gertie, my landlady, shrugged when I told her how rent payments would be made. She'd get my portion on the first, I explained, but the other part wouldn't come until the tenth.

"Yeah, I guess that's fine," she said, then smiled at Mia, who tucked her head into my shoulder. "Does she need a crib or anything?"

I wanted to say no. My instinct was always to turn things down when people tried to help us. Someone else would need it more. But then I thought of the hole in the side of Mia's Pack 'n Play.

"Yeah," I said. "She does."

"Oh, good," Gertie said. "The last tenants left some things, and I didn't know what to do with them." She walked around to the back of her truck and took out a white crib like the ones they had at Mia's day care. Inside the crib was a little red shirt. I reached down to pick it up and handed it to Gertie.

"You can have that if you want it, too," she said. "It's a costume or something."

I shook it out with my free hand and saw the hood had a couple of eyes sewn on, and there was a stuffed tail coming off the back. "Is it a lobster?" I said, smiling a little.

Gertie laughed. "I guess that's what it's supposed to be."

Mia didn't have a Halloween costume. It was September, and I hadn't given it any thought yet. My mind had been totally preoccupied with finding us a different home.

Gertie helped me get the crib inside, then left us to it, keys in hand. We had the ground-floor apartment, with a porch that led out to a little strip of grass. Beyond that was a large field. The dining room off the kitchen had wrap-around windows. My brother had built me a computer, and I set it up on the built-in desk off the kitchen counter, then dropped a CD into the disk drive. Mia danced a little, then ran around the table, to the living room, face-planted on the couch, then ran down the hallway before running back to do it all over again.

My books filled up shelves in the living room. I hung a few pictures and artwork my mom had given me—the paintings of snow-covered fields by Alaskan artists that I'd grown up with. I'd just hung up my last painting, a birch tree, when I saw that Jamie was calling. I'd left him a message earlier.

"What do you want?" he said when I answered.

"I, uh, I have a chance to work on Saturday and wondered if you could take Mia for a little longer?"

"How long?" He had her for a few hours on Saturdays and Sundays, except the last weekend of the month.

"It's far out of town," I said. "The job will take forever, so as much as you can do."

Jamie didn't say anything for several seconds. I heard him take in a sharp breath. He must have been smoking a cigarette. I'd asked him to take Mia for longer periods of time a lot lately, in an attempt to get as much work done as I could before the season ended.

"No," he finally said.

"Why? Jamie, this is so I can work."

"I don't want to help you out," he blurted. "You're taking all my money; you don't send her over with diapers. I have to feed her dinner. So no." I kept talking, trying to change his mind.

"NO!" he yelled again. "I'M NOT HELPING YOU WITH SHIT!" And he hung up.

My heart started racing in the irregular, pounding way that it did after these types of conversations with him, the ones that ended in him yelling the way he used to. This time my chest started to get even tighter, making it hard to take in a full breath. My therapist at the domestic violence program, Beatrice, told me to breathe into a paper bag when it happened. I closed my eyes and breathed in through my nose for five counts, exhaling through my mouth for the same amount of time. I tried it two more times before I opened my eyes to see Mia standing in front of me—staring at me. "Whadddssss-dddttt you doing?" she asked me, her voice garbled through clenched teeth that held her binky.

"I'm fine," I said and reached down to pick her up, making my fingers into claws. The tickle monster. I roared, and Mia squealed in delight, running around the kitchen table with me close behind. I caught her at the couch, tickling her so much that the binky fell out of her mouth from laughing. That's when I bent my arms around her, picked her up, and hugged her little body close, feeling her warmth, smelling her skin.

She started squirming. "No, Mama!" She laughed. "Again! Again!"

She ran to her bedroom with me close behind, without anyone yelling at us or hitting the underside of our floor with a broom.

5

Seven Different Kinds of Government Assistance

My hand reached for the hood of my raincoat to pull over my head, but the late-summer rain had started so heavy and fast my hair was already soaked. I walked over to the cobblestoned wall where my partner stood, his face engulfed by his raincoat's hood. "Well, what do we do now?" I shouted, straining for my voice to carry through the pouring rain.

"We go home," said John, my friend Emily's husband, who had hired me to help him with landscaping six months earlier. He gave me a shrug and attempted a half smile, even though his forest green raincoat was still peppered with the hail that had pelted us before the rain started. He took off his glasses, wiping the fog and drops of rain from them before putting them back on.

I drooped my head in defeat. We'd been doing that a lot lately, cutting our jobs short due to rain. The season's end was near, and so was my main source of income.

We loaded the garbage cans, trimmers, and rakes into the back of John's yellow pickup, and he smiled at me again before getting in and driving away. I watched him go, before my eyes returned to my car, parked on the side of the street. The front windows were open. *Shit.*

When I got home, I balanced on one foot in the linoleum square that marked the entryway, struggling to pull off my rubber Xtratuf boots. I unbuttoned my Carhartt pants and pushed them down to my knees so I could step out of them. They were so thick with mud and rain they didn't fall flat to the floor and remained standing in their accordion-like shape. Real Alaskans have a saying that that's when, and only then, a pair of Carhartts are ready to wash: when you've taken them off and they still stand on their own.

Mia was with Jamie that evening until seven, and I wasn't quite sure what to do with my time. A few textbooks sat on my kitchen table, reminding me of the homework that had become part of my daily life. I had begun the painstakingly slow process of earning a degree and had registered for twelve credits: two online classes and one that met in a building close to Mia's day care. When I'd met with the admissions counselor, I'd told her I just wanted to get an associate of arts transfer degree. Most of the classes I'd taken in high school through the Running Start program, which allowed me to take college classes for high school credit, and at the University of Alaska counted toward that. A two-year degree at a community college would be the easiest place to start, and I'd have my core classes completed in the cheapest way possible. Then, I could transfer to a four-year university with some ease. But, like most single parents with not much support, it would take me years to get to that point.

Since I'd already claimed Mia on my taxes, getting a government grant to pay for school was sort of an easy process. Claiming her as a dependent, and having the tax forms to prove it, was the simplest way to show I supported a child with my minimal (nonexistent) wages.

The Pell Grant, a federal program that offers financial aid to low-income students, paid more than my full-time tuition for the quarter, leaving me with $1,300 extra. With $275 a month in child support, and $45 a week from cleaning the preschool, that meant we had about $700 a month to float us through. Food stamp money was a little less than $300, and we still had the WIC checks. Thanks to TBRA and LIHEAP, housing expenses hovered around $150, which left my expenses for car insurance, phone, and Internet. With the winter season, I wasn't working anymore, so the grant for Mia's day care ended. Getting an education, going to class, didn't qualify me for childcare assistance, so I had to find people to watch Mia for a couple of hours twice a week during my French class, which was not only required but met in person. Even though I kind of hated everything about it, most weeks it was the only time I sat in a room with other people.

Many nights I'd make a large cup of coffee after Mia went to sleep and stay up until one or two in the morning to finish homework. Mia didn't take naps, and she hardly stopped talking or moving. She needed my constant attention and care. I couldn't find work to fill the gaps in my schedule, so we went for long walks through the woods and by the ocean shore, like I'd longed to do when I was working, only now I walked with the heaviness of only four hours of sleep and a lot less money. It had been easier when Mia was younger, before she started walking and her protests lasted only as long as it took to bounce her to sleep. Now, her strong-willed nature started to really come through. Mia definitely had an independence to her spirit; so much that she wore me out in a single morning.

But after she'd gone to bed, I stared at my textbooks in the stillness of our kitchen. The tedious task of reading assignments and end-of-chapter discussion questions in front of me only magnified my loneliness. That summer had been a period of constant movement as I focused on getting secure housing. Now that everything was in place, my mind could settle a bit, and the realization that I was taking care of a child all alone creeped into my mind like a thick fog. With so much drama revolving around Mia's time with her dad, and because his visits were only two or three hours at a time, I never felt like I got a break. Mia's energy knew no end. On walks, she insisted on pushing the stroller herself at a snail's pace. At parks, she insisted on me pushing her for what felt like forever on a swing, or me watching her as she went down a slide, over and over and over again. I was almost thirty, and many of my friends were getting married, buying houses, and starting families. They were doing everything the right way. I stopped calling them completely, too embarrassed to admit how bad things had gotten. If I had stopped to add it up, the Pell Grant, SNAP, TBRA, LIHEAP, WIC, Medicaid, and childcare would total seven different programs I'd applied for. I needed seven different kinds of government assistance to survive. My world was quiet amid the constant chaos of a toddler, of shuffling, of stress.

For the first time, my birthday came that month without anyone in my family noticing. Jamie must have felt sorry for me and agreed to take Mia and me out to paint our own ceramic mugs. Over dinner at the Olive Garden, I watched him hold Mia in his lap while she shoved handfuls of pasta in her mouth.

When we pulled up to my apartment, I sat there for a few moments before opening the door.

"Will you come in?" I asked.

"Why?" he asked, tapping the steering wheel.

I fought back tears for wanting, needing his company. "Maybe you could put Mia to bed?"

He pursed his lips in frustration but reached for the keys to turn off the car. I watched him, then looked back at Mia with a smile. Jamie and Mia were the only family I had.

I wanted Jamie to stay the night, even if it was to sleep on the couch.

On a normal day, every time I thought about going to bed alone, it felt like there was a monster in my chest clawing at me from the inside. I'd curl up as much as possible, and sometimes I hugged my pillow tight, but nothing soothed the deep pit that echoed inside. I desperately wanted it out, but every night it was persistent; it remained there. Now on my birthday, my first birthday in years without someone to snuggle me to sleep, I fought that feeling.

"Maybe you could stay?" I mumbled, looking at the floor instead of Jamie.

"No," he said, almost laughing. He walked out the door without saying goodbye or happy birthday. I regretted asking.

I sat on the floor and called my dad. It was almost ten p.m., but I knew he'd still be up, watching *Countdown with Keith Olbermann* on MSNBC with his wife, Charlotte, like they did almost every night. I'd liked that about living with them. After Jamie kicked us out, I stayed at their place for a few weeks when I had nowhere else to go.

"Hey, Dad," I said and paused. I didn't know what to say; I needed him but could never say it. The secret language of my family was that no one ever spoke.

"Hi, Steph," he answered, sounding a little surprised. I never called anymore. We hadn't seen each other or talked since Mia's birthday party three months earlier, even though he lived a few hours away. "What's up?"

I took a breath in. "It's my birthday." My voice quavered a little.

"Oh, Steph," he said, releasing a deep sigh.

We were both quiet. I couldn't hear the TV in the background and pictured their dark living room, lit by the paused image on the screen. Maybe Charlotte had gone out for a cigarette. I wondered if they still didn't drink wine on weekdays.

In the beginning, just after I left Jamie and took refuge with my dad, he watched me sit at his kitchen table late into the night, surrounded by piles of paperwork and court documents. I imagined that Dad was trying to make sense of what was happening in my life. All he knew was that I had no money, no home, and Mia was only seven months old. He had no idea how to make it better. He could feed me but couldn't really afford to. The housing crash had already impacted his occupation as an electrician. It was 2008, and developers struggled with not having anyone to develop anything for. I'd tried to ease the burden of having us there by purchasing food for everyone with my food stamps. I made dinner or breakfast and tried to clean the house during the day—but I knew it wasn't enough. I was asking a lot of Dad and Charlotte, who were already working hard to make ends meet. They'd moved to the property four or five years ago and had planned to live in a mobile home while they built their dream house. Then their property value dropped drastically; their plans vanished. Charlotte worked from home as a medical coder for insurance companies, something for which she'd had to go back to school to get a special certificate. Dad had been an electrician since he graduated high school.

Charlotte had purchased the trailer after her divorce, where she was left to raise her son alone on a modest salary. Dad, in his best effort to make it a home, built a large porch off the back, where they had about a dozen different bird feeders. Mia loved watching from the living room window as the blue jays swooped in to grab peanuts, flapping her arms and squealing with delight. Dad laughed whenever she did. "She looks exactly like you did when you were that age," he'd say with a sort of awe.

One night, Dad came home late, his arms draped with bags of groceries. After putting Mia to bed, I sat in the living room with Charlotte, watching TV. Dad slipped outside to the hot tub with a bottle of wine. Over the noise of the TV, Charlotte and I began to hear what sounded like sobbing. A grown man sobbing. I'd never heard anything like it. Charlotte kept going out to the porch to check on him.

"Stop it!" I heard her finally yell. "You're scaring your daughter!"

I'd never seen or heard my dad cry, yet, as a child would, I assumed it was my fault. I'd burdened him by asking for help at a time when he couldn't afford it. Earlier that week, he'd told me that I needed to move out. When I told Charlotte, she'd reassured me I could stay as long as I needed. I wondered how much they argued about me.

Dad's breakdown felt ominous in that we'd have to live somewhere else. As much as I tried to feel compassion for him, the thought of Mia and me living in a place where I'd have to pay rent was so impossible without me being employed, I couldn't even imagine what it looked like. I hadn't had any time to recover from the shock of being homeless with a baby. Charlotte was right. He was scaring me, but probably not in the way she thought.

When Charlotte came back inside for the third time, she returned to her seat on the couch, and we didn't say anything to each other. She unmuted the TV and we continued watching *Countdown with Keith Olbermann*. I couldn't turn my head to look at her but I tried to remain still. Calm.

Finally, I stood up to go to bed. My uncle had brought over a short camper trailer and parked it in the driveway. Mia and I had made a temporary home there. The roof leaked over the door, and we couldn't use the teeny kitchen or bathroom, but it had an electric heater and a space for us to sleep.

"You goin' to bed, Steph?" Charlotte asked in an attempt to act like it was a normal night.

"Yeah, I'm pretty tired," I lied. I paused at the door and looked at her. "Thank you so much for letting us stay here."

Charlotte smiled, like she always did, and said, "You can stay as long as you want," but now we both seemed to know that was no longer true.

When I peeked my head inside the door of the trailer, I saw Mia sleeping soundly on the fold-out sofa bed. I crawled under our blanket, teetering on the outer edge beside her. I wasn't tired, I just wanted to lie there and listen to her night-time noises, to forget everything else in our new world. I turned over to my back, then to my side, but I couldn't get the sound of my dad's sobbing out of my head. Maybe I could rent a lot in an RV campground for a while and park the trailer there. Or maybe we could move it back behind my grandpa's house in Anacortes, but I couldn't imagine living so close to Grandma, who I'd heard had taken to feeding fifty feral cats.

An hour later, through the thin walls of the trailer, I heard doors slamming at the main house. Dad and Charlotte were having a fight, and I heard a series of crashes and thuds. Then silence.

I slipped into the house to see what had happened. In the kitchen, magnets from the fridge were scattered on the floor. The table had been moved out of place. There was an un-easy stillness. And then I heard them on the back porch. My dad was still crying but now apologizing to Charlotte over and over again.

When Mia and I went in the next morning for breakfast, Dad had already left for work. Charlotte sat at the kitchen table, still in its off-centered place. I sat down, then instinc-tively reached for her hand. She looked up at me, her eyes puffy and dull.

"He's never done anything like that before," she said, her gaze locked on the opposite wall. Then suddenly, her eyes met mine. "He's such a teddy bear."

The events of the previous night began spilling out: how she had told Dad that she was leaving for her sister's and started packing a suitcase, how she'd even said that she was taking the dog. I looked at her in admiration, wishing I'd had the strength to leave when Jamie's outbursts started once I was pregnant. To be as strong.

"That was my mistake," Charlotte told me, looking down at Jack, curled up on the floor by her feet. "That's where

I went wrong." She put her coffee cup down on the table and carefully rolled up her sleeve, exposing deep purple bruises.

I looked down at Mia, who was playing happily next to the dog on the kitchen floor, patting his back, saying, "Dog, dog" with each one. Her hair was mussed from sleep, and she still wore her footie pajamas.

I closed my eyes. I had to leave.

That day I started calling homeless shelters. A shelter would, at the very least, be a roof over our heads for a certain length of time, and at best it would allow my daughter and me to live without fear of someone's violence. By the time Dad called from work to tell me to leave, I'd already packed our car to move.

When I tried to confide in my aunt and brother about the bruises Charlotte had shown me, Dad had already talked to them and told them I'd made it up for attention, that I'd made up everything that'd happened with Jamie for attention, too.

"I'm sorry, Steph," Dad repeated over the phone on the night of my birthday. He started to say that he'd been busy at work, but I stopped listening, regretting that I'd called.

He tried to make up for my forgotten birthday. A week later, I got a card in the mail with a check for $100. I stared at it, knowing it was a lot of money for him to just give away. Unable to fight my anger toward him for kicking us out, I decided to do something reckless with the money. Instead of saving it to put toward a bill or necessary toiletries, Mia and I went out to lunch at the new Thai place in town, the one that had little bowls of rice sweetened with coconut milk and mangoes for dessert. Mia got rice so embedded in the strands of her fine baby curls that she needed a bath. I put her down for a nap afterward, sat in front of the computer at my desk area in the kitchen, and then decided to do something solely for myself.

Match.com's website had been open on my browser for several days. I'd already filled out the profile, uploaded pictures, and looked around at the profiles of men my age. My parents had both found their current significant others on there, and so had my aunt. While I wasn't totally sure I would find that, one thing was certainly lacking in my life: a social outlet. Most of my friendships had faded over the past year because I'd isolated myself and hidden from the embarrassment of my daily life. In the hours at night, long after Mia had gone to sleep, when I sat still for the first time all day, I longed for company, even if it was just someone to email or talk with on the phone. Not my friends who knew about all the drama that surrounded my circumstances; I was tired of hearing myself talk about that. I wanted to flirt, to escape into the person I'd been before all of this, to that tattooed girl with her chin-length brown hair under a kerchief, who'd danced to bands with a sweatshirt tied around her waist. I wanted to make new friends.

It seemed entirely too desperate to be on a dating site in my situation, but I didn't care. I talked to men as far away as Salt Lake City, Utah, and Winthrop, Washington. I preferred men who lived a good distance from me, because there wasn't any risk of me developing feelings for them. There was no way for me to travel to see them or for them to come stay with me, since Mia saw her dad only for short visits. All of that felt like too much work, anyway. I really just needed to laugh and remind myself of the person I was before motherhood and poverty had taken over every aspect of my personality. I'd completely lost that person, the one who'd been so free to come and go, meet friends or not, work three jobs to save up and travel. I needed to know that person was still there.

If I'd been honest with myself, I would have admitted to looking for a partner or that I secretly hoped to find one. My insecurities, or possibly my rational, realistic side, knew there was a very slim chance of that happening. I was on government assistance, having regular anxiety attacks, still unable to process much of the emotional abuse I'd just experienced or know the depth to which it had affected me. My life was at some sort of standstill in its new identity; in being consumed with motherhood, which I wasn't sure I really even liked. I mean, who in their right mind would want to take a person like *that* on?

After only a month on the site, to my utter dismay, one did travel to see me. He lived close by, in a town called Stanwood, one I'd driven through several times on the hunt for a place to live that was anywhere but Port Townsend. Stanwood was a tiny farming community just south of Skagit County, where all of my family lived. It was close but not too close, and next to Camano Island, with countless, mostly untouched hidden beaches. This man not only had location going for him, but his emails read like John Steinbeck had written them when he talked about living on the property his great-grandfather had built a house on, and eventually shot himself in.

Travis spoke of the farm he lived on with a surprising amount of admiration, considering he'd moved from it once for a short period of time. He said he had pictures of himself as a baby, bathing in the sink he now stood next to at night to brush his teeth. His parents, who'd bought the farm from his grandfather, still lived and worked on the property, running the horse-boarding operation completely on their own. Travis's mom did the bookkeeping between caring for her five grandchildren during the weekdays. That, more than the promise of riding horses whenever I wanted, drew me to him enough that I accepted his offer to buy me dinner.

He had to ask his dad to feed and water the horses for him that night and was more than willing to travel to Port Townsend. When I met him at the ferry terminal, he had a wide-eyed look to him.

"I've never been on that boat before," he said, a little breathless. "I didn't even know this town was here." He laughed nervously, and I suggested that we walk down to Sirens. It was only four o'clock in the afternoon, so there wouldn't be anyone in there. I knew if someone saw me eating out with a strange, unfamiliar-looking guy, it would get reported back to Jamie. A couple of months earlier, after a long day of landscaping, I'd gone downtown for a much-needed minute to sit alone with a beer. Someone there tipped Jamie off, and he accused me of being tipsy when I picked up Mia. I tried to stay out of bars completely after that.

We found a table inside and both ordered burgers and beers. I glanced at the table on the deck where I'd sat with Mom and William six months earlier, the last time I'd been inside that building. I didn't get the impression that Travis went out to eat very often, either, judging from how he fumbled over ordering. I assumed he was nervous, too intrigued by him to care.

"So, what is it you do, exactly?" I asked, even though he'd told me through email and over the phone.

"I clean stalls in the morning, feed at night, and fix anything that needs it during the day." Travis didn't seem to mind my interest and constant questions, and he laughed easily when one of us tried to be funny. "But hay season, that's when you work all the time."

I nodded like I understood. "So you guys grow your own hay to feed the horses people board there? How many horses do you have?"

"My parents have a couple in their barn, plus a few others they keep in there for friends." He took a large bite of his burger, and I waited for him to continue. He'd worn what seemed to be his work clothes—blue jeans with holes and grease stains on them, brown leather boots, and a hooded sweatshirt over a faded t-shirt. My outfit sort of matched his, only I'd worn the nice pair of Lucky brand jeans I'd bought over the summer at a consignment store. "Then Susan, the woman who rents out one of the arenas, has her barn where she gives lessons. The main barn holds about 120 horses, but we only have half that now. People who boarded with us lost all their money and can't pay for horses anymore. Can't even pay for someone to take them."

I'd never thought of a horse being such a large expense, but I knew they were a lot of work. When I was really young and we lived close to my grandparents, I'd spent many summer days at the property down the long dirt road where my dad had grown up. My grandpa had been a logger before he retired and took lines of packhorses into the woods. He'd put me on a horse at Mia's age. I could ride bareback better than I could run on my own legs. My head filled with visions of Mia doing the same.

It was starting to get dark when I walked Travis back to the ferry terminal. We hugged goodbye, and I caught myself wanting to bury my face in his chest and not let go. He smelled like horses, hay, grease, and sawdust. He smelled like work, which my mind translated to stability. The combining scents brought up an amount of nostalgia that overwhelmed me. Working on cars, riding horses with Grandpa, handing nails to my dad as a kid. Travis's embrace reminded me of all of those moments, comforted me, and somehow brought me home.

6

The Farm

I closed my single-blade Gerber knife and put it back in the pocket of my Carhartts. The fall air was moist on my face as Travis and I worked to throw dozens of seventy-pound hay bales into a grinder, which chopped it to half-inch pieces so we could mix it with the wood chips for horse bedding. I wiped the dark yellow dust off my forehead before returning my fingers to the work glove I'd shoved in my armpit. I paused to take a breath, then yanked the red twine toward me. If I cut the twine holding the hay bale together in front of the knot, I could pull it out smoothly, and the entire bale wouldn't move, making it easier to pick off the flakes to throw into the grinder. Cutting the twine behind the knot made it snag, stubbornly catch, sending the flakes tumbling to the ground in a heap, slowing us down.

"You're not doing it right!" Travis yelled again as the bale's flakes piled at my feet.

"Sorry!" I yelled back, trying to sound sincere. I did this over and over, through a mountain of bales, turning them into an even larger mountain of finely cut, dry grass.

We moved to Stanwood to live with Travis just four months after our first date, when Mia was nearly two. It had been a rough nine months since then. Travis worked extremely hard on the farm and outside of the house. Inside, he barely looked away from the TV. Our relationship provided stability; a home. But perhaps more important, it provided me with an invisible stamp of approval. With Travis, I was part of a family unit. I was complete. But I didn't anticipate the loss of my independence, not realizing how much that had given my identity as a mother value. In Travis's eyes, my value relied on the work I did outside of the home on the farm, since the work I did inside—the cleaning and cooking—had no value to him. But I couldn't find a job, so my worth amounted to the work I did to help him. The problem was, I had only the small amount Jamie paid in child support and food stamps to use in caring for Mia. I'd watch Travis get paid for the work I did a decent part of and not get a share.

In the beginning, it was fun to go out every evening to feed and water the fifty or so horses that clients boarded there. When the weekend stall-cleaners quit, Travis volunteered to take over and earned an extra $100 a week in addition to the $100 his parents paid him for feeding. During the weekends Mia was with her dad, I got up at seven a.m. to go out and help muck stalls in addition to the feedings every evening, and I watched Travis pocket the wad of cash his parents gave him for the work, not offering me any.

"Travis," I said the second time it happened. "Shouldn't I get some of that? I helped."

"What do you need money for?" he snapped. "You don't pay any bills."

I stifled tears from the built-up humiliation and managed to squeak out that my car needed gas.

"Here," he said, flipping through bills and handing me a twenty.

We started fighting. Every time I refused to help feed. Every time dinner wasn't on the table. Every time I opted to sleep in, knowing I'd get the silent treatment as punishment. I desperately applied for almost every job vacancy posted on Craigslist or in the local newspaper, submitting anywhere from a few to a dozen applications a week, but I rarely got a call back. Then a friend gave my number to a woman needing a new employee for her cleaning business, and I was hired on the spot. The job felt promising. I would be paid $10 an hour, and Jenny, the owner of the company, hoped to have twenty hours of work for me each week: $200 a week of my very own money. And I could maybe even quit working on the farm.

"It's a great job. All of the houses they clean are in Stanwood," I told Travis as he climbed down from the tractor. "I don't think they even have a training period. I just go to work and get paid under the table." I tried to smile sweetly, even though we hadn't said more than a few words to each other in days. "It all feels kind of meant to be." Mia, now almost two and a half, was incredibly happy living with Travis. If I were honest with myself, I was, too, but mostly because in being with him, a shroud of stigmas from being a single mom fell off of me.

"What?" Travis asked, looking annoyed and like he'd heard only half of what I'd said. He had on the same outfit that he'd worn when we first met. I tried to remember what it had felt like to hug him that first time. A year ago, I'd felt safe, comforted in his arms. Now they were too full of resentment to embrace me.

"If I work part-time in the mornings," I reasoned, following him as he connected the trailer to the hitch on the back of the tractor, "then Mia could stay in day care for the rest of the day, and I'd be able to help on the farm?" I'd convinced myself that working on the farm was like working off my share of the rent and bills. It was the asking for gas money that I couldn't handle.

He looked at me without expression.

"I'll work hard. I'll clean stalls," I said, ignoring my lack of dignity in almost begging. "I'll feed and water horses. I'll try my hardest to cook dinner, even though I hate it."

"I don't care about dinner as long as you work on the farm," he said. Then he sighed.

I waited.

"Help me grind up these loads of hay," he said, climbing back into the tractor.

"So you think the job's okay?" I yelled at him over the tractor's engine. He glanced at me roughly but didn't respond. My only choice was to sulk behind, following the trailer piled with bales of hay to the barn.

It was early winter of 2009, during the recession, when people couldn't afford horses for recreation or for anything else. Travis and his parents' boarding operation was at an all-time low, while the cost of alfalfa and wood chips they used for bedding had increased. Most of their equipment was ancient and failing. His parents had wearied of keeping the business afloat and relied on Travis to run the bulk of it. He worked around the clock during hay season, spending up to twelve hours a day on the tractor, and in the cold months, he tended to repairs and frozen pipes while mucking out anywhere from forty to eighty horse stalls every morning.

I looked up through the hay dust floating in the air, surprised to see Travis smiling at me. We were about halfway through grinding the second load. Hay covered the top of his red baseball cap and the shoulders of his hooded sweatshirt. When he reached out a gloved hand to rustle my hair, I ducked and then threw a handful of twine at him. Travis laughed, his blue eyes lighting up his entire face.

Jenny's cleaning company seemed pretty well organized, from what I could tell. She rotated a lot of clients in a datebook she carried like a purse. My first day on the job, she gave me a cleaning kit and a roll of paper towels. I met her and a few other women outside a client's large brown house that looked over the valley. Jenny barely introduced me by name, instead saying, "She's the new girl," and the women nodded without stopping to shake hands or make eye contact as they unloaded their trays from the back of their cars. The client who answered the door was an older woman, with white hair in curlers, who smiled like we were dinner guests. Everyone walked inside to designated areas of the house, and I stood there, waiting for some kind of instruction.

"Just clean the master bathroom and the bedroom if you have time," one of my coworkers, the oldest one, said. Tracy, I thought her name was. She pointed to a room with a large, overstuffed pink chair next to the bed and left me standing there before I could ask any questions.

When I was about halfway done, Jenny came and checked my work, for a second her face showing no expression; then she smiled and said, "Looks great!" and disappeared again. Everyone was packing up when I walked outside, and Jenny said, "Just follow us to the next one." For my entire first week, it was the same. A whole team of us descended on a house for an hour, each of us spreading to different corners and rooms, working our way back to the front entrance. Then we'd get back in our little convoy of old cars and move on to the next.

In the center of it all was Jenny, her strawberry-blond hair pulled tightly into a ponytail. She carried herself like she'd been popular in high school and expected people to still appease her. When she instructed me on how to clean a room, whether it was a bed or bath, she'd smile and say, "Just make it shine!" I sprayed cleaning liquid and wiped it with paper towels, dusted with fluorescent-colored feathers, and sprayed rooms with air freshener as I left.

Every girl seemed to have a different preference for the part of the job they enjoyed doing most. Some liked cleaning kitchens; others seemed to prefer the vacuuming in living rooms and bedrooms. No one liked cleaning the bathrooms. That job went to the new girl.

A bathroom could seem clean or pretty, draped with pink toilet seats, rugs, and towels to match a shower curtain covered in roses, but that didn't mean the toilet wasn't horrific. At first, it was the stray pubic hairs that most disgusted me. But their quantity eventually dulled my shock. I figured out how to dump the small trash bags while avoiding—even with gloved hands—the tampons, condoms, tissues full of snot, and wads of hair. People left bottles of prescription medications all over the counters, by the toothpaste, or next to a glass. I was there to clean, obviously, but I kept expecting people to be a little tidier or to clean up their clutter. I spent at least five minutes picking up various objects, wiping them off, wiping underneath them, and putting them back in a neat way.

After that first week of following the group around, I eventually got paired with a woman with brown, shoulder-length, wavy hair about ten years older than me whom everyone complained about under their breath so Jenny couldn't hear. Angela had yellowed teeth and fingernails from smoking, and I hadn't been properly introduced to her until Jenny told me we'd go to the next house on our own.

"Angela knows the house," Jenny said. "She'll tell you where to go. Then you can drop her off and pick her up in the morning. Angie, I'll text you tonight and tell you what houses you're doing tomorrow, okay, girl?" Jenny waved and got into her car with two of the other women, and that seemed to be the end of my training period.

At the house, Angela chatted with the clients, a middle-aged couple dressed in ironed khakis, while I cleaned the kitchen and bathrooms. It didn't seem like she was actually working until I heard her running the vacuum for a bit before I came out from the master bathroom to join her.

"You done?" she asked, turning off the vacuum and smiling.

After Jenny had paired me with Angela, another coworker waited for her to leave and whispered that I should keep an eye on her when we cleaned. "She steals sponges and paper

towels from the houses," she whispered, items we were supposed to supply ourselves with our own money. Sometimes
after we finished a house, Angela would grab snacks out of
the cupboards and jump into the car with a half-empty bag
of chips or a sleeve of saltines. I'd watch her tear into them,
knowing she didn't have them before we went in.

"Do you want some?" she asked, pointing the bag toward
me, so oblivious to my contemptuous glare I wanted to
scream.

"No," I said, waiting for the two other cleaners we'd
teamed up with that day to pull out of the driveway behind
me. Tracy, the driver, whose short black hair had an inch of
gray roots, stopped to light up a cigarette.

"Hey, can I smoke in here?" Angela asked me for the third
or fourth time, like Mia did when she knew I was tired and
might give in.

"No," I said bluntly.

"Then I'm gonna see if I can ride with Tracy," she said,
opening the door, rushing to the car behind me as it started
to back out.

I never mentioned Angela's behavior to Jenny. I kept my
head down and didn't complain, humbled and grateful to have
found a job. But I also needed more hours. Jenny spoke about
her employees in a caring way, and I got the feeling that Angela had been cleaning with her for a long time, possibly the
longest of any of us. I wondered what the story was, why Angela had fallen to the place she had. I wondered that about all
of my coworkers. What had happened to bring them here, to
this place of cleaning toilets for so little money?

"She used to be one of my best employees," Jenny told me
once on a rare occasion that it was just the two of us driving
to the next job. Her voice softened. "She's going through a
hard time. I feel for her."

"Yeah," I said. "I can see that." But I most certainly did
not. In the houses Angela and I cleaned together, she'd mosey

around, looking through magazines and cupboards, while I'd go at almost double speed. After a while, my fingers began to crack along the sides. I reeked of ammonia, bleach, and that powdered shit we sprinkled on the carpet before vacuuming.

The winter weather hung with a dampness that filled my lungs. A few weeks into the job, I came down with a horrible chest cold; I tried my best to hide it with cough drops and cold medicine, but it kept getting worse. One morning, as Angela and I turned down a gravel driveway to a navy-blue house neatly nestled in the woods, I had a horrible coughing fit. It was so bad it felt like I couldn't catch my breath.

"Oooh," Angela said with a morbid sort of interest. "You're sick, too?" I tried to take in a deep breath, but I might as well have been doing it through a wet washcloth. I looked at her, annoyed, obviously sick. "Maybe we should call Jenny," she said. "These people inside are old. I don't think we should clean their house." Angela pulled out her phone and started looking for Jenny's number.

She turned her back to me and walked a few paces away. Before I could stop her, she'd already dialed. I waved my hands at her and shook my head and mouthed, "*No*," but she continued to talk to Jenny.

"Stephanie's really sick," Angela said in a lowered, raspy voice, similar to what a kid does to get out of school. "And I think I might have caught it, too." She held the phone to her shoulder and pulled a pack of cigarettes out of her pocket, frowning when she saw it was empty, and threw it into her cleaning supply tray.

I didn't want to lose a day's pay or call in sick as a new hire. I needed this job and didn't want Jenny to think I was a slacker. Angela ignored me as I got out of the car and stubbornly started to unload my supplies. "Thursday afternoon would work great for me," Angela said, looking at me with a huge smile, giving me a thumbs-up, happy to have the rest of the day off. "Great," she said into the phone, still smiling, forgetting to change her voice so she sounded sick. "Okay, we'll talk to you then."

"I told you not to do that," I said when she came over to join me at the back of the car. My head started pounding. I'd explain this to Travis, knowing he'd be upset to find me home early. But I felt the sting of a lesser paycheck even more. "I can't miss work. Do you not understand that?"

"It's okay, girl," she said, lifting her near-empty tray of supplies back into my car. "There will be more work tomorrow."

We drove the rest of the way to her house without speaking, and I reached over to turn up the radio to keep it that way. Angela moved her head to the music, drumming the tops of her legs a little. I couldn't believe she wasn't stressed about missing out on those wages. There were questions I wanted to ask her about her kids and living situation, to get a better picture of what it was like for her, since I'd also walked the path of being a single mom, homeless, and in poverty. It was part of the reason I was with Travis, though I'd never admit it to anyone. Angela's house, which turned out to be right around the corner from ours, had been condemned, and though she'd been evicted, she refused to leave. She lived without running water or electricity.

But my compassion or curiosity had faded in losing twenty bucks in wages that day. When I stopped in front of Angela's house, I kept my head down, trying not to stare at the several notices taped to the door, deeming it uninhabitable.

She paused before getting out. "Can you lend me money for a pack of smokes?"

"That's an hour's pay," I said, wincing a little, knowing she'd try to pressure me to give it to her anyway.

She nodded instead, possibly understanding how upset I was. Maybe even understanding I didn't really have all that much money, either.

I waited for her to grab her tray of cleaning supplies and tried to not look over toward her house. I didn't want her to feel embarrassed, remembering what it was like when I lived at the shelter just the previous year. Some of the other cleaners whispered that she'd lost custody of her kids by that point. I didn't know for sure, but they weren't around much anymore when I dropped her off.

"I'm good," she yelled over to me after closing the trunk door. I nodded, trying not to wonder what the rest of her day might be like. I just hoped she'd be ready when I came to pick her up the next morning.

When we returned to clean the old couple's house later that week, I saw two people who'd built a life together, surrounded by photos of family, who were now ending their time with each other. The husband laughed and joked with Angela while I watched him pick up his wife's cereal bowl, fetching her favorite blanket before she could sit down on the couch, and ached at the image of one of them being gone. It was hard not to be struck by the role I'd taken on in my clients' lives.

I became a witness. Even odder was my invisibility and anonymity, though I spent several hours a month in their homes. My job was to wipe away dust and dirt and make lines in carpets, to remain invisible. I almost felt like I had the opportunity to get to know my clients better than any of their relatives did. I'd learn what they ate for breakfast, what shows they watched, if they'd been sick and for how long. I'd see them, even if they weren't home, by the imprints left in their beds and tissues on the nightstand. I'd know them in a way few people did, or maybe ever would.

7

The Last Job on Earth

After a month, Jenny's promise of more work hadn't come through. It didn't seem as though she really liked me, for whatever reason. Maybe I wasn't chatty enough, didn't care enough about who went out on a date with whom. Maybe my grumpiness over the irregular work schedule, which made it impossible to budget and plan childcare, showed too much, or maybe I was just too grumpy in general.

Still, I took as many jobs from Jenny as possible, putting up with her poor management skills. Angela had become so unreliable, Jenny started to text me jobs in the evenings instead. I craved a normal work schedule, especially as Jenny's original projection of twenty hours a week had turned into ten or fewer, depending on whether Angela showed up to work. But that never seemed to be addressed. I couldn't complain about sitting outside Angela's house for fifteen minutes in the morning, waiting for her to get dressed, making us late to our house. Jenny took complaints as not being a team player. When Angela boasted about how happy she was to get paid under the table so she could get more government money, the knuckles of my hands, already firm on the steering wheel, turned white. Her level of comfort with that bothered me. It started to feel as if we were supposed to take care of each other, but I was more concerned about caring for Mia and what was ahead.

Meanwhile, Travis treated my new job like it was a book club, something that kept me from doing the important work at home on the farm. I struggled to keep up with caring for Mia while keeping the house clean, and I grew angry whenever Travis looked at me expectantly to feed the horses. The more tumultuous my life at home grew as "the farmer's wife," the more uncertain and the more insecure I became over whether or not our time in Travis's house would last. My ability to work, to earn money, was my only safety net in case the floor dropped out from under us again. And Jenny wasn't offering enough to support us, not by a long shot.

Classic Clean, a licensed and bonded cleaning company, almost always had an ad in the local classifieds. "Cleaners Wanted!" it read in bold type. I had always planned to inquire if Jenny's jobs didn't work out. Now the time had come.

"Hi. Stephanie, right?" the woman who answered the door said. "Did you find the place okay? I know it can be kind of confusing with all the buildings."

I tried to smile warmly, even though I'd just argued to the point of tears with Travis about the mud he'd tracked all over the kitchen. "Your directions were perfect," I said, and the woman looked pleased.

"I'm Lonnie," she said, extending her hand. "The human resources manager at Classic Clean."

I reached out to shake her hand, then handed her my résumé. Lonnie looked surprised, like she didn't see too many of those.

"Oh, well, look at you," she said, seemingly pleased. It was like the last job on earth. Any money I could make kept me out of ever needing to call a list of homeless shelters again. It unnerved me and made me angry with myself that I'd found us in that position. A regular schedule and a real job would be my ticket to independence, and ultimately our survival. Our future depended on my getting it.

Lonnie nodded to a table in the back of the rectangular office area, built into one of two large outbuildings. She had told me on the phone that the business operated from an office, on Pam's, the owner's, property. "Why don't you take a seat and start filling out our application. We need you to agree to a criminal background check, too, okay?"

I nodded and did what I was told. After a while, Lonnie came to sit down next to me. "You can probably tell by the accent that I'm from Jersey," she started. It was true. She sounded like Danny DeVito's kid sister. Lonnie was short and squat, with curly black hair shaped in a fluffed-up mullet—the kind of person you wanted to be on the good side of. She was direct and businesslike, spoke fast, and she'd pause to give me time to process what she said, raising her eyebrows to hear my "okay" before she continued.

"This is our schedule," Lonnie said, referring to a bulletin board behind her desk so large she needed a step stool to reach the top. "Each client's name goes on the laminated label, and they rotate through A, B, C, and D weeks. As you can see by the arrow here, we're on C week currently. Some clients are monthly, some weekly, but most are biweekly, so twice a month. Each cleaner gets a colored dot assigned to them, so we know what cleaner has who." She stopped to look at me. I stood next to her with my hands clasped in front of me. "You get what I'm sayin'?" she asked, and I nodded. "So, if your background check goes through, not sayin' I don't think it will, but you know sometimes you'd be surprised what we find." She stopped to chuckle to herself. "But anyway, so after that goes through, then we'll have you come in and get your tray and vacuum and some shirts. What are you, a small or a medium? You probably don't want a small. It's good to have some room to breathe. I think we have some mediums. Anyway, do you have any questions?"

I had a lot, but everything I wanted to know about how much I'd make or how many hours I'd work or if they offered health insurance or sick leave seemed unimportant. All that mattered was that the person I was going to replace was a yellow dot, which meant all the yellow dots on that board were now me, which meant I'd work every other Wednesday and Thursday and Friday and once a month on Monday.

Lonnie pointed to a poster on the wall that read "$8.55 an hour," which was Washington State's current minimum wage. "We gotta start you there while you're training," she said. "But it goes up to nine after that." That would be $18,720 dollars a year if I eventually worked full-time, which wasn't possible to achieve. The company's policy prevented working more than six hours a day. Any more than that and employees would risk injury from fatigue, she said. I would also not be paid for travel time. Jenny had factored in the hours I spent driving from one house to the next in my pay, giving me a buck or two extra per day. With the new job, I'd spend sometimes as much as two unpaid hours a day driving from job to job, then have to wash the rags I'd used for work at home with my own laundry detergent, along with the black Classic Clean t-shirts with a tiny red bird embroidered next to the company name.

Lonnie didn't seem to mind my standing there, studying the calendar, while she continued to explain their system. Many houses were two- or three-hour cleans. A few took four hours. Some took six. Each house I'd be assigned to came with a printed sheet, detailing each room and the instructions for cleaning it and how long that should take. She pulled one out to show me. Most rooms had added notes to warn cleaners of loose tiles, to dust in places often missed, and where clean bed linens were if the client forgot to set them out. Everything not only expected of me but also what I needed to expect was meticulously detailed in black-and-white. There'd be no late-evening conversations, planning through text. If I wanted, I could plan ahead and know that three months from now on the second Wednesday of the month I'd be changing sheets at one house before driving three miles to the next. It hadn't struck me how much I'd needed this sort of stability, this dependability; I almost hugged Lonnie. I had to hide the tears welling in my eyes.

Lonnie called me the next day. I'd just finished cleaning a house with Angela and sat in my car impatiently while she finished inside, trying to ignore a real possibility she was taking something that wasn't hers.

"You checked out," Lonnie said. "I knew ya would, but we have to check these things."

"Oh, I know," I said, wishing I could tell her how happy it made me to see them doing that.

"Are you available to come in this afternoon to get some things?" she asked. "Pam the owner's not around, but I can get you all set up and ready to go. Then maybe we can head over to my place—it's just down the street from here—and I can train you a little by cleaning my bathroom and dusting around a bit."

I tried to absorb what she said. So that meant I was hired. And I'd start working that afternoon. I had a job; a real job with paystubs and a regular schedule. "Yes! That sounds great!" I said, suddenly breathless, almost yelling. Lonnie laughed and told me to swing by the office after noon.

Growing up, I spent Saturday mornings deep-cleaning the house. Mom wouldn't change out of her bathrobe until it was done. I'd wake up to the smells of pancakes and bacon or sausage wafting into my bedroom, George Winston's piano music playing. After breakfast, we'd all get to our various predetermined and reluctantly agreed-upon duties. Mine was bathrooms. For a while it had been the only one I shared with my brother, but my skill was so great and Mom praised me enough that I wanted to do the master bathroom, too. Mom would brag to her friends about how well I could clean a bathtub, so much that my chest filled with air as I stood a little taller.

Appearances had always been important to my mother. "You'll just get it dirty," she said to any clothes I wanted that were white. I wasn't allowed to paint my nails when I was little because she said whenever she saw girls with chipped nail polish it looked trashy. One Saturday night that I spent at my grandparents' around age five or six, I watched Grandma paint her toenails and fingernails a deep pink before she carefully painted mine, even though I told her it would make Mom mad. At church the next morning, whenever we had to fold our hands in prayer, I laced my fingers on the inside of my hands to hide them.

Classic Clean's approach to their clients' houses was much different than Jenny's. I'd instead become a nameless ghost, appearing either at nine a.m. or before one p.m., depending on the clients' schedule and whether or not they wanted to be home, but not after. It was rare that I'd ever work after three-thirty. "You know, Mom hours," Lonnie had said. "When the kids are in school." I had to clean the house in a specific way, the exact manner and amount of time as the person before me, to prevent any differences between cleaners being noticed. I had to be diligent and have a sharp eye. Kitchen stovetops had to be impeccably polished, pillows fluffed each visit, and toilet paper folded into a little triangle the exact same way every time.

My initial training test was to clean the kitchen and master bathrooms in Lonnie's and Pam's homes, which I had absolutely no worries about acing. They both had pretty nice places, two-story houses in the woods. Not huge by any means, but not small, either. I followed Lonnie's Kia Sportage to her place with my freshly stocked cleaning supplies, which had been meticulously inventoried and logged in my employee file. Two spray bottles, one container of powdered Comet, two sponges, one pair of yellow gloves, fifty white rags, two dusters, one Oreck vacuum, two mop handles, and so on. Lonnie instructed me to only use the products given to me and to return to the office for refills when I needed them. We'd chatted a little while she found all the items I needed to get started, and I mentioned needing to drop Mia off later that day to visit her dad for the weekend.

"Oh, yeah," Lonnie said. "I know how that is, believe me, I know." Her daughter had been ten when she'd remarried, she told me. "And Pam, you know, she went through the same thing. In fact, she started this business as a single mom. I bet you and her will have a lot to talk about." Jenny had been a single mom, too. I wondered how normal it was for housecleaners to be displaced mothers, stuck in between the domestic work they did at home and seeking jobs that could pay a decent wage. The job seemed like nothing but a last resort.

Lonnie had me call the office from her home phone to officially clock in. "Hi," I said once the outgoing message stopped and I heard a beep. "This is Stephanie Land, and I'm starting at Lonnie's house," I said before hanging up.

"No!" Lonnie said so earnestly I jumped. "You're supposed to say the date and time!" Then she quickly seemed to correct herself. "Well, it tells the date and time after the message plays anyway. But you'll need to do that every time you start and finish, and it has to be from their landline so it shows up on the caller ID. It's just a way for us to keep track of things." I nodded, my eyes a little wide. She'd said all of this to me before, when she'd given me my binder full of client sheets I'd been assigned to, but it had been lost with all of the other information. With all of these instructions, I got the feeling she had to repeat herself a lot normally.

Lonnie pointed me to her bathroom across the hallway from the small, box-sized kitchen. "Now the thing about this bathroom is you need to pay special attention to the countertops and the wall behind the sink." Lonnie used a lot of hairspray, she said, as evidenced by the two cans of Aqua Net placed carefully on a mirror. "Everything else in here is pretty standard, you know, you got your toilet and bathtub and shower." She patted me on the shoulder. "Just do your best and come get me later to check your work."

Years before I got pregnant with Mia, I'd applied for the local branch of Merry Maids cleaning service, desperate for work outside of coffee shops. My first day was spent in the office watching four training videos; a blond woman wearing a hunter green polo shirt neatly tucked into khaki pants, who smiled as she put on knee pads while the smarmy female narrator said, "And how do we clean floors? That's right. On our hands and knees." I cringed, but part of the training video had proved to be incredibly useful: every space, every room, every floor, took on a gridlike map laid over it. Merry Maids instructed their cleaners to work in one direction: from left to right, top to bottom. Whenever I cleaned anything from then on, I could never get the video out of my mind, starting in the upper left corner, working my way across and down until the job was complete.

Almost instinctively, I did the same to Lonnie's bathroom, starting directly to the left of the bathroom door, the left part of the top of the mirror, and went from there. Any spray that didn't quite make it to the mirror landed on a surface that would be cleaned anyway. It also made it hard to miss spots. A maid's job is, essentially, to touch every square inch of a house's surface. With some homes having four bedrooms; two full bathrooms; two half baths; a kitchen; and dining, living, and family rooms, it's easy to feel overwhelmed by how many inches there are, and how to make sure they're all clean.

When I told Lonnie I'd finished with her bathroom, she pursed her lips as she prepared to inspect my work. Just a few seconds after she'd disappeared into the bathroom, she shouted, "Stephanie!"

I ran in after her. Facing the mirror, she bent over to a pike position, then stood up quickly, then bent over again, then asked me to do the same. Her finger pointed at spots on the mirror I'd missed that could only be seen from a lower viewpoint. She then ran a hand over her countertop. "You need to redo everything," she said, shaking her head. "Soak the hairspray on the counter and the wall."

My eyes widened. I'd forgotten the wall.

She had me run my hand over the counter to feel the sticky surface and told me to feel for that all over the bathroom. The hairspray film was indeed everywhere, even on the back of the toilet, another spot I'd missed.

"The bathtub and shower look great, though," she said, patting my shoulder again before leaving me to it.

As I stood in the empty bathroom, staring at my image in the mirror, I thought of my mom bragging to her friends. "Stephanie sure can make a tub shine," she'd told them. My reflection now showed someone humiliated, hunched over, wanting to run from not only cleaning another woman's toilet while she sat in another room looking at a catalogue, but that she'd told me to do it again.

Just when a decent amount of work hours started to light up on the horizon, Jenny fired me. Through text, of course, sent at eight p.m., after I'd turned down a house she'd scheduled me for the next day. I had a different house to clean for Classic Clean, which she knew and had forgotten, but she used it against me anyway.

"I got this client just for you because you said you needed more hours," she wrote. "This isn't going to work out. I need someone who's a team player."

I didn't defend myself, knowing Lonnie would be pleased to have me all to herself. The pay at Classic Clean was lower, but their organized, businesslike nature made up for it. For now, at least. It needed to. They were all we had.

8

The Porn House

For the first couple of weeks, I shadowed Catherine, the girl I'd replace. She was tall and older than me but drove a newer-model Jeep Cherokee. She said she was going to start working full-time as a bookkeeper for her husband's construction business instead. This had been an additional job for her while business was slow. She seemed tired but happy to be visiting her clients' houses for the last time.

I followed Catherine's Jeep to different houses for two weeks, trying to mimic her in the easy, calm way she approached them. In the days before Christmas, I noticed that she often got a little card from clients with $10 or so inside. They had no idea there were two cleaners or that she'd be replaced by me. Every time a client left one, she acted like it was a pleasant surprise, and I got the feeling that it was her Christmas bonus and not a regular thing. I'd have to work an entire year, scrub each toilet out by hand two dozen times, to get a $10 tip.

We were instructed to enter most often through back doors or through a side door off the kitchen. We'd walk in with our neatly organized caddies full of sprays and brushes, a large bag of square white rags, a vacuum, and mops. I had little experience on how to use it all in the beginning. Classic Clean was much different than working for Jenny—we were there to scrub everything by hand. My work was no longer about just dusting and polishing to make things smell nice and shine. And we did it all with a plethora of sponges and brushes and organic soap and vinegar.

I'd fumble my way in, trying to carry my supplies from the car all in one trip, and set up a "work station," just as I'd been told to do. I opened the binder to my timesheet and wrote in the last name of the client, then called the office to leave a voice mail to clock in, noting the start time. In the beginning, it was a race down to the minute as I fought to finish each house in its allotted three or four hours and clock out.

My days started to have some regularity again, beginning with dropping Mia off at the day care around the corner from our house. I never felt great about that day care, but it was the only place that would accept my childcare assistance money. Not only did I think the facility was cold, crowded, and its workers looked like they hated their jobs, Mia came home with a new illness immediately after getting over the last one. I needed her to be there so I could work, even though I sacrificed her well-being. My ability to earn wages was the only thing that mattered to us now. Once, I stood at the entrance to the day care, holding Mia's clammy toddler hand. I knew that she needed me. She needed us to be home, but I couldn't explain that I might lose my job if I stayed home with her, and what that could mean for us. We paused before going through the doorway. I looked down at her, her upper lip thick with ropes of green snot.

"What is coming out of your nose?" asked a dark-haired woman, who I assumed was the day care assistant, one I'd never seen before, as she sauntered over to us. She directed the question at Mia, but she was really talking to me. As Mia reached up for me, the assistant turned away from us, shaking her head. I felt terrible that I had to leave Mia there. After doses of Tylenol, after her throwing up the night before, I didn't have a choice.

Mia's day care only called for me to pick her up if she became listless and lethargic, if she threw up repeatedly, or if she had a high fever. Some days, by the time I got her home, I parked her on the couch in front of the TV, under her blanket, half holding a sippy cup of juice, and she didn't move until it was time for her dinner and bath before bedtime. Travis would sit next to her, and they'd watch cartoons while I cooked and cleaned.

Despite my building resentment, I saw that Travis truly loved Mia. He liked having a little buddy to accompany him on the four-wheeler or sit next to him on the couch to watch TV. But I think I loved what we represented more than what we were. He was a wonderful father figure, more than making up for what Jamie lacked. A working man, like my dad was. When work slowed down, he was goofy and made pancakes. For me, the goofiness didn't make up for the listless, somewhat constant gaze at the television screen, but I saw Mia's eyes shine when she looked at him. I envied that. I wanted to be smitten with him, too. Seeing them on the couch like that, after I'd worked a full day, made me feel a little safer—maybe even that things could possibly be okay.

At work, after Catherine had gone, Lonnie and I developed a ritual. With each new clean, she went along to "introduce" me to the house, as if each home had a spirit that I had to get to know.

This was the happiest I'd see Lonnie. She really seemed to find some personal connection in these homes. "You can get to know each other," she'd say with a wink.

Much of what Lonnie told me in these meetings about each house wasn't on the printed-out document we received for each client. There were unmentioned notes that clients would never see, like, "You'll really need to get in and scrub that shower because it gets so grimy in there" or "Watch for the pee that gathers on the floor in the half bath off the den." But it opened my eyes to my job in a new way, that beyond the professional front, we secretly acknowledged the disgusting nature of our job.

At Classic Clean, I rotated as the sole cleaner among only a handful of houses to start. Wednesdays were long, six-hour days, cleaning two smaller houses that stood next to each other on the edge of a bluff overlooking the ocean.

Many of my clients lived on the neighboring Camano Island, which was a thirty-minute drive from Mia's day care. A lot of the clients commuted to work in Everett or Seattle, at least an hour away. I really had no idea but just assumed they must have been big-city doctors and lawyers to afford the property taxes for the places they called home. Camano Island was wedged between the mainland and Whidbey Island, so most of the houses I cleaned had a view of the ocean. My Wednesday houses were two of my smallest, with detached garages that were twice the size of the clients' living space.

Lonnie told me to clean the married couple's house first, giving the other client time to leave before I started on his house. The morning we walked up to the first house, Lonnie nodded toward the house next door. "We'll give him some time to get up and moving. He's very sick." I asked what from. Lonnie shrugged. "His wife passed away," she said. "You'll see. It's sad."

From then on, I called it the Sad House. I couldn't think of it any other way. Other houses earned their nicknames the more I got to know them: the Cigarette Lady's House, the Farm House, and so on.

When I started, it seemed so odd to me that neither of my Wednesday clients knew they had a new cleaner, but the house and I were properly acquainted. I don't think Lonnie had to give them a heads-up unless instructed because of our invisibility. It would look bad if clients knew what a high turnover rate the company had. Perhaps they would feel weird knowing how many strangers rotated through their homes. I wasn't a personal maid, but part of a company. They had hired and trusted the company, not me. I spent a half dozen hours in their house a month, and I don't think they even knew my name.

The Porn House, as I'd come to calling it, was that first Wednesday home. The house really had only three rooms, with large windows facing the bluff and a rose garden in the back. Two people with a dog and a cat in a small space meant dust, hair, and dander. I had to pay close attention to places like mantels, tops of televisions, and the laundry room.

"This shower," Lonnie said, opening the slider to reveal a stand-up shower in the shape of a square covered in hair, shampoo bottles, and what looked like a wad of green snot. "You'll need to soak it."

Our cleaning supplies were extremely minimal. In my tray, I had one refillable bottle of half water and half Dr. Bronner's castile soap. In another was a quarter white vinegar and the rest water. I had one container of powdered Comet, one pumice stone, a toothbrush, a few green scrubby sponges, and two sizes of handheld scrub brushes. For this shower, with its visible film of soap scum and grime, there was a protocol.

The first thing I'd do is take out all the shampoo bottles, washcloths, and loofahs and neatly set them outside the door. Then I'd spray the entire shower with what Classic Clean called the all-purpose cleaner to soak it. After cleaning the counter and toilet, I'd fill a small milk jug that had been cut in half with water and set it in the shower. I'd need a sponge, a scrub brush, both of my spray bottles, and a few rags. I'd spray the inside of the glass doors again, sprinkle Comet on my sponge, and scrub it all, left to right, top to bottom.

Then I'd rinse with the vinegar water, dry it with a rag, scrub any missed spots, and call it good before turning my attention to the rest of the shower, which needed to be scrubbed in the same manner. During my first visit, I spent an entire hour getting the shower clean, wishing I had a "real" all-purpose cleaner. Classic Clean didn't advertise as a "green" cleaning company. They used natural products to keep costs down and relied on the cleaners' "elbow grease" to get things clean. Though I'd never tell my manager about it, nerve damage in my spine prevented me from gripping a sponge or brush with my right, dominant hand. I'd had scoliosis, a condition that made my spine curve from side to side, since I was a kid, but recently due to the cleaning work it had pinched a nerve that went down my right arm. To scrub that shower, I had to ball my right hand into a fist, placing the sponge between it and the wall, and press down with my knuckles as hard as I could. To get the shower floor, I'd lock my elbow, make a fist, and put all of my upper body weight onto my right hand to get the soap scum and grime off to prevent hurting my hand. My left hand took over whenever the right one got too tired, but in those first months of six-hour days, when I got home I could barely hold a dinner plate or carry a bag of groceries.

I went overtime for the first few visits, and Pam was livid. Classic Clean couldn't charge the client more and had to eat the cost of paying me extra. It wasn't much money, but Pam complained about the financial burden, like I had hurt her personally by going fifteen minutes over. I stressed about taking so long, and it boggled my mind how an entire house, even a small one, could be cleaned in just three hours.

The Porn House didn't earn its name until I'd been there a few times. One time, I walked into the bedroom, where I had to change the sheets, and saw a bottle of lube sitting on the nightstand in front of a digital clock. It was illuminated by the bright red numbers, and I watched it like it was about to pounce on me. I inched to the corner of the bed to avoid it. Below it, the nightstand drawer was left slightly open, revealing a *Hustler* magazine. By my feet were a discarded pair of dirty socks.

I recoiled as I reached to pull back the covers. I removed the sheets quickly and used them to scoop up the socks.

Everything went in the washing machine. Clean sheets went on the bed, just like I'd been trained to do them—with crisp, diagonal corners at the bottom and the flat sheet pulled all the way to the top. When it came time to dust, I decided to leave the nightstand for last to avoid the lube. Though I'd never fault someone for masturbating while looking at porn mags, I would fault them for leaving it out in the open for the cleaning girl to see.

Maybe he forgot it was Wednesday, I thought.

But over time, I realized the lube was only a symptom of a larger story occurring in the Porn House. The lives of the married couple in that house seemed to be separate. The woman was a nurse and worked odd hours; I knew that from the scrubs carefully placed over a chair in the back room. I couldn't detect what he did for a living. Though I assumed they were husband and wife, there weren't any wedding photos on the walls—just portraits of the two of them wearing matching sweaters. The house felt dim, as they seemed to favor earth tones, like navy and dark green. On the window ledge above the kitchen sink sat a frame in an easel with a quote that read, "We're staying together for the cat."

The garbage in the Porn House bathroom overflowed with wads of toilet paper, tampons, panty liners, and webs of floss. Their medicine cabinet, left ajar, revealed rows of prescribed antibiotics. Judging from the tissues and snot in the shower, it seemed possible that one of them had an ongoing sinus issue, much like I did, as did Mia, and probably most of the people who lived in the damp climate of the northwest, where patches of black mold appeared overnight in homes, basements, and window ledges.

In the living room were a couch and a couple of chairs that faced the box television and fireplace. The nurse seemed to favor the spot on the couch, next to the lamp, where their cat often sat. Her husband obviously sat in the chair where a basket of outdated issues of *Hustler* was tucked between stacks of travel magazines. For about a month, the dining room table was covered in brochures for several all-inclusive resorts, but I don't think they ever went. Clients usually canceled a clean if they left on vacation.

In the back room, adjacent to the laundry room, a twin bed was neatly made, with folded nurse scrubs on the chair next to it. Behind it was a nook, stacked with romance novels, the kind of books lined up on grocery store racks with illustrations of muscled, shirtless men embracing long-haired women. I wondered why she slept back there. There was a king-sized bed in the bedroom, along with a narrow dresser that had an urn with a dog collar wrapped around it. Maybe he snored. Or maybe she had to get in and out of bed at irregular hours.

But the porn and romance novels struck me. I imagined them sleeping in different beds, in different rooms, each fantasizing about a different partner and possibly a different life.

Travis and I had started to resemble this. Not to that extent, but he'd come in from work, eat the food I'd made, then sit on the couch watching TV for four hours before moving to our bed to watch more TV, the tiny one with the timer. He usually set it for sixty minutes.

When I first moved in with Travis, he had a TV the size of a queen mattress sitting on a homemade entertainment center. He'd leaned it forward to get the angle straight and secured it to the wall with large chains. I'd gawked at it when I first came to his house. He'd upgraded since then to a regular flat-screen with a store-bought entertainment center. But the screens were about the same size. I seethed at it all the same.

Travis bought me a laptop for my thirty-first birthday. After Mia went to bed at night, I sat at the kitchen table, writing in an online journal I had started keeping because my right hand was so weak, I couldn't hold a pen. Sometimes I did homework or chatted with friends online, my back to Travis while he watched TV.

9

The Move-Out Clean

Mothering, for me, so often meant learning to say goodbye in the hope of gaining trust in my return. Many things I learned from therapists throughout the turmoil Mia and I endured with Jamie said that, in order for children to develop emotional intelligence and be resilient, it's important, if not vital, for them to have one stable caregiver in their life, one adult person who doesn't waver in being there when they say they will. It didn't matter how many caregivers came in and out of their lives, appearing and disappearing, as long as one pinnacle person remained. Through Mia's earliest years, when the real shuffle started between day care and going to her dad's for the weekend, I became incredibly strict in keeping our schedule, our life at home, a predictable pattern. Every bathtime's end began a series of movements: a towel laid over the toilet, lifting Mia to stand in the center, drying her body and head with another towel, tickling her in the same way. Every bedtime story, kiss, saying, "Goodnight, I love you, see you in the morning," fell into the same niche of familiarity. As a mother, this became my biggest gift to her, because it required so much of me to always be there when I said I would and never, ever falter. My hope was, if everything else in her life was chaos, at least she knew that wherever we called home, there'd be pancakes cut in the same way.

Saying goodbye, like learning to share my daughter with a man who'd been horrible to us, never rose above anything but hard. Dramatic scenes of morning drop-offs at day care began as soon as we pulled into the building's parking lot. By the time we'd walked to her classroom, a worker had to peel Mia off me as she screamed, kicked, and cried out for me as I abruptly turned and walked away after saying, "Goodbye, sweetie. I love you. I'll see you after snack." Some day care workers took her from me and held her for a bit, but most extracted her from my body and put her on the ground, and I'd have to look at Mia as she cried at the window, banging on the glass.

Bringing Mia to a day care integrated in an old folks' home had seemed like a good idea, since she hardly ever saw her grandparents. But twice a day, I walked through the halls, watching the staff line up the residents for medications and complain to their faces about the way they smelled. It felt like I was witnessing, firsthand, the end of life, and, in contrast to the Sad House, it might have been one of the most miserable ways to go.

The Sad House didn't get dirty. Sometimes I had to scrub blood droplets off the bathroom floor, and the toilet was a disaster. Other than that, everything had a thin layer of dust on it. The old man was there most of the time unless he was in the hospital, but he seemed to use very little of his house.

Judging by their photos, his wife had died in the late eighties. At first, I had assumed she'd died recently, but I couldn't find any photos of her that appeared to be from the last several years. Trinkets she'd collected remained on the windowsills: little worry dolls and bird nests, neatly lined up. Tacked to the corkboard over the desk in their kitchen fluttered to-do lists in her handwriting. The bathroom had two sinks, and hers still had a hair dryer plugged in and hung on a hook that I dusted during my visits. His had a cup with a comb and his medications—which were different every time I came. I'd checked the medications, wondering what his illness was. It felt more like a broken heart.

On a shelf in the bathroom, directly behind where he stood to look in the mirror, were the ashes of his wife and their son. In a photo, the son stood on top of a mountain and gave a peace sign. He wore a green bandana and had a long beard. Inside the frame was a familiar poem:

Do not stand at my grave and weep.
I am not there. I do not sleep.

Below, two small boxes rested side by side: one pink clay with molded roses and the other dark pewter. His wife's picture leaned behind the pink one. I opened it to see what was inside. The boxes held ashes, and tags and statements from the funeral home.

He ate pastries and sandwiches from a grocery store deli, drank coffee with a lot of Kahlúa. He was probably in his late sixties or early seventies and still liked to golf and gamble at the Indian casinos. In the garage moldered a nice-looking speedboat and a Jeep CJ. On the living room wall was a picture of his wife in front of the Jeep, smiling and wearing sunglasses. He smoked unfiltered Camels in his bedroom, standing in the frame of the sliding glass door, or on his front porch when the weather was decent. His younger son, who lived a couple hours away, didn't seem to visit much. He was alone, dying slowly in a shrine that hadn't changed since his wife had passed away. He'd done everything right—good job, gorgeous house, married a woman he loved and traveled with—but despite all this he was still dying alone.

When I went home the first night after cleaning the Sad House, I couldn't stop thinking about my client. It had just been a mindless job and something to pay my bills, but now it felt like the work had an unexpected imprint on my life, and the vulnerability I was exposed to somehow relieved me of my own. Though I never met or spoke to any of them, though many did not know that I existed, my clients began to feel like family members or friends I worried about, wondered about, cared for from a distance. I wondered what my clients did in the evenings. Where they sat. What they ate and watched the day before. How they felt day to day. My life had become so quiet. These people gave me something to look forward to, people to hope for and want good things for other than myself.

Mia kept getting switched from one classroom at the day care to the next because of the high turnover among employees paired with the ebb and flow of enrollment numbers. For a couple of weeks, every time I saw her morning teacher, she actively wiped away her own tears before taking my child, who was bucking and screaming and reaching out for me. I overheard her talking to a parent once about how hard it was to work somewhere that paid her so little. "I went to college for this," she'd said angrily. I hated leaving Mia with her, hated that I couldn't afford to support a place that paid the workers at least close to a livable wage.

One morning, after a particularly difficult goodbye, I got in my car and cried, allowing myself a couple of minutes to give the sadness the love, attention, and affection it deserved. I'd had to drop Mia off a little earlier than usual, but the struggle to get out the door had made us late. My frustrations showed, and I walked away without blowing a kiss goodbye. Nightmarish thoughts of my own mortality consumed me. Like, what if I died in a car accident and her last memory of me was walking away, leaving her screaming and crying with strangers?

Those thoughts crept into my mind that morning more than usual. I knew I'd spend the next two days working at a house in a pocket of Camano Island that lacked cell phone reception. I didn't like being away from Mia, didn't like leaving her in a day care that didn't seem like a warm and caring environment, and I especially hated the thought that if anything happened to her during the day, no one would be able to contact me. But the job had been too good to pass up.

"It's a move-out clean," Lonnie had told me on the phone. "We don't do those as much anymore."

For most cleaning jobs, Classic Clean gave the potential clients an estimated rate. They'd meet with the owner, inspect the level of work that needed to be done, and make their best guess on the amount of time (and sometimes people) it would take to do it. Regular clients, who had weekly, biweekly, or monthly cleans, had set numbers of hours and rates, but the construction and move-out cleans normally had a budget to work around.

My schedule had about five or six houses rotating on it, but those were all bimonthly or even monthly cleans, meaning most of my paychecks had about twenty hours total for two weeks. I couldn't get another job because my schedule varied from week to week, so I got caught in a bind of waiting for more hours to become available, no matter what the job might be. When Lonnie called to ask if I'd be interested in doing a move-out clean, I gave her an enthusiastic yes, even thanking her for asking me to do it instead of her other employees.

The job was a double-wide trailer just down the street from another client's house that I had started to call the Chef's House, because of the gigantic stovetop. The owner, on the one rare occasion he'd been home, stood in his kitchen next to it, taking up the entire space between the stove and the island in the center. "I had to take out a personal loan to pay for it," he said, running his hand gently over the outer edge. "It's probably worth twice as much as your car!" Though I didn't doubt the truth of that statement, I tried not to frown at him pointing out that I drove an older Subaru wagon and instead asked if there were any special instructions he had for cleaning it. In two weeks' time between cleanings, the entire stovetop area would get completely covered with grease, thanks to his affinity for using the deep fryer on the counter and the countless bottles of infused olive oil. He must have used the fryer several times a week because the entire house was drenched in its oily stench. "Yes," he said, pointing for emphasis. "Do not use the scrubby side of sponges!" so I wouldn't leave any scratches, and I'd have to go through five or six rags instead.

When I pulled into the driveway of the double-wide for the move-out clean, I was already ten minutes late. Pam was there, along with the coworker I'd have for the duration of the day. I rushed over to join them. "Sorry for being late," I said quickly, trying to sound sincere. "Mia didn't want me to leave her this morning."

Pam huffed a little, mumbling about kids needing to understand and respect their parents' need to work. I didn't ask her to repeat herself or clarify what she said, imagining that she'd been in my shoes before, feeling as if she hardly ever saw her children due to work, and gotten through it just fine. Pam nodded toward the other cleaner, a gruff-looking, heavy-set blond woman with her hair in a scrunchie, who looked grumpier from boredom than from my lateness. "This is Sheila," Pam said. "She's leaving us this week." Sheila and I looked at each other, giving a nod and half smile. We were already unloading the van, which was stocked with a wide assortment of unfamiliar sprays, not used for the weekly cleans. These were the heavy-duty cleaners to remove mold, grease, and stains. She handed me supply trays and bags of rags, impatiently waiting for me to juggle my coffee, which I kept in a recycled jar.

"Before we go in, I need to explain a few things about this

house," Pam said as we stood outside the trailer. She asked Sheila and me to lean in close. Sheila looked at Pam, but I kept looking at Sheila, wondering why she'd quit, swallowing my burning envy.

Pam looked over her shoulder into a tall grassy field. She motioned to it and said, "Through there is the house of the Barefoot Bandit's mom."

The Barefoot Bandit was a household name at the time. His real name, Colton Harris Moore, was rarely used, but I knew we had the same birthplace in Skagit County. The Barefoot Bandit was only nineteen years old and had been wreaking havoc around the area lately, breaking into wealthy homes while the owners slept, once leaving behind bare footprints in the dust of a garage. He had broken into the Chef's House the week before to use a computer and procure my client's credit card information to order bear mace and night-vision goggles and look for unattended small aircraft. I could picture him sitting at the desk I dusted every other week, knowing how easy it would have been to find credit card numbers amid the scattered piles of papers. Local news outlets called him armed and dangerous and said he was possibly hiding out at his mother's house.

Though I doubted he was there, the whole scene felt like the setup for a perfect horror story. After all, we were in an abandoned trailer down a long dirt path in the woods. Move-out cleans have a haunted feel to them anyway—like you're cleaning up a crime scene, erasing all traces of any human interaction.

As we walked to the front door, Pam continued to prepare us for what was inside. She explained that the house belonged to a couple who had divorced. The wife had moved out while the husband had stayed with a couple of roommates. "The owner is under a tight budget, so we need to work very efficiently," said Pam, turning to face us before opening the front door. "I'll be here for a few hours today to get you started, and Stephanie—you'll return tomorrow to finish up."

I wasn't sure what "very efficiently" meant. We already weren't allowed lunch breaks, as it was assumed that we would take a "break" when we drove from one job to the next, stuffing apples and peanut butter sandwiches in our faces. But there would be no traveling today. I'd be here in this double-wide trailer for six to eight hours a day for the next two days, deep in the woods, in a house that didn't get cell phone reception, so I couldn't call anyone or even be on call in case of an emergency with Mia.

"Be sure you stay hydrated," Pam said, fumbling with the lock. She put down the mop bucket she'd filled with extra cleaners and paper towels. "And make sure you take small breaks to rest whenever you need."

My eyebrows went up at this comment. This was the first time I'd ever heard of our time on the clock having any allowance for breaks. Maybe move-out clean bids included short breaks and regular cleans didn't. Up until then, I'd assumed we weren't allowed to sit down.

Most of the houses I had cleaned up until that point were owned by people who could afford to keep them up, and it was rare that I was the first maid to clean it. Move-out cleans are deceptive. The house is empty. There's no dusting around lamps on tables, or books and knickknacks on shelves, so at first glance it looks like an easy job. Instead, they're the longest, most unforgiving, the filthiest. Most often, the owner has decided to sell, after the house has been rented and gone without regular cleaning for years. In these homes, a film of dusty grease, like rubber cement, covers the kitchen. The floors around the toilets are stained yellow; hair is embedded in all the crevices. Each time you wipe a surface, the original color is revealed, which makes the remaining discolored surfaces look even dirtier.

Walking into the trailer, I noticed the blackened tiles in the entryway first. The carpet had a visible dark path that led into the living room. When we stood in the dining room, we peered up at a chandelier, barely touching our heads, draped with dusty spider webs.

"I'll do the guest bathroom," Pam offered, making me like her a little more. "It's pretty bad in there." She put her hands on her hips, gazing up at the spider webs. "Sheila," she called over to the woman inspecting the corner of the blinds in the living room that were bent and black from dirt. "You can dust. Make sure you get those blinds, too." Pam looked at me, took in a deep breath, and said, "I want you to do the kitchen."

I followed Pam as she walked into the next room, peering into the fridge that she'd unplugged and left open during the walk-through. She made a face, like a grimace. It would be the only time I'd ever see her react to grime; usually she kept a pleasant-looking cheeriness to her, even when she was reprimanding us. "You'll have to pull all the drawers out and soak them," she said, her head turned toward me, but her eyes were still fixed on the inside of the fridge. I came closer to peer over her shoulder. "Take out all the glass shelves and soak those as best you can." She stopped to pick apart the accordion-like rubber on the door. "I would use a toothbrush on the seal around the door. Make sure to get the crusted-on food stuck in the crevices. Let me know if you need help," she said, patting my shoulder and smiling. "Those dried-up puddles from packages of meat can be hard to get out."

We continued to walk around the small kitchen, Pam pointing out the thick, brownish-orange layer of grease under the hood above the stovetop. We stood under the stains, our mouths open to gawk. There were splatters of what looked like chili on the ceiling. The burner control knobs were also covered in crusted bits of brown food. Every square inch of that kitchen, even inside the cupboards, had to be scrubbed and wiped down.

When I stood at the sink, I could just barely make out the corner of the Barefoot Bandit's childhood home through the window. I couldn't stop looking to see if his head would pop out of the grass. I felt protective of my beloved Subaru, the car I depended on to get me to and from work. I imagined him demanding my keys at gunpoint, then driving away in it.

To clean the ceiling, I had to stand on the kitchen counter. Pam came over to check on my progress and watched me with a wary eye. She asked me to let her know when I'd finished so she could show me what needed to be done in the master bathroom. She was still working on the guest bathroom. I could hear her coughing from the bleach fumes, even though she'd put on one of the white disposable masks. They didn't do much to shield us from toxic fumes. Pam wore them to set an example and reminded us to do the same. If any injury resulted on the job, the first question would be whether we'd been wearing any safety equipment provided by the company.

Pam caught me resting my arms when she walked into the kitchen. I'd been standing on the counter for almost thirty minutes in an attempt to remove the spotted stains from the ceiling. And I was failing.

She motioned for me to follow her, and we walked toward the half of the house I hadn't seen yet. The master bedroom still had its furnishings, and the closet was only half emptied. A thick fleece blanket with wolves on it covered what looked like a waterbed. I couldn't help but grimace, imagining scenes of the man—whose kitchen I'd just spent two hours scrubbing dried food from—entertaining women in the bedroom. I wondered what kind of woman would join him on the waves of his fuzzy wolf blanket.

These visualizations or hypotheses I made about clients were what got me through days of personal dread, fatigue, and loneliness. The imagined occupants of these houses walked around with me. I saw them sitting up in bed at the dawn of a workday, using a wet washcloth in the shower—the one balled up on the floor, which I gingerly handled, even with gloves. They also left traces of themselves and their actions.

I could see them standing at the kitchen window, drinking their morning coffee, while I wiped away the ring their cup had left behind.

When I was sixteen, I worked at a pet shop cleaning out animal cages—rats, mice, gerbils, hedgehogs, ferrets, and birds. The owner spoke in a voice that dripped with passive aggression, a tone high enough to make me wince. One morning, I showed up at work already stretched thin from the duties I endured at the job, knowing I could not make it through another day of sticking my hands into bird cages, the birds' wings frantically flapping, triggering every flight response in my body.

"The job is just too stressful," I said after marching into my boss's office. "I have to quit."

"Well," she said sarcastically from her desk, which sat next to cages for male breeder rodents, "I better let you get out of here before you get too stressed out!"

It took weeks to get my final paycheck in the mail. I had never walked out on a job since, but the master bathroom of the Trailer nearly broke me.

On the second day, I came back to the Trailer alone. I parked in the driveway, stopped to lock my car doors, then locked myself inside the house. I avoided peering out the windows, afraid that I might see the Barefoot Bandit walking by. That morning, I'd left Mia at day care after dosing her with Tylenol for a slight fever. The day before had proved there was absolutely no cell phone reception at the Trailer. If Mia became sicker, I wouldn't be able to be reached, period. My uneasiness in being left alone, locked in the Trailer, without a phone, crawled over me, and I couldn't shake it off. It was compounded with the stress of disappearing into some kind of void for the duration of the workday. As a parent, I always wanted to be, at the very least, on call in case something happened.

We'd finished most of the house the previous day, but I had

to go over Sheila's work. The drawers from the fridge were still soaking in the sink. The linoleum floor in the kitchen—a well-worn brown path that connected the sink, stove, and fridge in a triangle—still needed to be scrubbed. But most of my day would be spent in the master bathroom.

The day before, Pam told me to pace myself between spraying and scrubbing. She suggested doing small doses of the bathroom and then moving to another part of the house, then returning to do another section of the bathroom. My left-to-right, top-to-bottom method didn't feel like a good enough strategy for the mess in front of me. Black mold covered a lot of the ceiling and the upper walls of the stand-up shower. I went through two bottles of mold-remover spray, soaking it and then scrubbing it off, wearing goggles and a facemask to avoid breathing it in.

Inside the shower, the corners and crevices were pink with mildew. The cleaner dripped in streams at my feet, brown and black rivers of dirt and mold. I'd make clean spots and then regret it, as it meant I would have to scrub as hard over every inch of the tiny shower. I kept my nose covered with the collar of my shirt instead of wearing the mask and I stepped out several times into the dark master bedroom to breathe in the clear air.

When I kneeled at the toilet and saw up close the condition it was in, I abruptly got up and went outside. I had had enough. I sat out on that porch, in the drizzling rain, for at least fifteen minutes. I almost wished I had a cigarette, or even a proper lunch to eat, or something to drink other than water. The coffee and peanut butter sandwich that I'd brought that morning were long gone.

On the porch, I went through a slew of emotions. There was anger, of course, over getting paid near minimum wage to hand-scrub shit off toilets. Triple the pay still wouldn't be enough to do what I did. Inside the master bathroom of the Trailer were pools of crystalized piss around the base of the toilet. The underside of the seat, the rim, and the top ridge of the bowl had speckled brown spots, which I assumed were shit, and yellow and orange flecks that looked like puke. I wore a pair of yellow dish gloves, and I was armed with Comet. But the man who'd occupied this bathroom had purchased those blue disks, perhaps seeking the façade of a clean toilet bowl, and they had left dark blue tracks at the water line and from under the inner rim where fresh water filled the bowl. I would have to reach in and scrub those dark lines with a pumice stone, again and again, until they disappeared.

"They don't pay me enough for this," I mumbled. Then I yelled it into the trees. I sat alone on the porch, with the rain dripping off the roof, and the rage in my voice surprised even me. I'd grown stoic by then, after enduring attacks from Jamie that came without warning, finding myself lock-kneed, my lungs seized, my chest tight like a large person had me restrained in their thick arms. The floor had dropped out from under me too many times already, and I still walked carefully on it, knowing one upset could bring me tumbling back to where we began, in a homeless shelter. I had to keep it together. Above all else, despite uncertainties in things I couldn't control, I should remain calm. Dependable. I'd go to work and do the job that needed to be done. "You must not let yourself fall apart!" I repeated to myself. It became my mantra that I repeated in my mind, sometimes even saying it out loud.

My maroon Subaru gleamed in the rain. The clouds suddenly broke over it, letting the sun shine on the body of my car. I'd never wanted to walk out on a job so badly. I felt disrespected by that toilet, by the man who'd left it in that condition, by the company that paid me minimum wage. I stared at the Subaru, imagining my escape.

I had no choice. Travis and I barely spoke now. He was angry with me on the weekends when Mia went to her dad's, when I slept in instead of getting up at seven a.m. to help him on the farm. I no longer cared, and he knew that. We coexisted in that anger for months. I had absolutely no means to afford a place to live. So I'd go back to that toilet. Walking out on that job would mean desperate months ahead without an income. The child support I received barely covered the cost of gas. The entire $275 a month went to the trips back and forth so Mia could see her dad. Losing my job would mean being indebted to Travis. It would mean losing respect for myself.

I balled up my fists. I stood up. I walked back into the house, clenching my jaw. This was not my fate. This was not my ending. I was determined to prove myself right.

The Trailer gave me nightmares. In my dreams, I'd be driving home, and my phone would start buzzing with voice mail notifications. Or someone would call from a number I didn't recognize. When I answered, the woman on the other end of the line spoke so frantically I couldn't understand her until she said "hospital." An image of Mia, lying on a bed with part of her bobbed, curly brown hair caked with blood, flashed in my mind before the woman started demanding to know where I'd been and why there wasn't an emergency contact listed. *It's only me!* I repeated in the dream. *It's only me.*

But the Trailer had its own way of coming back. After I spent twelve hours cleaning it, Lonnie called a couple of days later. Her voice lacked its usual robustness. The client wasn't happy with the clean, she said. Something about dust on lightbulbs, or blinds, or spots on mirrors, or all of it. "I need you to go back and fix it," she said softly. "And as written in your employee contract"—she paused and took a breath— "we don't pay for that."

My heart started racing, beating against the walls of my chest in huge thuds. "There's no way I can do that," I said, choking on the words. The drive was forty minutes one way, which meant gas money that would not be reimbursed. Saying no to Lonnie meant risking my job, but I risked quitting entirely if I went back. "I don't think I can go back there. That toilet made me want to quit."

Lonnie sighed. She knew how desperate I was to work, how I truly couldn't afford to waste gas. "I'll figure something out," she said and hung up the phone. I never found out whether or not she had someone return in my place. Maybe they called Sheila to go back, but Pam was probably the one who had to finish the job. If she did, she never mentioned it to me.

10

Henry's House

Lonnie and I stood on the concrete porch for her to introduce me to my new client's house. We had knocked on the red wooden door and then stood for at least a minute, listening to a chorus of barking and someone shuffling around inside trying to calm the dogs. The man who swung open the front door wore a bathrobe, white shirt, navy blue sweatpants, and slippers.

"You're here!" he said, his voice booming. The dogs, two exuberant Australian shepherds, wagged their stumpy tails and jumped in excitement.

"Henry," Lonnie said. "I'd like you to meet our very best cleaner, Stephanie."

"Well, come in," he said, and then motioned to help carry my supplies. Lonnie smiled and thanked him, and Henry closed the door behind us. He set down the bag of white rags folded into quarters and said, "Let me show you how things should be done."

Henry had asked for a new cleaner. Lonnie talked me up quite a bit and convinced him I'd do a better job than his previous one. I'd been instructed to clean the house only to his specifications. In the order he wanted. To never be late. To never go overtime. To always, always do my best. The clean would take four hours every other Friday. "Be prepared to sweat," Lonnie told me.

Henry already intimidated me. When I finally saw him after Lonnie had told me how picky he was, I shrank back involuntarily. He stood almost a foot taller than me. He was straight-backed and confident, and his large belly stuck out in front of him.

We started in the front sitting room, which Henry and his wife used as an office. They both had large, shiny mahogany desks. Henry's desk sat by the front window, where most people would put a fancy couch. Shelves on the wall were filled with western novels, travel books, and computer programing manuals. He had two computer monitors on his L-shaped desk. They'd moved here after he'd retired from some sort of tech job in Hawaii. The surface of his desk was hidden under piles of bills, cameras, and manuals. In contrast, his wife's desk was smaller and neater—a scanner, a laminator, piles of clipped magazine articles on recipes and scrapbooking tips, and photos of their dogs and cats.

Henry would be home while I cleaned, and he needed me to clean the house in a certain order to coincide with his routine. I'd clean the office and formal dining room while he finished his breakfast and watched the news. By the time *The Price Is Right* came on, I would move to the other end of the house, pausing on my way to the guest bathroom to clean the laundry room, and then on to the master bath.

In the guest bathroom, I'd first pile the four rugs outside the door to be cleaned later. I would clean the toilet first, which sat across from a large, double-headed standing shower lined with river rock. Henry said he'd clean that himself. After refolding the towels, I'd wipe down the corner Jacuzzi tub, which, as far as I could tell, they never used. They used the hot tub on the porch, Henry explained, gesturing to the swimsuits hanging on the door. After the tub, I would clean their mirror, big enough that I had to kneel on the counter to reach the top, and dust the lights, double sinks, and cluttered counter. The wife's side had several clear plastic drawers and stands with various shaped holes to hold brushes and other beauty tools I didn't recognize. Henry's side of the sink had multiple medication holders—the compartmental kind with the first letter of the day of the week on top. He had several toothbrushes, and there was splattered toothpaste everywhere.

Before vacuuming the rugs, I had to spot-clean the walls and mop the floors. When I placed the rugs back into the bathroom, I was careful not to disturb the vacuum lines. I'd then dust the many shelves of their walk-in closet before cleaning their bedroom, vacuuming my way out.

On that first day at Henry's, we paused in the hallway to admire a glass showcase. Henry's hobby was woodcarving, and he interrupted the tour to say most of the pieces were done by artists with far greater talent than his. Half of his garage was a wood shop, he said a little sheepishly, but he rarely made furniture anymore.

I remained silent through the walk-through, trying to take in the many instructions, wondering if Henry would get angry if I didn't follow them correctly. In the family room sat a television bigger than my car. The cupboard below it had several different electronic boxes to play DVDs, or for cable, power, and volume to the many speakers placed around the room. I'd only seen setups like this in stores. In the other wall was a fireplace, complete with a brick mantel and bench. I'd have to move the two heavy leather chairs on sliders, and the table in between them, careful not to disturb the five remote controls on top of it. When I began to run a vacuum over the red carpet, I realized it was more of a brick color without the thin veil of dog hair. After the family room, I cleaned the breakfast nook, the stainless-steel refrigerator, marble countertops, and floors in the kitchen, and finally, the half bath in the entryway.

The first few times that I cleaned, Henry's voice made me cower. I worked constantly, pausing only to fiddle with my iPod Shuffle or to glance at my watch to make sure I was on schedule. I went overtime the first couple of Fridays, which worried Lonnie so much she called Pam to discuss her concerns, prompting Pam to call me and ask if everything was going okay. But after a while, I knew where the hair collected, which spots needed a quick wipe, scrubbed, or wouldn't come off. Everything melded into mindless movements, and I spent the time worrying about other things happening in my life.

When I got to Henry's house in the mornings, we always chatted a little bit. Then he'd putter around in the kitchen, making his breakfast, usually two thick slices of bread with tomato and avocado. Later, I would clean the wooden table he ate breakfast at, wiping away the crumbs he'd left, moving the lazy Susan, filled with different salts and hot sauces, to wipe under it. By the time I cleaned my way down the hall, he'd be working at his desk, remaining there until I left.

One Friday he asked if I could do an extra day the following week.

"I can't, unfortunately," I said. "I have a house I clean on Fridays opposite of yours." The Farm House was also new and, I realized, strikingly similar to Henry's in that the client had gone through almost every cleaner in the company before me. Both houses were sweaty, fast-paced four-hour cleans with horrible carpets and many animals. I held in an involuntary shudder thinking about vacuuming the navy-blue carpet that covered the stairs.

"Oh," Henry said, looking down.

"I could come this weekend, though," I said. "If that works, I mean. My daughter goes to her dad's every other weekend, and I drop her off after I leave here."

Henry stood up straighter and looked pleased. "Great, because I'm having a dinner party!" he said. He motioned for me to follow him. We walked out the sliding glass door to the covered patio behind his house. "And I want this grill to shine."

I nodded at its filth and noticed the hot tub with an empty

bottle of champagne sitting in the corner. My body ached, yearned for even a chance, just one opportunity, to drink champagne in a hot tub.

Inside, I returned to vacuuming the formal dining room. Henry had an old video poker game setup in there and a half-empty bottle of fancy gin sitting by the little sink at the bar. I caught myself wondering what my retirement would look like, if I would even know one. I'd never own a house too big for me to clean on my own, that was for sure. What a waste of space it seemed to hire someone to run a vacuum over the same visible lines they'd left two weeks ago. I tried to follow the same pattern, deep in thought, music blaring in my ears, when Henry tapped my shoulder. Flustered, I fumbled to turn off the vacuum and yank out my earbuds.

"Do you like lobster?" he asked.

I blinked.

"I usually do a surf-and-turf kind of dinner on Fridays," he said. "I get a couple of lobsters from the market."

I nodded, wondering why he had stopped me from vacuuming, trying to think if I'd ever seen someone purchase a lobster out of one of those tanks.

"How many people are you cooking for tonight?" he said.

"Two," I said.

"Well, I'll pick you up a couple," he said. "I appreciate you doing the extra work for our party."

I stammered out a thank-you. I had never encountered a client being so kind to me, treating me like a human being. I didn't know how to receive it. Besides, I'd eaten whole lobster only once or twice in my life and had no idea how to cook one. I already felt guilty that I would most likely screw up this generous gift with my less-than-savvy cooking skills.

Henry left a few minutes later, bringing the dogs with him. It was the first time he'd left me at the house alone. I beamed in his trust for me. I was so used to feeling distrusted. I thought about the woman at the Farm House, who had been home the first time I cleaned, puttering around, circling back to where I was. It felt like she was trying to bait me by leaving jewelry sitting out instead of inside the drawers.

When I stuck my hand into my pocket to get my phone, I looked around, even though the house was empty and no one would be watching me. I dialed Travis's number, and when he answered, I excitedly told him about the lobsters. I asked him to pull a couple of the steaks I'd found on clearance out of the freezer. There was something about sharing good news with him, this good fortune, that made me feel hope for us again.

But he did not acknowledge the lobster or the steaks. Instead, he said in a flat voice, "Did you check your car's transmission fluid?"

"Yes, it's low," I said, feeling deflated. I stopped looking at the painting, one of those metallic-looking ones of a lighthouse, in Henry's hallway and glanced down at my stocking feet, smudging one sock into the shiny wood floor.

Perhaps Travis's way of expressing his love for me was to ask about my car, but I couldn't hear it. Communication with my family was sporadic, and I needed him. "I love you," I said, just as we were ending the call, but he didn't say it back.

After we hung up, I started on Henry's bathroom, disappointment from the conversation with Travis lingering. Henry came home just as I reached to stick a rag in the toilet to scrub it out.

"Do you know how to handle these things?" he said, his voice echoed off the walls, making me jump. When I turned around, he motioned for me to follow him to the laundry room. There, on top of the washer I'd just cleaned, were two of the biggest lobsters I'd ever seen. They were brownish red. They were alive. And they were mine.

Henry handed me printed-out cooking instructions and a set of shiny shell crackers.

"You know," I said, rubbing the silver of the utensil with my thumb, "you could be saving my relationship."

"Oh, yeah?" he asked, looking at me with a mixture of interest and amusement.

"Yeah," I said, then shrugged, like it wasn't a big deal. "We've been arguing a lot. Money and all that."

"Well," he said, crossing his arms, "I'm sorry to hear that." He looked me square in the eyes, squinting a little, pointing a shell cracker at my nose. "When it stops bein' fun, it stops bein'."

Those words stayed in my head for the rest of the day. Travis and I didn't have the same type of fun. He liked to drive recreational vehicles in fast circles, while I liked drinking small-batch brewed beer accompanied with conversations about politics and books. We tried compromising. He often sat outside with me at night to have a beer and gaze at the huge garden we'd built in the corner of the yard. Between our differences was Mia—bouncing, happy, wrapping her arms around both of us. In those moments, we felt like a real family, and I fought to feel the love and joy that she felt. But I knew I would never understand Travis's lack of desire to wander, or wonder, or learn. We'd reached the point of resentment, blaming each other for our differences.

Because of Mia, I tried to cling to the dream. The farm. The horses. The tire swing in the front yard, the endless fields to run through. I had been secretly apologizing to her, whispering it since I'd watched her hold up fistfuls of carrots that she yanked from our tended soil last summer, wearing only underwear and little cowboy boots. *I'm so sorry this isn't enough for me.*

When I finished Henry's house, he helped me carry my supplies out to my car. I hugged the bag of lobsters to my chest, but I wanted to hug Henry for being so kind, for treating me less like a maid and more like a person deserving of love and laughter and the occasional lobster dinner. When I thanked him, Henry smiled broadly and puffed out his chest. "Get on home," he said to me, though I was beginning to realize that "home" was something fleeting, a ticking time bomb, an explosion waiting to happen.

At the stop sign at the end of the street, I pulled over to the curb. I leaned forward, pressing my forehead against the steering wheel. The interaction with Henry made me miss my dad.

This had happened often in the last year. Whenever I felt the pain of the loss—my chest caving in right at the hollow spot in the center—I found it was best to stop and wait, to give the feeling a moment to pass. The pain didn't like to be ignored. It needed to be loved, just as I needed to be loved. As I sat in my car, the bag of lobster next to me in the passenger seat, I breathed in and out, counting to five each time. *I love you,* I whispered to myself. *I'm here for you.*

Reassurance of self-love was all I had.

Mia was asleep when I picked her up from day care to drive her to Jamie's. It was getting close to two o'clock, and the traffic would get bad if we left any later. She protested as I scooped her up, put on her coat, and strapped her into her car seat. We stopped at home, and I left the car idling in the driveway while I ran inside to drop off the lobsters and pick up Mia's special backpack for her weekends away. I threw in some clothes, a blanket, the photo album we'd made, and her Curious George. Mia drifted off while we drove, giving me a chance to listen to a CD I'd made a while ago. This ridiculous country song about being a hay farmer came on. Travis had always played the beginning of it loud whenever Mia was in his truck because it started with a revving engine noise that rumbled your chest from the low bass. I smiled, remembering Mia asking for him to do it again, her pink boots with the brown horses kicking up and down as she laughed. When the ocean came into view, I reached back to wiggle her leg and wake her up.

It was six o'clock before I returned home. Alone in the kitchen, I salted a pot of water and set it on the stove. As it bubbled and spat, I used my body to block the lobsters' view of it while I read the instructions for the fifth or sixth time. Travis chose to stay out on the porch with the grill, probably burning the steaks. Dropping the lobsters in the pot to their death was up to me.

My pot wouldn't fit them both. I had to cook them one by one. My dad used to make his huge batches of chili with this pot, and for some reason I had inherited it after my parents' divorce. It was enamel with a liner that was a strainer. In my early twenties, I lived with my then-boyfriend in a cabin in Alaska. The cabin did not have running water, and it sat on five acres of permafrost. When my dad came to stay with us for a visit, he brought a handwritten recipe for the chili. He even wrote "Dad's Chili" on the top. I slipped the paper into a clear pocket, clipping it into a binder of recipes I'd collected.

It wasn't a fancy recipe—hamburger, onions, pinto beans, some cumin. I'm pretty sure he copied it out of a Betty Crocker cookbook. But as a kid, I loved when he made it. We'd sit around the table with our steaming bowls, grinding saltine crackers in our hands and then dusting the crumbs on the floor to make my mom gasp. When Mia and I showed up at my dad and Charlotte's the first time, about a month before Jamie punched the door and kicked us out, Charlotte pestered Dad until he made a batch of chili for me. I loved her for that. As I stared into the pot of rolling water, the lobsters awaiting their deaths, these memories came flooding back. I thought of Charlotte, how I couldn't think of the last time I'd seen or even talked to her.

When I lowered the first lobster into the boiling water, it didn't scream or move frantically like I thought it would. Its shell turned bright red almost instantly, and then a green foam formed on the surface. After it was done, I scraped the foam off before cooking the second.

The table was set—two steaks, two lobsters, two beers. I wondered how different our dinner table looked from

Henry's. They probably had dishes they used only for the occasion and large linen napkins draped over their laps. Travis and I ate in silence. I tried to smile at him, to ignore his displeasure at such a complicated meal. While he started a movie, I cleared the table, loaded the dishwasher, cleaned the larger dishes, and wiped down the table and counters. We sat next to each other on the brown leather couch he'd inherited from his parents, but we didn't touch. Halfway through the movie, I went out to the porch and lit a cigarette, something I now did when Mia wasn't home. I had bought the pack a few weeks before, after cleaning the Trailer. It was becoming more and more of a ritual. Travis came out to smoke half a cigarette before telling me he needed to go to bed.

"Do you want me to join you?" I asked, tapping away ash from the cigarette.

He paused. "I don't care," he said and went inside.

I thought maybe he wouldn't be as mad that I wasn't cleaning stalls with him that weekend, because I had to work. I even hoped we might make love, rather than the usual way he reached for my hips—my little spoon pressing into his big spoon—sometime in the night, our faces never touching, the darkness and silence interrupted by headlights from a passing car.

The next morning, Henry met me at his big red door. "How did it go?" he asked, smiling as I handed him back the fancy utensils.

"They were the best thing I've ever eaten," I said, beaming at him, then paused, suddenly realizing what he meant. "But they didn't save my relationship."

"Ah," he said, looking down at the silver utensils. "Maybe that's for the best. You don't seem like the type who needs a man around to save you. You're one of the hard workers."

While Henry offered praise, I knew that I could never work hard enough. Between school, the house, Mia, and trying to earn enough to make a living, work had become relentless and never ending. My paychecks made me feel like I didn't work that much at all. But Henry respected me. He was the first client who I knew with certainty did.

Soon after the lobster dinner, Travis and I broke up. That evening, I came home from work to make dinner, clean up, give Mia her bath, and put her to bed. I set up my books and laptop on the kitchen table, put my earbuds in to drown out the television, and began to do schoolwork. And then I saw that the kitchen trash was overflowing. I got up from the table and stood in front of Travis, blocking his view of the TV.

"Can you please take out the trash?" I said, hands on my hips.

Without hesitating, he said, "I think you should move out." Then he stood up, physically moved me out of the way, and sat back down again. I stood, stunned, looking down at him. A laugh track erupted on TV, and Travis, his face lit up from the screen, smiled. I returned to the table and sank into the chair, the weight of those words heavy, pressing me into the ground, into a hole I wasn't sure I'd ever be able to climb out of.

PART TWO

11

The Studio

Travis gave us a month to leave. I didn't tell Mia—in part because I didn't want to upset her and in part because I didn't have a plan. I posted ads online for a roommate or a barter arrangement or a room to rent. Nothing came to fruition. Every apartment I looked at cost more in rent than I received in wages. With my earnings, which hovered around $800 a month, there was no way to come up with a first and last month's rent, as well as a deposit. There was no way for me to earn enough to pay for gas, utilities, and rent, even a room. Apartments ranged around $700, at the least. The thought of more than one bedroom was impossible for me. I had no savings or credit to fall back on, nor even an ability to apply for a loan. I'd never be able to pay it back. Additionally, I'd have to set up electricity and Internet to do schoolwork. I'd have to get a router. I'd have to get so many things.

After I reached out to a few friends, they encouraged me to set up a PayPal "donate" button and embed it into a blog entry with a simple explanation:

Travis has given me until the end of June to move out. Unfortunately, I don't have the money for a deposit. I have set up a PayPal account. If you can donate even five bucks, it would help tremendously. Thank you.

I hated asking for money. I hated admitting that I'd failed again at making a relationship work. Most people didn't know Mia and I had lived in a homeless shelter, but it still felt like history was repeating itself. Then, the messages from friends through Facebook started coming, full of encouragement and love. People sent $10 or even $100. Every donation, no matter how small, made my eyes wet. I made a wish list through Walmart that I shared through a Facebook post. Soon, boxes started showing up at Travis's with pots, pans, clothes for Mia, and silverware. I'd sunk to a new low, but I wouldn't let it sink me. I couldn't go back to being homeless. After my dad told my family I'd made up stories for attention, asking for help was the hardest thing I'd ever done. It opened me up to judgment. It held me accountable for my actions, especially for involving Mia in what I felt like I should have predicted was a doomed relationship. I feared what people might think. But each friend who reached out lifted me up to a newer height. I'd rise above this.

When I'd moved into the homeless shelter, I had called Melissa, one of my oldest friends, and she listened as I went through my plans for rebuilding my life. Nearly all of those plans involved the help of some form of government assistance: food stamps, WIC checks for milk, gas vouchers, low-income housing, energy grants, and childcare.

"You're welcome," Melissa said pointedly.

"For what?" I asked, peeping through the shelter's worn blue curtain at a deer walking through the backyard. Mia napped in the next room.

"My tax money's paying for all of that," she said, then repeated, "so you're welcome."

I didn't say thank you. I hadn't said thank you. I wasn't sure what to say.

"Hey," I said, with false urgency. "Mia's crying. I should go."

Mia's door creaked when I opened it. I sat on the edge of the bed, watching her chest rise and fall. Melissa had, at first, sounded so happy to help, but I knew that wasn't the case. I had heard her talk negatively about people who took advantage of welfare before. She didn't like the mother of her stepdaughter complaining about how she had supposedly abused the system.

I wished I'd had the courage to speak up for myself, to speak up for millions of others who were struggling through the same hardships as I was: domestic workers who worked for minimal pay, single parents. Instead I hid. I silently blocked Melissa on Facebook and turned my back on any comments or media that spoke poorly of people on welfare. "Welfare is dead," I wanted to say. There was no welfare, not in the sense they thought of it as. There was no way for me to walk into a government office and tell them I needed enough money to compensate for the meager wages I needed in order to pay for a home. If I was hungry, I could get a couple hundred bucks a month for food. I could visit a food bank. But there was no cash to buffer what I actually needed to survive.

Every little bit of donated money from friends started to add up, and I found myself with nearly $500, and Travis offered to match it. Finally, I could afford a studio apartment in Mount Vernon in an old house that had been divided into three apartments. Our studio had once been the front living room and an attached sunroom. For $550 a month, we had a bathroom with a tub, a tiny kitchen with a full-sized fridge, and a view of the whole city through a wall of windows.

The landlord, Jay, and I emailed back and forth about the place, and he said I could drive over and look at it. I stopped by after work that day, before I had to pick up Mia, to check it out. I'd known it was small—a studio apartment implied that. But standing in there, in that room smaller than the one I'd used to watch movies with Travis for the past year, for a moment I wanted to turn away and refuse. I thought back to the apartment Mia and I had had in Port Townsend, the one by the fairgrounds with separate bedrooms, a dining room, and a washer and dryer. This place had none of that. This was a grimy room above a freeway that I would struggle to afford.

Where I stood, the floor was old, possibly the original wood, with large cracks in between the planks. Through French doors was the sunroom that looked over the city. Under the windows, there was a bench with tops that lifted up so I could store things in there, but someone had left a bunch of blinds and curtain rods. There was a dark green carpet, and I mentally tried to imagine where Mia's bed and toys would go and wondered if my dresser would fit. In the other section, L-shaped cabinets with an electric stove, fridge, and sink served as a kitchen. I walked from one wall to the other. About thirty paces.

"It's great," I said to Jay on the phone. "I'm here right now. It'll work for us, I think."

"Your daughter's three?" he asked. I hoped he wasn't rethinking his offer to rent to us.

"Almost," I said. "But I work a lot, and she goes to her dad's on the weekends." I walked over to the windows off the kitchen, looking down at the cars speeding by. "We probably won't be here very much." I involuntarily held my breath. That was only halfway true.

"Okay, that's no problem," he said. "Did you want to stop by to get the keys this weekend? You can drop off the rent and deposit then."

"Can I make payments on the deposit?" I asked, surprised at my boldness. Maybe standing in that space brought on a nothing-to-lose feeling. "I can do fifty or a hundred bucks a month. I just, uh, this move is kind of sudden and I don't have anything saved up right now."

There was a silence. I pulled at my lower lip with my teeth. "Sure, that's fine. A hundred bucks extra for the next five months' rent would be fine."

I breathed out, almost laughing. "Thank you so much. I really appreciate that."

When I met Jay at the apartment to give him a check for the first month's rent and get the keys, he and his wife were just beginning to paint the ceiling of my new living room and kitchen. He was a plain-faced, brown-haired guy about my age. His wife, who introduced herself as Mandy, was much smaller than me in just about every way. They looked like they were good people. Nice. Trustworthy. Probably hard-working and honest. I hoped, anyway.

"Looks like you guys have your work set out for you," I said, watching them piece a long pole together.

"Yeah," Mandy said, rolling her eyes. "At least the grand-parents agreed to take the kids for the day."

"Exactly what we wanted to be doing on a sunny Saturday," Jay added. They both looked at each other. He let out a sigh.

I smiled, waved, and thanked them for their understanding about the deposit. I imagined spending a Saturday next to my spouse, painting the walls and ceiling of an old house that we owned and rented out, while my parents watched the kids. *That's exactly how I'd want to spend a Saturday,* I thought as I drove back to Travis's. I had to start packing our stuff, had to figure out what major things we lacked— like bedding, bowls, cups, and something for me to sleep on. It would be a couple of days before the apartment was ready for me to move in, but they said I could come over in the evenings to clean it up if I wanted. Scrubbing the grime off the cupboards and floors of our new home was my version of a sage smudging ritual.

When my friend Sarah saw my posts about needing help, she sent me a message to ask if I needed anything. I brazenly listed off several items, nervous I would have to do without. She wrote back, offering her daughter's twin bed. Travis came with me to pick it up. His face remained blank, emotionless, through all of this. He'd disappear into the barn if he walked into the house and saw me in tears, struggling to come to terms with my fate. We didn't speak except out of necessity, but I figured any way he could help us get out of his house would be something he'd want to participate in. I'd been to Sarah's house a couple of times to eat snacks and drink wine at her table on weekends when Mia was with Jamie. Now, standing on her porch, I couldn't keep my head and shoulders from hanging low.

"It's in here," Sarah said, eyeing Travis. We followed her down a hallway, into her daughter's room. "We're getting her a queen-sized bed. She's sort of grown out of this one."

Maybe she thought the bed would be for Mia instead of me, but I didn't correct her.

Before I left, she gave me a hug. "Oh!" she said. "I have something for you." She disappeared into the laundry room and then came out with a box, setting it down on a bench in the entryway. It was a set of brand-new dishes, the color bright and blue like the robin's eggs that Mia and I found all over the farm in the spring. My hand went to my mouth in shock as I took in the four dinner plates, salad plates, coffee cups, and bowls. New. For our new start. I threw my arms around her and thanked her, and then I took a deep breath and carried the box of dishes to the truck.

This was a start, but I had so much work to do—not only in moving but in the work it would take to afford staying.

For two weeks, I put Mia to bed at Travis's and then packed my car with as much stuff as I could cram into it. At the new studio, I scrubbed the counters, sinks, and tub. Even the walls got a good wipe-down before I hung up the few paintings from the artwork my mom gave me. My favorites were two Barbara Lavallee prints from the book *Mama, Do You Love Me?* that I'd had since I was little. The iconic Alaskan illustrations reminded me of a happier time, when my family spent our summers fishing, filling the freezer in the garage with salmon and halibut. Our studio was tiny, just

over three hundred square feet, with ten large windows—
eight in the sleeping area and two in the section with the
wooden floor—so I had to be choosy about what ended up
on the wall. I tried to avoid looking at everything critically,
like I had with the homeless shelter. This was yet another
tiny beginning for us. I feared Mia would not see it the same
way.

I'd return to Travis's at almost midnight, after he had
gone to bed, to crawl under the throw blanket on the
couch. A week before Mia's third birthday, I took the final
hauls of furniture and got everything set up at the studio. I
picked a weekend to move when she'd be at Jamie's. Travis
and his friend helped move the bigger stuff, even disas-
sembling and putting together the loft bed his parents had
handed down to Mia. They did it while I was cleaning the
Farm House. I'd dropped Mia off at day care that morning,
knowing I'd pick her up, deliver her to her dad, and never
return her to the home she'd known for the past year and a
half. I wanted to do it all myself and not have to ask Travis
for help, but I'd hurt my back at work that week in a stupid attempt to move a bed. I had to take 800 milligrams
of ibuprofen two or three times a day to get through work;
the physical pain provided a distraction from the heartache
I felt for Mia.

By Saturday night, I had everything moved in. By Sunday
afternoon, her toys were in the correct bins, and our clothes
were neatly folded and put away. When I picked Mia up
and brought her into our little studio, I hoped, as any parent would, that she'd like the new space. I hoped she'd feel
a sense of home, of belonging, but she looked around for a
bit, checked out the bathroom, then asked to go home to
Travis's.

"We're staying here, sweetie," I said, stroking her hair.

"Travis coming home?" she asked. She sat in my lap, on the
twin bed Sarah had given me.

"No," I said. "Travis is staying at his house. He's sleeping there. We're sleeping here. This is our house."

"No, Mama," she said. "I want Travis. Where's Daddy Travis?" She started wailing, sinking into me, heaving under the weight of her tiny crushed heart. I apologized, and I cried right along with her. I promised myself to be more careful. I could be as reckless as I wanted with my heart, but not with hers.

12

Minimalist

One of the greatest things about a willingness to get on your hands and knees to scrub a toilet is you'll never have trouble finding work. To supplement where Classic Clean's hours lacked, I started looking for more clients on my own. I posted ads online and on Facebook. I picked up Donna's House, a biweekly, four-hour clean on Friday afternoons when I didn't have to drop off Mia with Jamie. Donna's House was deep in the hills of the Skagit Valley, toward the Cascade Mountains and the backcountry where my family had lived for six generations.

She was involved with the local Habitat for Humanity and mentioned a few families who'd recently been granted the ability to own their first home—much of it with what the program called "sweat equity," where family members and friends performed physical work like hammering nails, painting, or landscaping in exchange for a down payment. If finding the time to meet those requirements sounded difficult enough, as an adult with one dependent, I needed a monthly net income of $1,600 to qualify.

"I don't know if I'll be able to do that," I said. She encouraged me to contact the program anyway. But when I really thought about it, I wasn't sure I wanted to own a home in the Skagit Valley. With the exception of Anacortes and Deception

Pass, which were unaffordable at my wages, it didn't feel like home to me. And Habitat for Humanity didn't offer a choice of where to live in the county.

"All your family's here," she said. "Can't be more 'home' than that."

"Well," I said, dusting the tops of the pictures in her formal living room, "I kind of want to check out Missoula in Montana. I'd been planning to move there for college when I found out I was pregnant with Mia."

Donna had been scrapbooking as we spoke and stopped going through the piles of papers, photos, and stickers on her dining room table and was looking at me now. "You wanna know how to make God laugh?" she said.

"What?" I asked, wondering how this related to my desire to move to Missoula.

"Tell him your plans," she said. "If you want to make God laugh, tell him your plans." And then she let out a bark of a laugh.

"Right," I said, turning to dust the molding that stretched down the hallway.

Donna paid me $20 an hour to clean her house and told me to never accept less. Classic Clean charged $25 an hour to have me work in a home, but I still only made nine. After taxes and expenses, I took home $6 an hour. Finding and scheduling clients on my own took a lot of time, especially when walk-throughs didn't result in a new client. But the unpaid labor of finding and scheduling clients was still worth it and helped to increase my overall wages. That is, if I never managed to damage anything.

The move from Travis's house added forty minutes to our daily commute. All but two of my Classic Clean clients were in the Stanwood and Camano Island area. But Mia's day care was still right around the corner from Travis's house, and driving past it was unavoidable. I almost involuntarily slowed down when I passed it, rubbernecking to catch Travis walking in the door with his muddy boots on. Besides missing the comfort of a partner, there was one thing I couldn't seem to let go. After a couple of weeks of passing it multiple times a day, I asked Travis if I could stop by to tend the garden. I hated seeing it so overgrown and wilted; perfectly good food going to waste.

"Okay," he said after a long pause.

"I could bring Mia with me to hang out for a while," I said. He seemed fine with that. Travis said he'd try to stay involved with Mia's life as much as he could. But summers meant hay season, and most days he worked from dawn until dusk. She liked to ride on his lap when he mowed. At least she could have a few more times spent in his lap.

Our new life began at seven o'clock each morning. I would climb out of bed, shaking the sleep from my body, and heat water on the stove for coffee. I made one cup for the morning and then poured a cup for the road in a jar. Mia usually ate oatmeal or cereal. Sometimes I'd add water to pancake mix and she'd watch me scoop steaming silver-dollar-sized pancakes onto a plate before adding a dab of butter and syrup. I made do with the usual peanut butter Clif Bar in the pocket of my Carhartts and a toasted peanut butter and jelly sandwich wrapped in a paper towel and tin foil that I'd reuse until it fell apart.

With rent, utilities, car insurance, gas, my cell phone and Internet, the Laundromat, and toiletries, my monthly expenses hovered around $1,000. When Mia or I needed new shoes or even toothpaste, I had to refer to my budget posted on the wall, with a list of each bill that was due and what date it came out of my bank account. That meant only $20 to cushion any unexpected blows, like an electric bill that was bigger than usual. Had I not received a government grant for childcare, I wouldn't have been able to afford to work at all. Since my income was higher, I had a monthly co-pay of $50. More in wages meant I received a smaller amount of food stamps—around $200 each month now—and it was still all the money I had for food. Even with the increase in money coming in, I had more bills and less supplement coming from the government. So most months we had only about $50 left over for activities or household goods. With the amount of time and energy I spent physically working, the burn of not being able to afford necessary staple items was even more painful.

The downtown location of our new apartment proved to be a blessing. There was a food co-op where Mia had her own "banana card," which earned her a free apple, orange, or banana every time we shopped. I could use our food stamps to buy one of their deli sandwiches on clearance, yogurt or hummus for Mia, chocolate milk, and her chosen fruit. We'd sit at a table by the big windows that faced the sidewalk. I'd get a drip coffee for a dollar. We sat, smiling at each other, appreciating the ability to go out to eat.

Down the street was a consignment store called Sprouts that had only recently opened. Sadie, the young, blond girl who owned it, was always there with her daughter either strapped to her chest in a carrier or in a playpen.

"Can you take another one of those travel cribs?" I asked her as she sorted through the bags of clothes I'd brought in. Sadie paused for a second to think.

"Is it in good condition?" she asked, bouncing a little to keep her baby asleep while she examined the items.

I had to tell her about the hole in the side of the mesh. "But it hasn't been used that much," I said, then decided to add, "I have a jogging stroller, too."

"I can only give store credit for equipment," she said, her nose scrunched up with disappointment. "Not cash."

"Okay," I mumbled.

She opened the cash register to give me $20 for the clothes. "There's a lot of nice stuff in here," she said, smiling.

"I know," I almost whispered. "I'd been saving it for…" I

sucked in my breath, looking at the newborn onesies I'd carefully packed away in the chance Travis and I ever had a baby.
"I'd been saving it for no reason."

Sadie somehow knew what I meant, or maybe she just
acted like she did. We'd gotten to know each other after she
saw my posts looking for work in a Facebook group for local
moms. She'd hired me to clean her house, since she'd ne-
glected it for so long after opening a business while also caring
for a toddler and an infant. When I asked if she needed help
at the store, she said no at first; then I asked if she'd be willing
to barter me cleaning the store's bathroom for some credit for
clothes. Sadie smiled, first at me, then at Mia, clutching her
new Thomas the Tank Engine footed pajamas I'd found in the
boys' section, and nodded. With the barter, Mia could walk
in and pick out a dress or something that caught her eye when
the need arose. I'd make an afternoon of it—going to lunch
at the co-op, then over to Sprouts for her to pick something
out. Her wardrobe was comprised entirely of used clothes and
Walmart stretch pants found on clearance. But she held her
head so high whenever it was time to pick out a dress, she
might as well have been in an upscale department store.

When we moved into the transitional apartment building,
my mom had given me boxes of antiques she'd displayed
around the house I grew up in. Now, with the lack of space, it
felt more like she'd burdened me with stuff she didn't want to
pay to put in storage. Most of the bigger stuff I took to donation centers or consignment shops because the studio's small
space, much like the homeless shelter where we had room for
only one bag, left me no room for any of it. My lack of living space afforded me room only for things that were useful.
I thought back to magazines I'd flipped through, with articles
featuring smiling couples who'd chosen to minimize their belongings or elected to move into a tiny house, boasting how
mindful they were about the environment. They could just
as easily choose to move back into a regular house with two

bedrooms, an office, and two-point-five baths. I'd feel differently about our studio apartment when I handed over my monthly rent check if I knew I could afford something triple its size.

During the weeks after I had moved from Travis's to the studio, Pam offered me part of the loft in her shop for storage until I figured out what to do with all of it. I'd gone into Classic Clean's office to refill my supplies, pick up my paycheck, and formally change my address.

"How's the new place?" Pam had asked in her cheery way, and I tried to give a positive response, or at least try to imitate her disposition.

"It's fine," I said. "I just don't know what to do with my stuff. Travis doesn't want me to keep anything there, and I can't afford a storage unit." I stopped myself there, trying not to unload all of my stress on my boss. She had such a sincere way of asking how I was, fully listening when I spoke, she had started to fill a maternal role that my life desperately needed.

Decisions over what to keep and what to donate or attempt to sell weren't easy. Things I stored were equally useless and priceless. Baby books, photos, old letters, and yearbooks had no value but took up valuable space. Then I whittled down my clothing, getting rid of winter and fishing gear I'd kept from Alaska, dresses and shirts I no longer wore regularly. Household things became the hardest to decide what stayed and what went. I not only had to decide what we had space for but what I could not afford to replace. My dad's chili pot no longer had significant use, but it had a heavy hand in the sentimental value department, along with the casserole dishes my parents got at their wedding. Things, they were all just things, and I didn't have space for much. So Mia and I each had two towels, washcloths, and sets of sheets. In my closet, which was originally built to house brooms and mops, I kept my entire wardrobe: two pairs of jeans, one pair of khakis, one nice button-up shirt, and a "fancy" dress I bought with my own money. The rest were my Classic Clean t-shirts and work pants. I didn't have the heart to get rid of many of Mia's things and found creative ways to store her stuffed animals, books, and toys so they looked part of the decor. There was so much stuff to go through. Decisions to make about what to keep and what to throw away, the amount of loss heartbreaking. I stored some of it in the basement under our apartment, but not much for fear it would get destroyed by the dampness and mold and mice. But I couldn't get rid of all of those things, either. They were our history.

There wasn't any way I could have verbalized any of that to Pam in that moment, but she seemed to understand intuitively as she stared at me. Maybe she'd once had the same dilemma as a single parent in compartmentalized space. Suddenly, her face got a kind of Mrs. Claus twinkle, and she told me to follow her.

We entered the door to the smaller shop that sat between the office and her house, and she pointed to a small hidden space at the top. "It's a really big space up there, and it's not getting used," Pam said, shrugging. The loft space had a rickety ladder I'd have to somehow hoist my stuff up to get to the top. On the floor where we stood were various assortments of old things—like the stuff you'd find at a garage sale that had already been picked over. "Whatever you need, take it." She gestured to the various pitchers and plastic shelves when she saw me looking at them. "Take from any pile. Our church is having a huge yard sale and needs the donations, but if you see anything, you can just have it."

I looked down and saw an old footstool. "I could use this as a coffee table," I said. Pam smiled and nodded. "And maybe this jar for kitchen utensils."

"If you need anything else, even if you need me to wash your work rags, just let me know," she offered. I wanted to hug her. I wanted her to hug me. I needed a hug from a mom so badly I could easily see myself choking on a few tears and asking for one. "And I do need some help with the yard, if you're available," she added.

"I have time next weekend I know for sure!" I said eagerly. "I can check my calendar if you need it done sooner."

"That's fine," she said. "There's no rush." She opened the door to a walled-off section under the loft where she stored her cleaning supplies. "Maybe you could organize this room, too." When she flipped on the lights, I saw a long hallway filled with spare vacuum cleaners, a floor polisher, and rows of mops and bottles.

I was already calculating the extra wages in my head.

Pam smiled at me. Her eyes twinkled a little more. Studying her short, roundish body and kind soul, I wondered if the other cleaners felt as close to her.

On free weekends, I started going through my stuff stacked in the loft at Pam's. I whittled down my papers, books, and keepsakes to two storage bins. Most of it either went in the trash or to thrift stores, disposing of things I'd once carefully folded to save. One afternoon, when I knew no one was on the property, I went through and got rid of the last of the baby clothes I had set aside—the special newborn outfits I'd saved for last, which I'd hoped, someday, another baby of mine would fill. At least I could exchange them at the consignment store to properly clothe the kid I already had, who seemed to need new pants and shoes almost constantly. But maybe that was the lesson there— appreciating the stuff you had, the life you had, using the space you were given. I wished it wasn't a forced journey, but I recognized it as an important part of mine.

13

Wendy's House

By my third visit to Wendy's, a new client's house, her health had started to abruptly and visibly plummet. "The cancer doesn't give me much time," she'd drop in conversation, her shoulders uncharacteristically slumping. No response ever felt right, so I mirrored her sage nods, agreeing with her in a grievous way. Yet Wendy's shirts were still starched. Her house was still so clean I was often confused why she paid to have me work there.

Sometimes, after I finished cleaning the kitchen, she made me lunch, insisting that I sit with her at the dining room table. We'd exchange stories about our children over a lacy white tablecloth, eating tuna sandwiches on white bread, cut into triangle quarters, with carrot sticks on the side. She served instant coffee that we'd nimbly sip out of teacups with cream and sugar packets and a silver spoon to stir. It all felt like tea parties I'd pretended to have with my grandma when I was a child, and I told her so. Wendy smiled, then waved her hand to brush it off. "It's good to use the fancy teacups while you still can," she said. Her hands shook enough to make the cups rattle on the saucers that were etched with pink flowers.

Wendy's house was filled with glass cases displaying knick-knacks, photos of her children and grandchildren, a portrait from her wedding day. Wendy caught me gazing at it once. I had been staring at it, thinking how young she and her husband looked, wondering how it is that people can suddenly become so old, how they stayed in love for that long, their heart and body growing together. She smiled and pointed to a glass bouquet of red roses, which sat on the shelf next to their wedding portrait. "My husband always wanted to make sure I had red roses," she said, and I felt an odd sensation of both envy and tears.

Wendy's house was such a typical "grandmother house" that being there made me ache for family or my own grandmother. The kitchen counters were filled with cookbooks and piles of papers—grocery lists and green smoothie recipes. She drank her coffee with packets of imitation sugar and had a basket of them next to the coffeepot, which always seemed to be turned on.

Wendy's house was, compared to my others, easy. I wiped down the counters, cupboards, and floor; dusted and vacuumed; and cleaned the half bathroom downstairs. She insisted on doing the one upstairs herself.

There was a spot on the floor in her kitchen, near the end of the bar, where the linoleum had been worn down and chipped away. I asked her about it once during our lunch together, and she said that was where her husband had sat to smoke cigarettes. She grimaced at the memory. "I always hated it," she said, taking a sip of her coffee. I nodded, thinking of Travis's muddy boot tracks across the kitchen floor. "But it's important to not let those things get in the way," she said, smoothing her white cardigan over a pin-striped shirt.

"It did for me," I said. She looked up at me, her white hair nearly glowing in the afternoon light like a halo. "My boyfriend and I broke up recently. We'd been living together for a little over a year. My daughter's only three and... they were close. Now we live in this tiny studio apartment I can hardly afford." I picked up my cup to drink the last gulp of my coffee and to hide my red cheeks. Saying those words all together like that not only made me ache with grief, it made everything real, like it was actually happening, and not just some nightmare we'd found ourselves in.

Wendy was quiet for a few moments. "I need a lot of help around here," she said, getting up from her seat at the table. She collected her dishes, and I jumped up to do the same. "You can leave those there. Come with me."

I followed her upstairs, past the mechanical seat she used to traverse them on her "bad days," as she called them. She didn't seem to get many visitors, and it made me wonder if she put on nice clothes and did her hair for me. I hadn't been upstairs, except once or twice to vacuum the stairs. Her bedroom was to the right of the landing, where she slept with her portly, snoring white dog, who knew to ring the bell by the sliding glass door to be let out. When she opened the door to the guest bedroom, light flooded into the hallway where we stood.

Dozens of shoe boxes, plastic containers, and rubber bins lined the walls. There were still more containers balanced in stacks on top of the bed. Wendy sighed.

"I've been trying to sort things into piles of what goes where," she said. "Because of the cancer." I nodded and looked at everything she had been doing. "Most of the things for my son are in the garage—the tools and all of that. But my nieces and nephews and their children will want a lot of this."

I admired her as she pointed to the piles, telling me what would be given to whom. In my time working as a maid, I'd seen various decluttering projects—garages parceled out in preparation for yard sales or downsizing. But this wasn't the same kind of project. This was an afterlife project—Wendy had been putting things aside for relatives to have after her death.

I'm not sure if Wendy knew how much time she had left to live, but if she did, she never told me. The extra work she hired me for during the month of July is how Mia and I survived the unexpected expenses from moving and a $300 car repair that would otherwise have sent me spiraling. I picked her weeds, sorted piles, and deep cleaned areas of her house to save her family from having to do it all. Wendy was so matter-of-fact about asking me to fulfill these duties. I admired her, as weird as it seemed, hoping I'd feel the same peace at the end of my life, calmly sorting piles instead of scrambling to make amends or cross experiences off of a list.

I spent most of the Fourth of July weekend in her yard, working my way around the weeds in her flower beds and beneath her evergreen bushes. It had been a while since I'd done that work, and I forgot how enamored I'd been of working outside. Most of my days were spent working in stuffy houses, the heat turned down or the air-conditioning turned off, as they sat empty while their occupants were away.

At home, I battled a relentless black mold. Our sleeping area, with its walls made up of large windows, became a sauna in the evening sun. If it had rained recently, it was more like a greenhouse. Sleeping was nearly impossible for Mia, who'd always slept through anything—even fireworks. Travis stopped by to visit with Mia one evening and, after balking at how hot it was, left suddenly in his truck, returning a half an hour later with an air conditioner he installed in the window for me. He turned it up full blast. Mia and I stuck our faces in the cool air. It felt expensive, like a luxury. Maybe I'd only use it when we got home or right before bed to cool the room down a little, so our electric bill didn't go up too much. It worried me that the air felt moist. Everything seemed to exacerbate the black mold growing on the windowsills that surrounded us while we slept.

Outside, I could breathe deep. When I worked, I listened to the noises of a neighborhood instead of music from my iPod. That Fourth of July weekend, many of Wendy's neighbors were already lighting fireworks or cooking meat on the grill. Occasionally, I'd get a whiff of steak or hamburgers, and my mouth would water. I imagined crisp lettuce and thick slices of tomatoes, cheese, ketchup, and mayonnaise applied generously, all washed down with a bottle of beer. From beneath the evergreen tree, I imagined kids in yards up and down the neighborhood, running around with sparklers. That weekend, Mia was with Jamie, and I found myself hoping that she was at a barbeque with her dad, surrounded by kids her age. I hoped that she would get to see fireworks that night.

Wendy wrote me checks with a shaky hand, insisting that I be paid my regular rate even for my lunch break. "Your time is valuable," she said, handing me the check with illustrated pink roses by her name and address.

After a couple of months, Wendy canceled her cleans. "I just can't afford them anymore," she told me over the phone, and I thought I heard regret even through her weakened voice.

I don't know when she passed, but I wondered if it was soon after I stopped visiting. I thought often about our conversations over sandwiches and coffee, how the carrot sticks in front of her went untouched, and that perhaps her plate was mostly for show; that, even though she didn't have the appetite to eat, we weren't eating a meal alone. Memories of those afternoons with Wendy reminded me not only that my time was of value but that even though I was there to clean a toilet or pick candy wrappers out of her junipers, I had value, too.

Weekends without work or Mia blared with silence. With the Pell Grant only covering enough tuition for the regular school year, I couldn't afford tuition for the summer semester due to rent, so I didn't have homework to catch up on, or a yard to putter around in, or any money to spend on a drink with a friend. Even driving to Seattle or up to Bellingham cost too much money, so I stayed home instead. I tried going to the park to read books on a blanket in the grass, but I seethed with envy for the families and couples eating lunch from to-go boxes, dads playing with kids while moms sat with babies in the shade.

Purchasing, preparing, and eating food became more of a chore than pleasure, since my diet was so unvaried. When I could afford them, I cooked a big batch of mashed potatoes on Sundays to form into patties that I'd fry with butter, then put an egg over for breakfast or an after-work snack. Besides the protein bars and PB & Js, I ate huge bowls of Top Ramen. I learned how to make my own sauce out of rice vinegar, Sriracha, soy sauce, a little sugar, and sesame oil. The initial cost of the sauces was expensive, about $20, but I couldn't bear to eat the flavor packets. Those huge bowls of Top Ramen and sauce were my version of a fancy dinner. I added sautéed cabbage, broccoli, onions, or whatever else was on sale, topped with hard-boiled eggs and sliced deli meat on clearance. Fresh produce became a sort of delicacy. I only bought vegetables priced at a dollar or less a pound and only at the beginning of the month.

For whatever reason—whether it was Mia eating more than usual from being home sick from day care, when I'd have to feed her breakfast, snacks, and lunch, or if she was experiencing a growth spurt—the second shopping trip of the month had to be for minimal foods that barely kept our bellies full and never satisfied. That's when I bought the cheaper bread and no-frills crackers, the jam I knew was full of sugar, artificial ingredients, and high fructose corn syrup and not much else, which I had to feed my growing daughter anyway, and cheap TV dinners or boxes of prepared food. For a couple of weeks, I couldn't afford coffee. I switched to black tea, and I wept. Though I knew it was available, I never went to a food bank or a soup kitchen. Our choices were limited, but we weren't starving, so I could never bring myself to go. There always seemed to be plenty of people who needed it more.

Mia, thankfully, never seemed to notice, since I was always the one who ate less. But one afternoon I picked her up from her dad's, and she spent the next twenty minutes talking about a birthday party she'd gone to. Not because of the friends or games but because of food. "They had so many berries, Mom!" she kept saying. "Strawberries and raspberries and so many berries and they let me eat as many as I wanted!" That night, after she went to bed, I looked for any photos that friends from Port Townsend might have posted of the party and found a few. Mia wasn't in any, but I could clearly see the berries. The whole table was covered with bowls and plates of them. I understood why Mia was so excited. A small package of berries, at five dollars, was an incredibly special treat for her, and she usually ate it in a matter of minutes.

A few other clients offered to pay me for additional work during those months, and I had steady interest in an ad that I'd posted on Craigslist:

I WORK 25 HOURS A WEEK AS A PROFESSIONAL CLEANER, BUT IT'S NOT ENOUGH TO PAY THE BILLS.

Most of the other, competing ads seemed to be husband-and-wife teams who had trucks for clearing out clutter to take to the dump. A few were businesses much like Jenny's had been: licensed, insured, and with a few employees to juggle bigger jobs. I didn't think my ad would stand out or bring in any extra income at all, but I got a half dozen calls every time I posted a different variation.

One short, bright-eyed woman, Sharon, hired me to clean out her rental property before the next tenant moved in. The apartment was grimy but not horrible, and during the walk-through she admitted that she'd never hired a cleaner before. She wanted me to clean out the oven and fridge but not the blinds. I tried to estimate how long it would take me, but I had come to the walk-through with Mia balanced on my hip, and it was hard to get a good look at the space.

"Four or five hours?" I guessed, distracted by Mia, who was steadily reaching for something on the counter.

"Oh, I just figured I'd give you a hundred dollars," Sharon said as we stood in the hallway. Then she handed me a wad of cash. I looked at her for a second, a blank expression on my face, unsure what to do. It was much more than I had been paid for any individual cleaning job before. But she motioned for me to take the money from her hand. "I liked your ad," she said. "I remember what it's like, to struggle when you have someone who depends on you." She looked at Mia, who, growing timid from the eye contact, pressed her head into my shoulder.

"Thank you," I said, trying to suppress the feeling that I was getting away with something. "You won't be disappointed."

After I strapped Mia in her car seat, I sat behind the wheel, staring at the dashboard. *I'm doing it*, I thought to myself. *I'm really fucking doing it!* I turned around to look at Mia, and I felt my heart swell. We had been through so much together, and yet I was still getting us through. "Do you want a Happy Meal?" I asked. The wad of cash bulged in my pocket. Pride swelled in my chest. Mia's face lit up, and she threw up her arms. "Yay!" she yelled from the back seat. I laughed, blinking back a few tears, and yelled out for joy, too.

14

The Plant House

My alarm went off for the third time only thirty minutes before we had to be at the specialist's office for Mia's ear tube surgery. They'd instructed me to give her a bath that morning and dress her comfortably. Instead I tried calling the office to cancel. Mia's head and chest were overflowing with thick, green snot. She'd even thrown it up the previous night, and once that morning, all over our floor. There was no way they'd do surgery on her when she was this sick, but I went through the motions, got her ready, and drove to their office on time.

Mia sort of knew what was going on. I'd told her the doctor needed to look at her ears again, but I couldn't be in the room with her this time. We'd been to the doctor several times for her ears by then and had seen the specialist once to determine if she was a good candidate for the surgery. My nervousness about it revolved around the anesthesia more than the actual procedure.

"I put ear tubes in my own son," the specialist had told me. "I'll give your daughter the exact same care."

When we arrived at the office at eight a.m., they ushered us into a room where they had already set out a gown, a hat to cover up her hair, booties, and a bag for Mia's clothes. My stomach dropped further with every nurse who came in to ask questions. Mia remained tense and silent, not making eye contact as they weighed her, took her temperature, checked her oxygen levels, listened to her chest, and even took her picture with a Polaroid camera.

"She's really sick," I said to the first nurse, who barely nodded. "She's had a bad cold. A cough, with green snot. I think it's an infection," I said to the next. "The specialist is going to check to see if she needs her adenoids out, he's not just taking them out. He's just going to check."

One nurse, an older brunette whose hands were so cold Mia had recoiled from them when she tried to listen to her heart, asked if we had a humidifier at home.

I shook my head no, thinking about the condensation on the inside of our windows, the seams with the spots of black mold that I'd scrubbed off before we moved in and which returned after it rained. "I can't—" I started to say.

"Well, you'll need to get one today," she said, writing something on Mia's chart.

"I . . ." I looked down. "I don't have the money."

The nurse stood erect, pursed her lips, and crossed her arms, looking at Mia instead of me. "Where are her grandparents? Doesn't she have grandparents? If it were my grandchild, I would offer to buy things like that."

"My family can't help with things," I tried to explain quickly, probably offering too much information to this stranger. "Or, my dad and stepmom can't. My mom lives in Europe and says she can't help, but my dad really doesn't have the money."

The nurse clicked her tongue. Mia's eyes had remained focused on her hands, which she'd folded and tucked between her legs. She must be cold. Or she needed to pee. Every time I asked, she shook her head no. "I don't know how any grandmother could live so far away from her grandbaby," the nurse said, then looked me in the eyes in a way that made me feel like I needed to answer, but Mia whispered in my ear.

"I need to go potty," she said. Her breath had that twinge of infected snot to it, different from how it normally smelled.

The nurse pointed us down the hall as she left the room. I carried Mia and sat her down on the toilet. She bent herself completely over, her chest flat against her legs, and threw up a large puddle of green snot. One of the nurses stood outside our room, asking the woman at the front desk where we went, and I waved her down to show her what had happened. *There's your proof,* I wanted to say. *My baby is too sick for this.*

"I'll take care of it," the nurse said. "Just go back to your room."

We sat in there for only five minutes, or about as long as it took me to get fed up and reach for the bag to start dressing Mia in her clothes.

There was a knock at the door, and the specialist came in. He didn't say hello—he never did—and sat on the chair in defeat. We all sat there looking at one another for a few beats, him sizing us up. "She's probably sick from being nervous," he said. "If you're nervous, then she's nervous."

"I haven't had time to get nervous," I mumbled.

He sat back, crossed his arms, then rose and stood over us. "If you don't want to do the surgery, then that's fine. It saves me time, that's for sure."

"No," I said, furrowing my eyebrows. I wondered if he'd speak to me this way if I was there with a husband or if Mia had insurance that wasn't Medicaid. "I didn't say anything like that. She's been sick. She's sick. I figured she was too sick to do the surgery today. I don't even know why I came here. I'm too tired to think about this."

"The surgery will help her," he said. "I'm trying to help."

I nodded. Frustrated, I tried not to cry, ignoring my overwhelming urge to drop down and sob into my arms, to give up and surrender to how hard it was to have a child this sick while fighting like a warrior to pay rent with a job that had absolutely no benefits at all, a job where if I didn't show up, it might not be there when I finally could. Not that I expected any of those things. A lack of benefits simply came with the territory for jobs that paid close to minimum wage; it just seemed like an exception should be made for those who had people to care for. "I trust you," I said, looking at Mia, my arm around her shoulders, knowing I'd have to let her go with him.

A different nurse came to take Mia into the surgery. Another came in the room with some paperwork for me: instructions on how to care for Mia over the next couple of weeks.

"You're Dan and Karen's daughter, aren't you?" she asked. I nodded. "I thought I recognized you. Boy, Mia is your spitting image! She looks exactly like you did when you were little." My confused expression prompted her to introduce herself fully. She was the wife of the lawyer who'd handled my lawsuit for a car wreck I'd been in at sixteen. "But I've known your parents since they started going to Bethany Covenant when you were still in diapers!"

"Still in diapers" made me think about the story my mom always told about the time they'd rushed to church one Sunday morning, getting there after the sermon started. Dad passed me to Mom, and her hand brushed past my bare butt. I was barely two years old, and they were only twenty-one. They'd forgotten to put a diaper on me in their hurry to get out the door and didn't have any with them. I wondered if this nurse had seen them. I wondered if she'd helped them, too.

Her small talk passed the time that Mia was in surgery. I'd read a lot of articles online about what to expect from little children waking up from anesthesia, but I still wasn't prepared for it emotionally. It was nice to have the distraction, someone to keep me company, to keep me breathing. Losing my child, her not coming out of anesthesia, something going horribly wrong, were all thoughts I had to keep at bay in order to stay strong, if not for me, then for her. Neither of us needed the added stress.

Mia came into the room at nine a.m., wheeled in on a gurney with gauze stuffed in her mouth. Her face was soaked in tears, red with anger, and her eyes looked around, wide with terror, like she couldn't see. They pushed the gurney she was on over to the fixed bed in the room so she could crawl from one to the next. I leaned over to her, placed my hand on her back, and started whispering into her ear, not knowing how well she could hear me, wondering if her ears were sore, what they'd done to her in there; what fear she must have felt without me there to hold her hand. "It's okay, sweet girl. It's okay."

Mia flexed her whole body, lying on her side, completely rigid, then started writhing, growling, and pulling at the tape holding needles in her arms. A nurse and I intervened as best we could. Mia went up on her hands and knees, spitting the gauze out of her mouth, then sat up on her knees. She reached for me, her arms lifting the tubes attached to them. I looked at the nurse and she nodded, allowing me to wrap my arms around my daughter, picking her up enough to put her in my lap so I could cradle her, rocking from side to side, repeating my promise that everything would be all right.

"I want some juice," she growled at me, collapsing into me at the effort and possibly the pain it took to form words and voice them. I heard her whimper. The nurse handed her a sippy cup. Mia sat up to drink half of it, then tucked herself back into my arms again.

Within an hour, I stood in the parking lot with Mia dressed but still wrapped around me, not ready to put her in the car seat to drive the few blocks to get home. They'd rushed us out, loaning us a humidifier that was shaped like Mickey Mouse. "Yup, we do things quick around here," the nurse said after placing it on the hood of my car. I stood there like that in the parking lot for another fifteen minutes, holding my daughter, staring at the building, feeling more alone than I'd ever felt before. We'd made it through that morning, Mia had survived the surgery, but in that moment a sort of cloak fell over me. This wasn't a moment of empowerment or a celebration that we'd done it; this was a saturation into a new depth of loneliness that I now had to learn how to breathe in and out in. It was a new existence. Where I'd wake up and go to sleep.

⁓

Before I arrived first thing the following Monday for her monthly clean, the owner of the Plant House moved everything she could off the floor. She rolled up rugs, put stacks of magazines on chairs, and piled books, workout equipment, and shoes on the bed. Her instructions were militant, the most specific of all my clients: deep clean all floors, the kitchen and the bathroom, and inspect windowsills and frames for black mold.

The Plant House owners were empty nesters. Their son's room hadn't seemed to change much since he moved out. His trophies still stood on the windowsill behind his bed. They'd moved in a desk and a large keyboard where the wife gave piano lessons. I wondered if it was easier to use than the upright piano by the front door. The husband was some kind of pastor or maybe worked at a church. They had prayers written out and framed instead of pictures on the walls.

The wife had huge plants on wheels that I rolled around to sweep and mop beneath. Each window in the living room had a half dozen spider plants perched on the sill or hanging from a hook in the ceiling. Christmas cactuses sat in pots near the spider plants, and she draped philodendron vines over the curtain rods. I'd sneaked to snip off a couple of baby spider plants and took them home to put in pots. I wanted to be surrounded by green growth, by life, too. I just couldn't afford to buy the starts from a store.

There weren't any plants in the bathroom. But there was mold. I stood on the edge of the bathtub to clean it from the crevice where the wall met the ceiling. The wife would leave the shower curtain rolled up and folded over the rod. She removed the rugs and towels to place them in the wash. By the time I arrived, the bathroom was bare, stark, white. I turned off the humidifier that she used to filter the air so that all of my movements echoed. I liked to sing in that bathroom with my voice reverberating off the walls.

As a child, I had performed in school swing choirs, fall plays, and spring musicals. I never sang a solo, but I liked being onstage. My friends and I would break into harmonies as we walked down the street. The empty houses gave me space to sing again, without fear of anyone listening. I'd belt out Adele, Tegan and Sara, and Widespread Panic.

That Monday after Mia's surgery, I stood in the Plant House's bathtub and sang loud, my voice booming, until I started crying and couldn't stop.

With the final wipe to dry the shower walls, tears brimmed in my eyes, and I immediately put my hand to my face to catch them. I pressed palms to my eyes, letting out a choking sob, lowered myself to my knees and remembered how we'd been rushed out the door from the recovery room. As soon as Mia sipped down some juice and went pee, we had to leave. I couldn't even sit with her in the waiting room. But I wasn't ready to stop holding her; I was unable to drive with the expectation to watch the road. I'd leaned up against the car, still warm from the morning sun, and let her body drape over mine, feeling for both of her pink flip-flop sandals, then moving my hand up to squeeze her calf, then thigh; then I wrapped both of my arms around her, burying my face in her neck. I'd been there for Mia, but I'd needed someone to hold my hand, be there for me. Sometimes mothers need to be mothered, too.

Mia rarely saw me cry. Crying meant admitting defeat. It felt like my body and mind gave up. I did everything I could to avoid that feeling. An inability to stop crying was my fear.

Of gasping for air. Of the way my mind tricked me into thinking that I might die. Crying like that, in that bathtub, felt almost the same, like I had lost myself in that uncontrollable way needed for my body to release. With all the things swirling around me that I had no control over, I could, at the very least, control my reactions to them. If I started crying every time something hard or horrible happened, well, I'd just be crying all the time.

As I was on the brink of feeling like I could give up, something shifted. The walls of the Plant House closed inward. I felt safety. That house had spoken to me. It had watched me go through its phone book to find churches that might donate funds to help me pay rent after I learned that the waitlist for Section 8 was five years long. That house knew me, and I knew it. I knew that the owner had constant sinus infections, that she'd stockpiled home remedies, that she worked out to old aerobics videos from the eighties in her bedroom. The house had been witness to my desperate calls to caseworkers, asking if there was any way I'd qualify for cash assistance. While cleaning its kitchen, I'd fought doggedly with Jamie. I'd cleaned the entire living room while on hold, waiting to renew my food stamps. For a few minutes, as I kneeled in the cradle of the tub, the walls of the Plant House protected me and comforted me with its stoic silence.

15

The Chef's House

When we lived in the homeless shelter, I sat up late at night, long after Mia went to bed. As the night stretched out before me, I created a vision of a "happy" life. There would be a large yard of freshly cut green grass and a tree with a swing hanging from a branch. Our house wouldn't be terribly big, but it'd be large enough that Mia could run around in it, maybe with a dog, and build forts beneath the rungs of furniture. Mia would not only have her own bedroom but her own bathroom, too. Maybe there'd be a proper guest room, or an office where I could write. A real couch and a matching love seat. A garage. If we only had these things, I thought, we would be happy.

Most of my clients had these things—the things I yearned for in those dark nights sitting up alone—and they did not seem to enjoy life any more than I did. Most worked long hours, away from the homes they fought so hard to pay for, with even farther commutes than mine. I began to pay attention to the items that cluttered their kitchen counters: the receipts for rugs that were as expensive as my car, the bill for the dry cleaner that could replace half my wardrobe. In contrast, I divided my hourly wages into fifteen-minute increments to add up how much of my physical work paid for my gas. Most days I spent at least an hour just making the money it took in gas to get to work in the first place. But my clients worked long hours to pay for lavish cars, boats, sofas that they kept covered with a sheet.

They worked to pay Classic Clean, who paid me just above minimum wage, to keep it all spotless, in place, acceptable. While they paid for my work like some magical cleaning fairy, I was anything but that, shuffling through their house like a ghost. My face had an ashen hue from a lack of sun, dark circles under my eyes from a lack of sleep. Usually my hair was unwashed, pulled back into a ponytail or under a kerchief or hat. I wore pairs of Carhartt cargo pants until the holes in the knees were unsightly enough that my boss told me to replace them. My job afforded me little money to spend on clothes, even for work. I worked through illnesses and brought my daughter to day care when she should have been at home. My job offered no sick pay, no vacation days, no foreseeable increase in wage, yet through it all, still I begged to work more. Wages lost from missed work hours could rarely be made up, and if I missed too many, I risked being fired. My car's reliability was vital, since a broken hose, a faulty thermostat, or even a flat tire could throw us off, knock us backward, send us teetering, falling back, toward homelessness. We lived, we survived, in careful imbalance. This was my unwitnessed existence, as I polished another's to make theirs appear perfect.

The Chef's House had two wings: the guest bedroom and office on one end and the master bathroom with a hallway that led to a converted garage, where their dogs, two white Westminster terriers, always left puddles of pee. They went with either Mr. Lund or his wife to work on the days I cleaned. I hadn't noticed one had also started pooping by the dining room table, and I'd accidentally walked through it. I groaned. Beige carpet. Light beige. Almost fucking white. There was no way I'd be able to rub out shit stains.

I'd still only met the owner of the Chef's House one time

in the six months I'd cleaned there for three hours every other Thursday. The Chef's House had been one of Pam's original clients. She used to clean it weekly in two hours, an ability I balked at because the house was huge. I would sweat hard, working that house, too busy to stop to text or take a call from anyone for fear I wouldn't complete the clean on time. I certainly couldn't pause to scrub out brown smudges of shit.

I had a second house that day—the Cigarette Lady's House—that was another three-hour job with about a twenty-minute commute in between. A full schedule of work was normally some sort of an escape. For three, four, or even six hours, I'd be in constant movement—from the left side of the counter to the right, polishing the sink, wiping the floors, dusting, cleaning smudges left by dogs on sliding glass doors, vacuuming down halls, scrubbing toilets, wiping mirrors without pausing to look at my reflection at all, ignoring the aching muscles that grew more to a constant burn throughout the day, sometimes shooting pain or tingling sensations down my limbs. After weeks of the same movement—from start to finish, at the same time, in the same way, every other week—I stopped having to think about what to do next. Movements became routine, automatic. My muscles became tight and trained. The movement and house routines were like a much-needed mindless respite when every other aspect of my life was one difficult decision after another that had been even harder. I guess the escape had gotten a little *too* mindless, so that I wound up in shit.

The Chef's House was one I envied, with its view, yard, trees that dropped apples to rot in the grass before the land-scapers mowed over them. I wanted their back porch with its matching polished wooden furniture and maroon cushions. I imagined the lazy afternoons they must have had on the weekends—the shrimp on the grill, the chilled rosé wine in stemmed glasses, sipped under the striped canopy that rolled out from the side of the house. It seemed like a dream; and these people, with their hallways lined with paintings of scenes from Paris, got to live it every day.

Their kitchen counters were piled with food, and the neatly arranged tins of fancy cookies made my mouth drool. At Christmas, their decorations had been impeccable. I'd stopped to inspect the Christmas tree ornaments. They had every year of this Hallmark series called "Frosty Friends," which my mom had collected for the years my family spent in Alaska. Mom gave them all to me after the divorce, but about half of them went missing in all the moving around. When I saw the ornament from 1985, our first Christmas in Alaska, I gingerly cupped it in my palm, remembering my mom unwrapping the red kayak with the Eskimo child and dog to let me put it on the tree. Christmas was half a year away now, and I realized I wasn't even sure we'd be able to fit or afford a tree big enough to hang ornaments on in our studio. Mia was usually with Jamie for Christmas, since I always got Thanksgiving. I wanted so much for her to have a life where the same exact ornaments went on the tree every year. Traditions so small they'd gone unnoticed when I was a child, and now they were all I wanted for mine.

A third of the time I spent at the Chef's House went to floors. Sometimes I shuffled to my car a little bent over with one hand on the bottom muscles near my spine. I wasn't a stranger to pain, but being hunched over for hours cleaning took its toll. My spine curved like a question mark; it had put me in the emergency room several times. I had to be careful not to upset it, and I popped 800-milligram doses of ibuprofen around the clock if I did. My latest mistake at work had been bending slightly to pick up the edge of a couch to push it closer to a wall. It felt as heavy as my car. The muscles in my back, prepared to lift something light, snapped back like a released rubber band and stuck. For days, I gritted my teeth through spasms, losing sleep from the pain. I couldn't handle painkiller pills very well. They made me loopy and sick, like I was half drunk.

When I saw the counters of the Chef's House starting to fill with large prescription pill bottles of hydrocodone, it was almost tempting to pocket a few. Prescription pills littered the bathroom countertops and the medicine cabinets of most of the houses I cleaned, but this one had giant bottles in almost every room, going from full to empty in the two weeks between my visits.

Lonnie and I never spoke of the secrets the empty houses revealed. Most of my clients had sleep aids, ones for depression and anxiety, or pain. Perhaps because my clients had easier access to doctors or health insurance plans with a generous prescription medication clause built in; perhaps access to medical care created a default to prescriptions as a solution. Though I could get coverage for Mia, I made too much money for me to receive Medicaid, so I couldn't see a doctor about chronic back pain or lingering sinus infections and coughs. Mia, thankfully, had always been covered, so I never had to worry about that, and the application process was simple, since they used the same paperwork I submitted for food stamps. It would have been impossible to afford her regular check-ups and vaccinations, let alone the surgery she'd just had, but I always wondered if doctors and nurses, after seeing the type of insurance I used, treated us differently because she had Medicaid. Even though I would have greatly benefitted from regular care, physical therapy, or even access to a gynecologist, I'd never be able to afford that for myself. I had to be careful not to hurt myself, not to get sick, and try to manage my pain on my own. But vitamins, over-the-counter cold and flu remedies, and even Tylenol or ibuprofen were a huge expense, or so low on the budget that I rationed what I had. Living with illness or pain was part of my daily life. Part of the exhaustion. But why did my clients have these problems? It seemed like access to healthy foods, gym memberships, doctors, and all of that would keep a person fit and well. Maybe the stress of keeping up a two-story house, a bad marriage, and maintaining the illusion of grandeur overwhelmed their systems in similar ways to how poverty did mine.

I drove with all the windows down on my way to the Cigarette Lady's House. It must have been in the eighties outside, meaning our bedroom would be close to ninety degrees by the time we got home. Sweat gathered in the creases of my skin. Most of the windows of her house faced north, so it would be cooler in there, but they'd all be closed, and the stuffiness combined with a mix of stale smoke and scented candles would make me nauseated. When I walked in, I went to place my binder on the counter, where she had the cordless phone next to her datebook that only contained appointments for facials and massages at a spa, and I saw she'd left a note. *Thought you might like a good-smelling candle for your home!* it read. I picked up the little silver tin and opened it to see bright orange wax, smelling of a perfectly ripe peach. My favorite scent. I smiled, inhaled the candle again, and tucked it away in my purse before calling to clock in.

The Cigarette Lady was a mystery to me. Our one brief encounter came after I barged into her kitchen two hours earlier than she expected me to arrive. She rushed out quickly, before we could have any sort of verbal exchange, but long enough for me to see that her hair and makeup were impeccably done, satisfying one of my curiosities. There were always new bags of makeup or anti-wrinkle cream or some tiny container in her bathroom. Each new product had receipts for at least $50, but I never saw evidence of empty bottles or others being completely used. Every other week, she'd get a massage, a facial, and a manicure and pedicure, and I had often wondered if they were products someone had talked her into buying but weren't ones she was necessarily interested in using. Her appearance proved otherwise. She looked flawless, even on a random Thursday afternoon.

Her house sat right next to a golf course, and golf seemed like a hobby she put a lot of time into. In the downstairs closet above the washer and dryer were framed scorecards and a photo of the Cigarette Lady standing next to Tiger Woods. She wore a white shirt to match her pressed white shorts, and her hair was piled on top of her head, separated from her face by a visor. The downstairs of the house felt stuck in time. When I walked down with my vacuum, rags, and cleaning tray, it felt like I was walking into the late eighties or early nineties, with outdated furniture on top of a thick white carpet. The guest bedroom had decorations of Canadian geese that I swore were the same ones I'd grown up with. In the office was a particle-board desk and an ancient-looking treadmill, which faced an old TV/VCR combo, like the one I had at home.

Upstairs, she'd done several updates—hardwood floors, new countertops, and a stainless-steel fridge that, from what I could tell, mainly held bottled water and lettuce.

The furniture was sleek and modern, and from the amount of dust that settled on it, untouched. In her closet, I coveted a tan cashmere cardigan so much, every time I vacuumed in there, I'd pause, unzip the front, and put it on, placing its hood over my head, wearing it so the sleeves covered my hands, and rubbed my face with its softness.

It was hard to tell the house was used at all, except for the small bathroom off the master bedroom and the guest toilet across from the kitchen. I always grimaced when I lifted those toilet seats to scrub the bowl. Under the rim was almost always splattered with vomit.

After a few visits, I began to get a vision of her time at home. Her husband owned and operated a construction company at least an hour outside of town. It was 2010, and building operations still seemed to be at a standstill. They were probably anxious about their security, wondering if they might be next. Their house always seemed to be set up for a dinner party, with fake candles lit and placemats set, but I could tell by the dust on the tables and chairs that nights with guests and fancy meals rarely happened. Most of her time at home she seemed to spend sitting on a bar stool across from the stovetop that was built into the bar. The stovetop had an air intake for the fan at the back, closest to her, and it was usually peppered with cigarette ashes. Next to her sat a tiny television, her datebook, and a cordless phone, with a few stray crumbs on the floor.

On a shelf, next to the dining room table, were several electric wax warmer air fresheners. Their combined smell gave me headaches. Once she left a lighter by her datebook, but other than the cleaned ashtray I found beneath the sink, there was no other evidence of cigarettes. Then, one day, on my way out through the garage, I noticed a freezer. I opened it to reveal stacked cartons of Virginia Slims. I stared at them, then smiled with satisfaction. Mystery solved.

I could picture her, with her chin resting in her hand, stamping out a cigarette, letting out a breath full of smoke carefully into the stovetop fan, then getting up, tossing her hair a little, and emptying out the ashtray in the garage before carefully rinsing it and wiping it clean. I wondered if she carried the cigarettes in her purse or if it was something she only did at home in that one spot in the kitchen. It wasn't about the smoking. I smoked off and on. I couldn't have cared less if she smoked. It was the secrecy that fascinated me, the amount of energy she put into appearing perfect and clean.

16

Donna's House

Over the summer, the idea of drug tests for welfare recipients had some new life breathed into it. Since the recession, millions had turned to the government for help. More struggling middle-class taxpayers voicing their anger over the injustice of others getting a handout caused tension between folks already on government assistance, using their food stamps, and those who didn't qualify. Demanding drug tests perpetuated a new layer of judgment for those of us receiving the assistance, creating a new narrative for how we took advantage, took money from the government in our laziness and now possibly addiction. Memes online compared people on food stamps to wild animals. One meme showed a bear sitting at a picnic table and read:

> Today's lesson in irony: The food stamp program, a part of the Department of Agriculture, is pleased to be distributing the greatest amounts of food stamps ever. Meanwhile, the Park Service, which is also part of the Department of Agriculture, asks us to PLEASE DO NOT FEED THE ANIMALS because the animals may grow dependent and not learn to take care of themselves.

Another popular one had an illustrated work boot that read, *"If I have to take a drug test to work, you should have to take one for welfare."* Another one read, *"If you can afford drugs, alcohol, and cigarettes, then you don't need food stamps."* One of my friends on Facebook worked at a grocery store, and she had started to post what people bought on food stamps to make fun of them: *"Funyuns? On food stamps? With soda?"* She encouraged her friends to make fun of what poor people could barely afford to eat.

Around forty-seven million families were signed up for government assistance along with me that year. EBT cards, distributed by the Department of Health and Human Services to utilize as food stamps or cash assistance, were a common sight at cash registers. Take-and-bake pizza shops now accepted EBT cards, but I rarely used my allotment of food stamps for that. Mount Vernon, Skagit County's largest city at thirty-three thousand people, became home to a large population of migrant workers through the growing season, and many of those families decided to stay year-round. But as the migrant population increased, the conservatism of the area was exposed.

Donna seemed to have a lot of grievances about this. I'd come to depend heavily on the $20 an hour with a ten-dollar tip she always left for me, but driving back and forth to her house would steal an hour from my workday. About half of the time, she was there when I arrived. One day she was on her way to the store to purchase ingredients for smoothies, since she'd just bought a special blender. "It's for a new me!" she cried. "But I'm going to the co-op this time. I don't like the big grocery stores anymore."

"Oh, really?" I asked, feigning interest. Donna enjoyed Mary Kay oils, which left a film that stuck to the side of the bathtub like Velcro, collecting every hair, every dead skin cell that came off her. It was hard to have conversations with her without seeing flashes of it. I never knew if she expected me to stop and talk or continue cleaning while having a conversation with the person whose pubic hairs and leg hair stubble I'd have to scrub from the ring of her jetted tub.

"Last time I went to the big store, I got in line behind a Mexican family," she said. "They used food stamps to pay for their food. And those kids were dressed to the *nines!*"

I continued to dust a windowsill in her front sitting room full of little angel statues with their hands together in prayer. Her words were sharp. I bit down on the tip of my tongue. I thought of how much Mia loved her fancy dresses and shiny shoes, which I purchased with credit from the consignment store. Maybe Donna didn't realize I was on food stamps, too.

I wanted to tell Donna that it wasn't her business what that family bought or ate or wore and that I hated when cashiers at the supermarket said, "On your EBT?" loud enough for people in line behind me to hear. I wanted to tell her that undocumented people couldn't receive food benefits or tax refunds, even though they paid taxes. They couldn't receive any government benefits at all. Those were available only for people who were born here or who had obtained the documents to stay. So those children, whose parents had risked so much to give them a good life, were citizens who deserved every bit as much government help as my daughter did. I knew this because I'd sat beside them in countless government offices. I overheard their conversations with caseworkers sitting behind glass, failing to communicate through a language barrier. But these attitudes that immigrants came here to steal our resources were spreading, and the stigmas resembled those facing anyone who relied on government assistance to survive. Anyone who used food stamps didn't work hard enough or made bad decisions to put them in that lower-class place. It was like people thought it was on purpose and that we cheated the system, stealing the money they paid toward taxes to rob the government of funds. More than ever, it seemed, taxpayers—including my client—thought their money subsidized food for lazy poor people.

Donna left for the grocery store, oblivious to my emotional reaction to her words. Grocery shopping made me feel twice as vulnerable after that. With the added posts on social media, I was certain that people watched my every move. I worried about buying items that were either too nice or too frivolous. In the chance I would ever need to get Easter candy or chocolates for Mia's stocking at Christmas with food stamp money, I'd go late at night, using the self-checkout. Even though I really needed it, I stopped using WIC checks for milk, cheese, eggs, and peanut butter—I never seemed to get the right size, brand, or color of eggs, the correct type of juice, or the specific number of ounces of cereal anyway. Each coupon had such specific requirements in what it could be used for, and I held my breath when the cashier rang them up. I always screwed up in some way and caused a holdup in the line. Maybe others did the same, since cashiers grew visibly annoyed whenever they saw one of those large WIC coupons on the conveyor belt. Once, after massive amounts of miscommunication with the cashier, an older couple started huffing and shaking their heads behind me.

My caseworker at the WIC office even prepared me for it. The program had recently downgraded their qualifying milk from organic to non-organic, leaving me with a missing chunk in my food budget I couldn't afford to make up. If at all possible, I tried to give Mia only organic whole milk. Non-organic, 2 percent milk might as well have been white-colored water to me, packed with sugar, salt, antibiotics, and hormones. These coupons were my last chance for a while to offer her the one organic food she ingested (besides her boxes of Annie's macaroni and cheese).

When I'd scoffed at losing the benefit to purchase organic whole milk, my caseworker nodded and sighed. "We just don't have the funding for it anymore," she'd told me. I somewhat understood, since a half gallon had a price tag of nearly four dollars. "The obesity rates are going up in children," she added, "and this is a program focused on providing the best nutrition."

"They don't realize that skim milk is full of sugar?" I asked, allowing Mia to climb out of my lap so she could play with the toys in the corner.

"They're also adding ten dollars for produce!" she added brightly, ignoring my grumpy attitude. "You can purchase any produce you want, except potatoes."

"Why not potatoes?" I thought of the large batches of mashed potatoes I made to supplement my diet.

"People tend to fry them or add lots of butter," she said, looking a little confused herself. "You can get sweet potatoes, though!" She explained I'd have to purchase exactly ten dollars' worth or less, and wouldn't be able to go over, or the check wouldn't work. I wouldn't get any change if the produce I selected rang in under ten dollars. The coupons didn't have any real monetary value.

That day at the store, with it being the last month of organic milk, I wanted every bit I could get.

"Your milk isn't a WIC item," the cashier said again. "It won't ring up that way." She started to turn to the young man bagging our other groceries and sighed. I knew she was going to tell him to go run and get the right kind of milk. It happened to me with the eggs all the time.

My checks weren't expired, but the store had already updated their system. Normally, I would have cowered, taken the non-organic milk, and run out, especially with two old people shaking their heads in annoyance. I glanced at them again and caught the man standing with his arms crossed and head tilted, eyeing my pants with holes in the knees. My shoes were getting holes in the toes. He loudly sighed again.

I asked to speak to the manager. The cashier's eyebrows shot up as she shrugged her shoulders and put up her hands in front of me, like I'd pulled out a gun and ordered her to give me all her money.

"Sure," she said, evenly and coolly; the voice of a customer service representative faced with an unruly shopper. "I'll get the manager for you."

As he walked over, I could see his flustered employee following behind him, red-faced and gesturing wildly, even pointing at me, to explain her side of the story. He immediately apologized and overrode the cash register. Then he rang up my organic whole milk as a WIC item, bagged it, and told me to have a wonderful day.

As I pushed my cart away, my hands still shaking, the old man nodded toward my groceries and said, "You're welcome!"

I grew infuriated. *You're welcome for what?* I wanted to yell back at him. That he'd waited so impatiently, huffing and grumbling to his wife? It couldn't have been that. It was that I was obviously poor and shopping in the middle of the day, pointedly not at work. He didn't know I had to take an afternoon off for the WIC appointment, missing $40 in wages, where they had to weigh both Mia and me. We left with a booklet of coupons that supplemented about the same as those lost wages, but not the disgruntled client whom I'd had to reschedule, who might, if I ever needed to reschedule again, go with a different cleaner, because my work was that disposable. But what he saw was that those coupons were paid for by government money, the money he'd personally contributed to with the taxes he'd paid. To him, he might as well have personally bought the fancy milk I insisted on, but I was obviously poor so I didn't deserve it.

Would my clients like Donna, the ones who confided in me like a good friend, who gave me coloring books and crayons for Mia, do the same if they saw me at the grocery store? How would they view a cleaning lady on food stamps? As a hard worker or as a failure? I'd become so self-conscious about these things that I tried to hide the details as much as possible. In the middle of conversations, I'd wonder if the person's view of me would change if they knew I was on food stamps. Would they assume I had less potential?

I found myself wondering what it would be like to have enough money to be able to hire someone to clean my house. I'd never been in that position before, and I honestly doubted I ever would be. If I ever had to, I thought, I'd give them a big tip and probably offer them food or leave them good-smelling candles, too. I'd treat them like a guest, not a ghost. An equal. Like Wendy, Henry, Donna, and the Cigarette Lady did with me.

17

In Three Years

As far as I know, only one of my clients—the one who owned the Farm House—used hidden cameras. She told me this so matter-of-factly, it caught me off guard. I tried my hardest to nod, as though hidden cameras were totally normal. The Farm House was two stories of navy-blue carpet covered in white hair from her cats and dogs. The stairs had carpet as well, and the hair would become trapped in the corners and creases of each step. Before I had started working there, Lonnie explained that she'd gone through every cleaner at the company trying to find someone suitable for the Farm House—I was their last chance at keeping the client.

It wasn't ever clear what I did so differently than the other cleaners, and since I rarely cleaned with them, I wasn't able to compare our skills or work ethic. I had a fear of being caught not working. Plus, I never could shake when, in an argument with Jamie, one of the many of its kind, he had said to me, "You sit around here all day, doing nothing but taking care of the baby, and the grout is filthy in the bathroom." I never forgot that feeling. Even though I felt like I did everything I could, I was never doing enough.

Subconsciously, I wore the social stigma of being on government assistance even more after the encounter with the old couple in the supermarket. It felt like a weighted vest

I couldn't take off, or like someone had hidden cameras on me all the time. People I talked to rarely assumed I needed food stamps to survive, and they always said "those people" in conversations. Yet "those people" were never people like me. They were immigrants, or people of color, or the white people who were often referred to as trash.

When people think of food stamps, they don't envision someone like me: someone plain-faced and white. Someone like the girl they'd known in high school who'd been quiet but nice. Someone like a neighbor. Someone like them. Maybe that made them too nervous about their own situation. Maybe they saw in me the chance of their own fragile circumstances, that, with one lost job, one divorce, they'd be in the same place as I was.

It seemed like certain members of society looked for opportunities to judge and scold poor people for what they felt we didn't deserve. They'd see a person buying fancy meats with an EBT card and use that as evidence for their theory that everyone on food stamps did the same. Surely, someone was keeping tabs on me. Sometimes I felt that way in what was supposed to be the safety of my own home. If I wasn't working or taking care of Mia, I had to be taking care of something. I felt like sitting down meant I wasn't doing enough—like the sort of lazy welfare recipient I was assumed to be. Time lounging to read a book felt overly indulgent; almost as though such leisure was reserved for another class. I had to work constantly. I had to prove my worth for receiving government benefits.

Every once in a while, though, to escape, I went on dates. I'd call up an old boyfriend or meet someone online, or my cousin Jenn would introduce me to someone. For a few awkward hours, I could return to the person I was outside of motherhood, outside of being a maid. It felt like make-believe, maybe more for me than for my date. I knew none of it was real. I'd talk about books and movies in a way that sounded foreign to myself. Sometimes, that parallel, other life was what I needed to mentally remove myself from my own. But dating soon became less fun, less of a game, making my loneliness or sense of isolation more acute. A text gone unanswered or a call going straight to voice mail meant rejection, proof that I was unlovable. I hated that neediness, and I was sure that men could sense it, that it lingered like a pungent odor. Additionally, socializing opened me up to the painful reminder that most people had normal lives. They afforded concerts, takeout, trips, all without losing a night's sleep. Despite Mia's constant touch and pull and her sticky hand finding mine, I ached for affection, for touch, for love. I never saw a time I wouldn't crave that. I wanted to be strong and not need it, but I always would.

I walked along a deep precipice of hopelessness. Each morning brought a constant, lip-chewing stress over making it to work and getting home without my car breaking down. My back ached constantly. I dampened my hunger pangs with coffee. It felt impossible to climb out of this hole. My only real hope was school: an education would be my token to freedom. It had to be, otherwise it was a waste to invest so much precious time. Like a prisoner, I calculated how long I had left until I'd completed enough credits to qualify for a degree. Three more years. The Pell Grant covered tuition but not textbooks, if my classes required any. Sometimes I could get by with purchasing a used, older edition off of Amazon. Three years of dark nights and weekends spent over books, writing reports, and taking tests. This life of working as a maid, of constant subservience, was temporary. I cried myself to sleep some nights, my only comfort knowing this was not how my story would end.

So I stopped trying to have a social life and filled my free weekends with work instead. I took on a new client, a four-hour clean forty-five minutes away on the Saturdays Mia was with Jamie in Port Townsend. This house, the Weekend

House, had clients who were always there, but we never got to know one another. A young couple lived there with their weeks-old baby. The grandma had been staying with them to help, and her parting gift was a bimonthly housecleaning.

They didn't want the housecleaner there when they weren't home, which was fine, but that made it difficult to clean around them while they obliviously used a kitchen counter I'd just wiped to make toast or walked through a floor I'd just mopped. They chatted with friends who came over for baby play dates, serving them food like I wasn't there.

On my second visit to clean, I drove out to find their front door locked. After knocking a few times on the door, I peered into the garage window, cupping my hands on the unusually clean glass, and saw it was empty. Even though it was a Saturday morning, I called Lonnie's cell phone.

"They're not here, Lonnie," I said, nearly yelling, showing my anger at how frustrating that was, something I rarely did. "Did they ever say anything about leaving a key?"

"No," she said. "The mother just told me they'd always be there. Let me call them and see what's up. Maybe they're just running errands and are on their way home."

Because I wouldn't get reimbursed, I tried not to add up how much that trip cost me in gas, but I knew without thinking too much that it would be around ten bucks, more than I made an hour before taxes and the cost of washing my own rags. When Lonnie called back to tell me they forgot, I pressed my lips together in frustration, trying not to cry.

"Do they want me to come tomorrow or something?" I asked. "I can do it if it's early."

"Nope," Lonnie said. I heard her sigh. "They canceled."

I was so quiet for a minute, Lonnie asked if I was still there. "Yeah," I said. She asked if I was okay, and I said no. "Can you ask Pam if I can at least get some gas money for this? I've already spent an hour of my time and money coming out here. I don't have a lot of that to spare, you know?" I wiped at tears that had escaped and trickled down my cheek and tried not to let my voice sound shaky. Lonnie said she'd see what she could do, but I could already hear Pam telling me how the recession had slowed business, and they had to be really careful with extra expenses. I started to regret asking.

Two weeks later, I returned to clean their house again. The husband approached me as I unloaded my supplies into the entryway. "I'm really sorry," he said. I nodded, taking out a rag to shove in my back pocket. "We're just not used to having someone come here to clean the house."

"It's okay," I said, grabbing for a spray bottle.

"Here," he said, reaching into his back pocket, and pulled out two tickets to a Seattle Mariners baseball game. "These are for tomorrow night." He tried to hand them to me. "You should take them." The tickets had graphics of the players throwing pitches or sliding into third. Fancy tickets. Tickets to good seats. I'd gone to games as a kid, and during the 1995 playoffs when Ken Griffey, Jr., Edgar Martinez, and Randy Johnson were on the team, but hadn't been since.

We stood on the stone tile in the entryway that his mother had asked us to buff. Pam had shown me how to do it before loading the buffer into the back of my car. I'd had it in there for three weeks, taking up half of my Subaru wagon's rear storage space. He apparently didn't want me to do it that day, either, because of the men walking in and out to re-grout the tile in their shower. I knew he couldn't possibly know how frustrating this was.

I looked down at the tickets again. There was no way I could afford the gas and parking that going to the game would require. I looked up at his tired but smiling face, and the blue receiving blanket over his shoulder, like he'd just burped his month-old son after a feeding. I saw the familiar exhaustion in his eyes. He might be living a completely different experience than mine with a newborn—the large house, nice cars, slew of swings and bouncing chairs, and relatives coming over to bring food and available arms—but his duties as a parent were universal. Even like mine.

"It's okay," I said, trying to believe that it was, trying to not be angry with him anymore. "You should use the tickets or give them to someone who can. I won't be able to go." I wanted to tell him I couldn't afford the gas to go, but I worried that he'd offer me money, too.

"Well, you could sell them," he said, pushing the tickets toward me again. "I'm sure they'll go pretty quick on Craigslist. They're front-row seats."

I winced. "Really?" Front-row seats to a Mariners game. It was a chance to fulfill a dream I'd had since I'd been Mia's age. I looked at him again. I wondered if he was the type of father who got up in the middle of the night to change a diaper. The type who bounced the baby in the kitchen while the bottle heated, then fell asleep on the couch with a tiny infant sleeping on his chest. I decided he was.

"Okay," I said, looking down at the tickets. He reached out to hand me the tickets again. When I took them, he put a hand on my shoulder and squeezed, like he wanted to hug me.

He was right; it was easy to sell the tickets. The next afternoon I placed an ad online. My buyer met me at the Laundromat and happily handed over sixty bucks.

"They're for my son's birthday," he said. "He's turning four. His first baseball game!"

I smiled and told him to have fun.

18

The Sad House

On Saturdays and Sundays, Mia and I got up at our usual time, even though we didn't have anywhere to go. I made her pancakes, sprinkling in blueberries I'd picked and frozen the summer before. I sat across from her at the table, holding my coffee close to my face, watching her gobble down bite after bite. She smiled at me with full cheeks, the blueberries staining her lips. I smiled back, trying to hide the tears in my eyes, trying to mentally record that moment, to meditate on it when I needed to. Our lives went by too quickly in the often chaotic dance of work, dinner, and bedtime. I knew she'd grow out of her Ramona Quimby bob. She'd soon stop playing with the My Little Ponies that she'd lined up in a half circle, facing her bowl. Whenever I ached for her, either at work or when she was at Jamie's, these were the moments I replayed in my head. The moments I wrote about.

I'd started a writing exercise whenever Mia took a bath or was otherwise preoccupied: ten minutes of constant typing of whatever was on my mind. Sometimes I wrote in the morning on weekends, and the paragraphs were full of good weather, plans to enjoy it, or a secret spot I felt excited to share with my daughter. Other times I wrote after Mia was asleep, after an exhausting day of her fighting me through every transition and turn. I'd try to pull out of my memory a sweet exchange, bring to the forefront a passing primal connection only a mother and a child could have, and write it down. It became more like a baby book for Mia than a journal. Most of all I knew, years later, I'd look back on this time as one with decisions and tasks too much for one person. I'd need to think on these times with a fondness, too, since she'd quickly be so grown up. Even though we lived in the place we did, and I worked at a horrible job, and we couldn't afford much, I'd never get this time with her back. Writing about it was my way to appreciate and create a nice picture of our life, our adventures. I figured, if anything, maybe I could print them out into a book for Mia to read someday.

Our favorite beach spot was at Washington Park, on the western side of Anacortes. We sat on the rocks, waiting for low tide, then looked for creatures in the little pools left behind.

"Look at that crab, Mom!" Mia would say. I'd squat down, pulling the yellow shovel out of the red plastic bucket, and try to scoop it in for a closer look. "Don't let it pinch you. It will pinch you, Mom!" Out in the distance, the ferries went by, and every so often we'd see a porpoise, sea lion, or eagle. I brought Mia's little bicycle in the back of my car, unloading it so she could ride the two-mile paved loop, forgetting how long that was, and ended up carrying both Mia and her bike for at least the last half mile. On the way home, we would stop by an ice cream parlor that had been there since I was a kid. I called it "Ice Cream for Dinner." Mia never got anything but chocolate, covering most of her face with its stickiness.

Other weekends, I'd go online in search of hidden waterfalls, creeks with swimming holes. I'd pack a leather-handled basket with a blanket, a change of clothes, a towel, and snacks for Mia, and in a few minutes we were out the door. The only cost was the gas to get us there and back.

These times were our happiest, perhaps because of the simplicity. I'd let her ride her bike downtown, with me trotting behind her, to get an apple from the store. On the off chance it rained, we'd stay in, do a puzzle, or build a fort. Sometimes we'd fold out the love seat and I'd let Mia watch as many DVDs as she wanted, like a weekend-long sleepover.

I didn't know it then, but those weekends, that still life with Mia, was what I'd look back on with the most nostalgia. Even though some trips were utter failures, ending in temper tantrums and screaming matches that left us both crumbled and hollowed out, those hours with my three-year-old were precious. She'd wake me up by crawling into bed with me, wrapping her little arms around my neck, soft curls framing the sides of her face, whispering in my ear, asking if we could be pandas that day. Suddenly, my week of teeth-grinding grit would fade. And we would drift, in a bubble, just me and this amazing kid.

Those were the only times I could quiet my mind, when I didn't worry whether I should be working instead or if I was doing enough. I didn't wonder whether someone might see us as a "welfare family," taking advantage of the system as we sat on a blanket at the park, sharing slices of cheese. I never cared about any of that on those days with her. For that afternoon, we were each other's moon and sun in our own little world.

By midsummer, I had been working with Classic Clean for six months, and I had a solid twenty-five-hour-a-week schedule with them. Additionally, I juggled several of my own clients on the side, cleaning their houses or yards once or twice a month. Along with the Cigarette Lady's occasional offerings, other clients started leaving me things on the kitchen counter. Henry always gave me something. He knew that after I left his house, I picked up Mia and drove her to her dad's. One time he gave me a box of donuts, another time a large jug of a fancy brand of apple juice.

Henry's health seemed to be failing him a little. The pills by his bathroom sink had multiplied, and, judging from the state of his toilet, they had upset his stomach quite a bit. His wife had been home a few times lately, too, but she spent most of the time on the phone, arguing with insurance companies or her mother, who, from what I could tell, had to be transferred from one old folks' home to the next. I loved seeing the two of them together. Henry's boisterous demeanor changed to a softness that I craved from a partner in my own life. He made her tea. They discussed what needed to be picked up from the store for dinner. Henry said he'd make "that one thing" she liked, and she gave him a fierce hug before rushing out the door. She always made sure to say goodbye to me, using my name and everything, with such sincerity sometimes that I almost expected a hug of my own.

I tried to carry these moments with me on the days when I cleaned the Porn House. That house had an air of anger to it, or disgruntlement. I didn't like being there. A note on the counter read simply, "Change the sheets, please." At least she said please.

Around Father's Day, I'd gotten into a huge fight on the phone with Jamie, and I was cleaning the Porn House at the time. After that, being in that house reminded me of him, no matter how hard I tried to sever the association.

The fight had been about Mia's last name. I wanted to change it to mine. She'd eventually start school, and every time I took her to the doctor, they asked me if I was her mother. It didn't make sense for her to have his last name if she lived with me nearly all the time.

Jamie vehemently disagreed with this. He argued I hardly spent any time with her, that most of her days were spent in "that disgusting day care." I regretted letting his mom pick Mia up one day I had to work late, as Jamie had used her judgmental opinion of the facility against me ever since. But I'd never do anything right either way. If I stayed home or worked less, he faulted me for not working, saying that his child support went toward me sitting on my ass. If I went to school, I was wasting my time. Now, apparently, working too much was also bad.

That day on the phone he said, "And you've never told me to have a happy Father's Day." I'd almost finished the kitchen, polishing away the grease splatters on the brick-red stovetop.

"What?" I said, not really asking. Jamie had never once wished me a happy Mother's Day. He'd never told me that I was a good mom. The closest thing he'd come to praise was to tell me that I was smart enough to push his buttons and manipulate him to get what I wanted. Even that summer we were dating, I don't think he ever praised my appearance. He called me ugly several times after I got pregnant, and especially after Mia was born.

"You've never called me a good father," he said.

"Jamie, that's because you aren't one," I said. "You blame everyone around you for everything. You never take responsibility. Everything is always someone else's fault. What's that going to teach Mia? What are you going to teach her?" I reached up to dust the chandelier above the dining room table.

"I'll teach Emilia lots of things!" he said, which made me wonder, again, if everyone in Port Townsend still called her Emilia. He refused to call her Mia because it was a nickname *I'd* given her. I tried to explain she'd given it to herself and that she got mad if I called her by her full name. He'd tried to talk her into a nickname that sounded like Mee-lah for a while, but it never stuck. Every time he said it, I wondered if she subconsciously changed identities when she was there.

"Jamie, you don't even know how to swim," I said. It was odd for me to speak this way to him. Working full-time, doing everything on my own, had empowered me. I no longer chose to allow him to make me feel bad about myself. "What about when she brings home math homework? Or has to write a report? How are you going to help her with that?"

I didn't say these things to him as a jab. These were actual concerns. Jamie always talked about studying for his GED, or he promised that this summer would be the one when he'd learn how to swim, but he never did any of the things he said he would. Instead, he always had an excuse or a rambling story about how it was his mom's fault because he had to help raise his younger brother. Now it was my fault for forcing him into fatherhood, into a life he never wanted.

"I know I'm a good father," he said. I could imagine his posture, puffing out his chest, probably pointing to it, maybe looking in a mirror. "I know I am because she needs me." I heard him take a quick breath. Ah. He was outside, smoking a cigarette and pacing.

It was my turn to point into the air, walking between the living room and the bedroom, duster in hand. I had watched him make a pouty face, pretending to cry until Mia turned to him and gave him one last hug whenever I picked her up. "You've manipulated her to need you."

That pushed Jamie over the edge. I knew his ranting and yelling well. "Everyone in town talks about what a fuckin' loser you are," he said. "All you do is whine about stuff online, on Facebook and that stupid website you keep a diary on. You don't have any real friends. No one's ever going to love you and your saggy boobs."

With that, I hung up on him. It always got worse after he turned down that road. He usually brought up how I was too fat, or too ugly, or too skinny, or too tall. The "saggy boobs" was a new one. "No one's ever going to love you" was his favorite line. I knew how his lips curled, almost in a smile, when he said it, and I could see it even when we were on the phone. When I lived with him in the trailer, he'd call me "stupid nut job" or "crazy bitch," but now he said those only when he really wanted me to hurt.

I finished the shower in the Porn House in record time that day, thanks to my angry scrubbing. After I wiped the floor by hand and waited for it to dry, before returning the rugs in front of the toilet and the sink, I stood out in the hallway to catch my breath. On the wall to the right of the door hung studio portraits of the family, both looking in the same direction with identical sparkles in their eyes.

I walked into the doorway of the bedroom. In some ways, this was close to the life I wanted—a sensible house with a big yard. It didn't necessarily have to sit on high-end property with views of the ocean, but it would be nice to be surrounded by a yard and a few towering trees. I stared at the bottle of lube on the nightstand by the alarm clock and couldn't help but wonder how often they had sex with each other.

But maybe it was the life I thought I wanted, and the life I really dreamed of was next door at the Sad House. After Jamie and I fought that day, I cleaned the Sad House for the first time in months. He'd been sick. Or in the hospital. Both of those things. From what I could tell, that guy had been married to the love of his life. Then she died too soon, and he was left alone to live out the years he needed someone to take care of him the most. The Porn House and the Sad House seemed to scream opposite life lessons, to illustrate that no matter what the circumstance, we all end up alone in some way or the other. The husband at the Porn House, masturbating while his wife worked nights or read romance novels in the other room. And the widower.

For me, being alone started not to sting as much. Mia and I had become a team. I loved not having to worry about if the other adult we were with was having fun or stressed over their bored sighs, obvious signs that they wanted to leave. I never had to ask anyone what they wanted to do for dinner. We could get ice cream for dinner without worrying if the person at home would feel left out or judge me as a parent.

Our studio had its downside. But it was our space. I could rearrange furniture any way I wanted, at any time. I could leave it messy or obsessively clean. Mia tap-danced and jumped from the couch to the floor without anyone telling her to be quiet. When I'd first started working as a maid, I thought I'd spend my days in longing or envy. At the end of the day, I went to a place I not only called home but that felt like it. It was our little nest that we'd fly from someday.

When I finished the Porn House, I tried to carry all my supplies over to the Sad House in one trip. Outside, it was damp and misting rain. It was weather that grew mold. Weather that made my skin creep with mildew or moss.

I opened the sliding glass door with my pinky because my hand held my tray of supplies. The door led to the kitchen, and as soon as I entered, I smelled the familiar wood chip and aftershave smells of the Sad House. I was about to set down the tray when I turned around and screamed.

His face was covered in open sores. I immediately regretted screaming; I wanted to cry. He'd never been there during a clean, and I'd never met him. And now I'd screamed at the sight of his face, which showed obvious signs of how much he'd been struggling.

"I'm so, so sorry," I said, nearly dropping my tray, the tote bag of rags, the garbage bag filled with used rags.

"No, no, I'm sorry to startle you," he said. "I was a little slow to get up this morning. I'll get out of your way. I was just on my way out."

I moved away from the sliding glass door so he could get by. Neither of us offered to introduce ourselves or shake hands. I watched him walk into the side door of the garage. From the window, I watched as his beige Oldsmobile pulled out of the driveway and away. I wondered where he went, where he felt he had to go for those few hours.

The kitchen looked the same as it always did, except for a few dishes in the sink and on the counter. The bar at the end was stacked with medical bills, instructions for medications, and hospital release forms. Lonnie had said, when she called to tell me to go to the Sad House that week, that the

woman from the Porn House had been looking after him—
maybe because she was a nurse, or because he just didn't have
anyone else.

The covers on his bed were pulled back like he'd left them
when he'd gotten up that morning. The other side was still
made, almost exactly like I'd left it the last time I cleaned,
the decorative pillows still in their places. The sheets were
speckled with blood. I pulled back the covers all the way and
carefully pinched the corners of the sheets to pull them toward the center, then took the cases off the pillows, stuffing
everything into one case. On my way to set them on the
washing machine, I went through the bathroom. There were
several drops of blood on the floor, a new rail installed by the
toilet and in the shower, and a seat in the bathtub.

Before she died, the wife collected rocks, birdhouses, and
nests, lining them up by the windows in the living room.
They'd spent a lot of time traveling in Central or South America. The wife had been a teacher. I imagined her bringing
the little dolls and artwork from their travels to decorate her
classroom or to show them to her students. I wondered if she
taught them Spanish.

The Sad House seemed like it had been a vacation house,
or an empty nester's way of not mourning vacant, stagnant
rooms no longer filled with children. They'd had two sons.
One had passed away, and the other lived in the area but
never seemed to visit. I often wondered if he'd lost them all
at the same time, if maybe his wife and son were killed in an
accident, and grief tore his other son away. I made up stories based on artifacts I saw around the house—photographs,
notes scrawled on paper, a framed card with a cartoon illus-
tration of a naked man and woman holding hands that read
"Cabin Rules: Save water. Shower together." The Sad House
seemed frozen in time—projects half done, artwork still waiting in the walk-in closet to be hung on the wall. His wife's list
of projects was still tacked to the corkboard in the kitchen on

now yellowed paper. *Get new hose. Fix latch on gate.* I imagined her pulling weeds from the flower beds outside, then coming in to grab something to drink from the kitchen, jotting that down before returning to her work. Underneath it was a receipt she'd signed for landscaping. There wasn't a date.

Just halfway through my six-hour workday, I let out a big sigh and hooked a spray bottle onto the pocket in my pants. I sprayed one rag lightly with vinegar water and stuffed it in my other pocket to use for dusting. Then I grabbed another one for wiping anything that needed to be sprayed. But the Sad House never got dirty.

The various medications in the bathroom seemed to increase every time I cleaned. I moved them to wipe the counter under them before turning around to move to the bathtub. There was that wicker shelf. I'd opened the boxes with the ashes purely out of curiosity the first time. Since then I couldn't help but revisit them occasionally to see if they were still there. I wondered if he'd spread some of them but kept these for himself. I wondered if it comforted him to have them there, behind him, while he combed his hair.

On the bar by the kitchen, the stack of photos had been partially hidden by the paperwork from the hospital. I looked for clues in the photos, thinking I'd see something different. But they were always the same—people standing next to grills full of burgers and fish and the Sad House man standing, proudly, with children dressed in red, white, and blue holding their sparklers high. Everyone puts on a smile for pictures, but the man beamed in his, like a child holding up the first fish he'd caught. He'd done everything right. All these trinkets and photos pointed to a person who'd successfully accomplished the American Dream. Yet here he was, alone.

He never left notes or cards on the counter for me. I didn't expect him to or think it necessary for him to spend any extra money on a tip or holiday bonus for me. It seemed weird to think of it this way, but the man had given me another gift.

The Sad House made me look at the small space I shared with Mia, at the room we lived in, and see it was a home, full of love, because we filled it. Even though we didn't have nice cars or a house on a bluff above the beach, we had each other. I could enjoy her company, instead of living alone in a place filled with her memories. My struggle with loneliness, for companionship, still tugged at me, but I wasn't alone. Mia saved me from that.

19

Lori's House

Summer started to wane, and the sun set slowly, filling the evenings in our studio with pink, orange, and purple instead of heat that left our bedsheets soaked with sweat. Mia started falling asleep before nine again, leaving me to sit at our little kitchen table. On those nights, I listened to the cars speeding by on the freeway and the neighborhood boys talking from their perch on the curb below, smoke from their joint wafting into my windows. I sat, too tired to read a book, with my day planner open in front of me instead, an attempt to memorize the twenty clients I rotated in weekly, biweekly, and monthly schedules. Most of the houses took me three hours to clean, and I usually had two or sometimes three houses a day.

Being a thirty-two-year-old single mother with several tattoos, I never felt like Mia and I fit into the conservative niche of our surroundings. Mia wore her monkey costume or tutus for days, her hair a disheveled mop of curls on her head. Walking through grocery stores, we were a sharp contrast to the well-put-together stay-at-home moms. Passing them in the cereal aisle, glancing at their large, sparkling wedding rings, staring at their toddlers dutifully in tow, their clothes unstained, their hair still smartly pulled into the ponytails and barrettes from that morning.

One woman, though, glanced in my direction, and her face

turned to a warm smile. I recognized her as one of my mom's old friends but didn't remember her name. She asked how we were doing and where we lived. When I told her, she asked if Mia went to the day care behind Madison, the elementary school where I'd spent a few short months in second grade before my family moved to Alaska. I shook my head.

"I'm a little limited to where she can go," I said, waiting for the confusion to show on her face before I explained. "The preschool would need to take a state grant I receive for childcare, and private schools don't accept it." I'd called local Montessori and other private schools, offering to barter the tuition for cleaning services, but none accepted. Mia would have greatly benefitted from the more enriching environment of a real preschool instead of a day care. I tried to make up for it by reading to her for at least thirty minutes every night.

"Grandma Judy's day care is through the YMCA, and I'm pretty sure they would accept the state grant," the woman said.

"Grandma Judy?" I asked, picking Mia up after her third attempt to hide under my skirt. The woman reached to gently touch Mia's cheek, but Mia turned away to look over my shoulder and stiffened.

"She runs the day care. She really is like a grandma to the kids," the woman told me. "My kids still visit her sometimes. The center is in one of those outbuildings behind the school, but Judy's so great it's almost like they're going to Grandma's house."

A week later, Grandma Judy did welcome us with loving arms. On one of our first meetings, she pulled me into her office so we could sit and get to know each other. Maybe she caught me on a rough day, or at a time when I felt so helpless and overwhelmed, but as I sat in her office talking about our daily life, I began to cry. Judy handed me a tissue and said, "You're a wonderful mother. I can tell. And I know a good mother when I see one." I looked at her, sniffled, and realized that no one had ever told me that before. Those words were all it took for Grandma Judy to feel like family.

With Mia spending the day in a supportive environment, I felt better about being away from her to work. I took on as many houses as I possibly could, filling gaps in the company's schedule with my own clients. I charged double the wages I made at Classic Clean. For a month that summer, the bills were paid. Mia and I were an inseparable twosome, singing to Sufjan Stevens's "The Perpetual Self" or, as Mia called it, the "Uh-Oh Song." *Everything is lost! Uh-oh!* We called it our happy morning song, making sure to listen to it before going to our respective places, and feeling pretty great about it. We had a routine. As fall started, I braced myself for adding a full load of online classes, for losing sleep. When school was in the mix, I drank a large cup of coffee in the evenings so I could finish homework. On the weekends, I studied. When classes began, I knew I would be exhausted, but in my mind, school was the most important work. It was the work that would get us places.

Pam and Lonnie estimated the time to clean a house based on their own speed. But they were middle-aged women and not in the greatest shape, and I'd become a ninja. After several months of working full-time, I had to find a belt for my pants. I couldn't keep weight on if I tried. If I finished a house faster than the allotted time, they'd tell me to slow down. If clients suddenly had bills that were less than the original quote, due to my shorter times, they'd come to expect that same amount. I had to keep with the expected times out of fairness to whoever eventually replaced me.

For some houses, that meant that I had time to stop and thumb through books sitting on nightstands or kitchen counters. I began looking through the rapidly growing stashes of alcohol, hidden chocolate, unopened bags from the mall that remained untouched for months. I became intrigued by understanding how people coped. I snooped because I was bored, and, in a way, it became my own coping mechanism.

I started to love the houses that didn't echo in vacancy. I appreciated my Friday mornings with Henry. I never snooped in houses where I wasn't invisible, where my name was "Stephanie" instead of "cleaning service" or even "MAID" on their calendar. And I never looked through the stuff of clients I met on my own outside of Classic Clean. We had a mutual respect for each other, and over time, some became friends. The snooping was like uncovering clues, finding evidence of the secret lives of people who seemed like they had it all. Despite being wealthy and having the two-story houses of our American dreams—the marbled-sink bathrooms, the offices with bay windows looking out at the water—their lives still lacked something. I became fascinated by the things hidden in dark corners and the self-help books for hope. Maybe they just had longer hallways and bigger closets to hide the things that scared them.

Lori's House was built just for her and the people who knew how to care for her Huntington's disease. She spent most of the day in a cushioned chair directly in front of the TV. She could hardly speak, but her caregivers seemed to be able to understand her. Her limbs had minds of their own; her legs occasionally shot straight up in the air. Lori's caregivers fed her, cleaned her, and helped her to the bathroom. While I dusted the TV and the shelves filled with photographs, Lori watched me with dark, alert eyes.

Every other Tuesday, I spent six hours in her house. It was large and had been designed by her husband, who had a loft apartment upstairs where he slept on most weekends. Lori had a rotating staff of caregivers, but Beth always seemed to be there on the days I was. She offered me coffee, and while I rarely accepted, we would often chat while I cleaned.

On the morning before my second or third time cleaning

Lori's House, the DVD player Travis bought Mia for her birthday broke. Mia started crying and kicking it from her car seat. We'd come to heavily rely on that thing during our long hours in the car. I'd listened to Elmo sing about ears and noses easily a hundred times. When I got to Lori's House that morning, I was a ball of nerves and rushed to get all my supplies into the master bathroom, a room bigger than my entire apartment.

I had to hide from Beth in that room while I regained some composure. It was the only space on the main floor with a door. The bathtub had windows all around it, and I had to climb into the tub to get the sills clean. *You can't even replace it* started repeating in my head, strong and fierce. My body tucked into itself, and I sat, gasping, holding my knees, and rocking. The DVD player didn't even cost a hundred bucks, but I couldn't afford to buy a new one. That thought triggered a spiral of all the other things I could not provide for my daughter: a decent house, a family, her own room, cupboards full of food. I hugged my knees tighter, not bothering to wipe the tears from my face, and started whispering my mantra to interrupt the negative swirl of fear that encased me. To comfort, to stop the downward spiral from going to a place of true panic.

I love you. I'm here for you. I love you. I'm here for you.

When I was homeless, a therapist had first introduced me to the idea of mantras; only then it'd been phrases like "nobody dies from a panic attack," or to envision my daughter swinging and match my breath with the speed of the pendulum. None of that worked. What my mind needed to know was that someone was there to make it all better. That summer, through gritted teeth, I'd decided that person was me, not a man or a family, and it would only ever be me. I had to stop hoping for someone to come along and love me. I had to do it myself, ducking my head and barreling through anything life brought.

After that morning of the broken DVD player, whenever I cleaned Lori's tub, I did it over a shadow in the shape of myself from that morning, rocking and whispering, waiting for breath to come easier. I stood there sometimes, looking down on that ghost, that former version of myself, with compassion, like an older, wiser self, offering a caring gesture of comfort. I learned to look to that wiser self in moments of panic, too. The one, ten years from now, who would have made it through hell. I just had to keep the faith that she existed.

One Tuesday I called Pam to ask if I could split Lori's House into two days or maybe get by with a three-hour clean just this once. Mia had been sick for several days with a sinus infection and had developed pinkeye on top of that. I couldn't take her to day care, and I couldn't afford to miss any more work. I called Jamie that morning to ask him to take her for a few days. I planned to take her to Urgent Care first thing and then drive to our meeting point at the ferry dock, only to turn back around to Lori's House, where I could work late to finish the job.

Mia and I shared my twin bed a lot, which wasn't ideal even when she was well. She thrashed in her sleep, kicking me, flailing her arms, throwing her fist into my eye. For the past several days, her plugged nose, fever, and general discomfort meant that she woke up throughout the night crying and wanting comfort. I hadn't slept well in days.

Since becoming a single parent I'd referred to the phases of our progress as "a whole new level of exhaustion." Most of my days seemed to drift, like a boat with a broken motor, through a thick fog. At times, the thickness would lift a little; I could see, I could think, I could joke and smile and laugh and feel like myself for an afternoon. There hadn't been many moments like that since we'd been on our own. Since we'd been homeless. Since I fought daily not to have to return to a shelter. Yet I mentally prepared myself for another level—

the addition of schoolwork on top of the schedule I'd fought to fill with work. I rarely questioned the how of things. I just knew what needed to be done. And I did it.

I called my boss and Jamie to update them on my progress from the parking lot outside the pharmacy. I told my boss I should be at Lori's in a few hours—it took just over an hour one way to meet Jamie to hand Mia off. His voice came through at high levels of irritation on the phone, but I ignored it. He didn't like giving her medicine, didn't trust doctors, and blamed day care for making her so sick all the time. I didn't have time to engage with him that morning, which upset him more. I cut him off, told him I'd drop her off with her medications and all the instructions, and to follow everything they said.

"Those antibiotics are only making her sicker," he said in a snide tone. He said it every time she had to take them for a sinus or ear infection. I didn't like giving her antibiotics, either, knowing they masked the real problem—that our lifestyle, our living space, was making her sick. But another choice didn't seem to be available.

"Just do it, Jamie," I said. I hung up and rolled my eyes. Then I turned to look at Mia in her car seat behind me. She wore a red t-shirt with a cartoon horse in a cowboy hat on the front and a pair of black stretch pants with a hole in the knee. In her lap was a new bath toy I'd gotten for five bucks at Walmart—a Little Mermaid doll whose tail changed from blue to purple in the warm water of the bath. She looked at me, dazed from her stuffed sinuses, eyes bright pink and collecting goop in the corners. I patted her knee, rubbed her leg a little, then faced front, took a deep breath, and started the car.

We headed west on Highway 20 to the coast. I'd traveled this highway between Mount Vernon and Anacortes since I was born. One stretch in particular reminded me of a night when I must have been close to Mia's age, looking at the stars on our way home from visiting my great-grandparents. It was

Christmas Eve, and I strained my eyes, searching for the red light of Rudolph's nose. Mia was the seventh generation of our family to be born in the area. I'd hoped those deep roots would ground us, too, but they hadn't. They were too far gone, too buried. My family's history remained elusive to us. I'd grown tired of asking family members if they wanted to see Mia, and I craved grandparents, aunts, and uncles who were like some of my clients—their houses covered in photos, their children's numbers first on auto-dial, a basket full of toys in a corner they kept on hand for the grandchildren. Instead I had brief moments of familiarity on a highway, memories ingrained in me so deeply they could almost pass as a belonging.

In the times when I'd scrape at the bottom of my despair for too long, I thought about these things. Though I was thankful that Jamie could take Mia for the week, I knew it would come at some cost. He would hold it against me, bring it up when he felt like shaming me for working too much, cite it as a reason Mia should live with him.

"Mommy," Mia said from the back seat. "Mommy."

"Yes, Mia," I said, my elbow pressed into the window and the top of the door panel, my hand cradling my forehead as I drove.

"Can I have my window down?" she asked, her sick voice squeaking a little. "I want Ariel's hair to blow like in the movie." I did it, not caring how ridiculous that seemed. I just needed to get to work. I needed to finish work. I needed to sleep.

We drove up and over the canal that separates the mainland from Whidbey Island. I glanced to my right as an older brown Ford Bronco passed us. I locked eyes with the other driver, and he gave me a smile, then pointed to Mia's window, just as I saw a flash of red hair in the back window behind Mia's seat.

"My Ariel!" she screamed, kicking her legs against the seat in front of her. She'd let Ariel out the window too far and lost her grip.

I set my jaw and faced forward. Mia wailed like I'd run over a newborn puppy. Over the next bend was a stoplight where I could do a U-turn. *I have time*, I thought. I could turn around, stop on the eastbound side of the highway, jump out, grab her doll, and then take the next exit, go under the bridge, turn back around, and we'd be on our way. Sound logic while driving sixty miles per hour through exhaustion's deep fog, amid the cries of a toddler in the back seat.

"I'll go back and get it," I yelled, to get her to stop making those horrible sounds. My head hurt from the lack of sleep and the two huge cups of coffee I had that morning to counteract it. It had been several days of caring for a sick child, and I desperately needed a break. I just wanted the screaming to stop.

After turning around, I stayed in the left lane, speeding up only to slow down again, merging toward the left shoulder. It was an unseasonably warm day in September. As I stepped from my car out onto the asphalt, the wind from cars speeding by felt hot, blowing through my favorite green t-shirt that had thinned over the years. I scoured the grass that divided the east- and westbound traffic, my ponytail smacking toward my face, so much so I used one hand to hold it against my head. I must have looked odd, searching for a doll amid the candy wrappers and soda bottles full of piss that had been dumped in the median.

Finally, I saw the wisp of red hair. I got closer; it was Ariel. But only her head. "Shit," I said under my breath and then glanced back at the car, wincing, feeling a sudden weight in my stomach. This had been a bad idea. Mia would cry the entire way to Port Townsend over a doll that was now broken instead of lost. Maybe her dad could fix it; he could somehow tape it together. Then I saw the shape of the tail, fanned into two sections, but no sign of her shell-bikini-clad upper body. "Shit," I said again. I bent down to pick it up, and heard it.

The sound of metal crunching and glass exploding at once.

It was a sound I knew from accidents I'd been in as a teenager, but I had never heard it like this.

A car. Hitting another car. My car. My car with Mia sitting in the back seat.

That sound was the window next to my baby girl's head exploding, popping like a glass balloon.

I dropped Ariel's head, screamed, and ran. *This isn't real*, I thought, running. *This isn't real*. By the time I reached the car, my scream had turned into a repeated *No. No. No-no-no*.

When I opened the car door behind the driver's side, Mia's car seat faced me, dislodged from its place. The rear window was missing. Her wide eyes locked on mine, her mouth frozen open in a silent scream. I breathed, and she reached her arms out for me. I moved the car seat. Beneath her, the floor of the car was bent, smashed inward and upward, almost to her feet. She held up her feet, which were protected only by light-up sandals.

I unbuckled her and immediately felt her arms around my neck, felt her legs push against the seat with enough force to back us both away from the car. Her legs wrapped around me, and I hugged her tight and sobbed, turning her away from the wreckage of the car.

The cars in both directions slowed down as they passed, the drivers' heads craning out the windows to see the damage. I stood in the grassy median, about ten feet away from the car we depended on, clinging to my three-year-old, feeling as if everything around us had begun to spin like a cyclone.

The other driver, a lanky teenage boy with spiked hair, walked up to us from where his car had stopped a hundred feet away. He had a gash above his left eye. His short-sleeved, white button-up shirt flapped in the breeze, revealing a ribbed tank top underneath.

"Are you okay?" he said. Then, his eyes fixed on Mia. "Oh, my God, was she in the car?"

"Of course she was in the car, you fucking idiot!" I yelled

in a new voice, nothing like I had ever heard before. It didn't sound like my own. "How could you hit my fucking car?" He didn't respond. "How could you hit my fucking car?" I repeated. I said it again and again, not really saying it to anyone, burying the words in Mia's shoulder. How could this happen to us? How were we standing in the middle of a highway, alone, with a smashed-up car that I still owed money on, that I needed for work, that we needed to survive? That was our *car*, as important as an arm or a leg to keep us moving.

The boy backed away, and I pressed my forehead to Mia's and asked her again if she was okay.

"I'm okay, Mama," she said, her voice uncharacteristically even and calm. "We're okay."

"We're okay?" I said, gulping for air. "We're okay?"

"We're okay," she said again. "We're okay." I held her tight, feeling my body starting to go from panic to grief.

A cool hand touched my shoulder, and I whirled around, ready to beat the piss out of that boy, before I saw that the hand belonged to a tiny blond woman. Her timid voice made it so I couldn't hear her or understand what she said, but her face showed concern.

"Are you okay?" she asked. I didn't respond. I stared at the woman for a second, so translucent she looked angelic. What kind of question was that? Was I okay? I had no idea. I almost lost my kid. This kid in my arms. This kid who'd placed her palm on my cheek that morning and whispered, "I love you." This kid who shared my bed and loved pancakes. This kid could have died.

"My daughter," I said out loud. It was all I could think to say, and I buried my face again in Mia's hair.

Another car had stopped, too, idling behind her black Suburban. The driver was on the phone. I could do nothing but clutch Mia. I couldn't stop crying. My car. My car was dead on the side of the road. My irreplaceable car. The car

I couldn't afford to lose. The car I was required to have in working condition, to keep my job, to survive.

The police arrived first to direct traffic and assess the scene. They asked me what happened, listening patiently between my huge gasps for air. A few policemen started examining the skid marks my car's tires made when it was bumped at least a foot to the left. The rear right tire jutted out to the side, the metal behind it twisted and smashed. Everything inside my car had shifted in the crash. The tape cassette in the player hung out of it, ready to fall at any second. But I couldn't stop staring at the back seat where Mia had been, at her car seat so incredibly close to the shattered window, to the floor that had been pushed up to meet her toes. In the impact, her car seat had moved to the side, away from the window, and somehow, she wasn't injured.

One of the policemen pulled out a small tape measure.

"What are you doing?" I asked, a new wave of panic crashing against my chest.

"We need to try to determine fault, ma'am," he said. "Please step aside."

Fault. My fault. Of course it was my fault. I was the one who had pulled over on a fucking highway, who had gotten out to look for a freaking doll and left my child in the car, in harm's way.

Two paramedics jumped out of an ambulance, one rushing over to the other driver and the other toward us. Another ambulance arrived, then a fire truck. Traffic crept by on the road, and I tried to ignore the gawking, the rubbernecking, the feeling like we were in a fucking fish bowl.

When I sat Mia on the bench in the back of the ambulance, she let her arms loosen from my neck for the first time since I'd unbuckled her. The paramedic asked her questions, asked to look at her bare chest. He handed her a teddy bear dressed in a nightgown and sleeping cap, its eyes closed and hands together in what looked like prayer.

"See how she does tonight," he said, his brown hair, eyes, and olive skin reminding me, for some reason, of my brother. "If you notice any bruising, or if she seems in pain for any reason, take her in immediately." He looked over at Mia again. "Or you could take her to the emergency room now if you want her to have X-rays." I looked at Mia, trying to register what he'd said, now seeing the entire scene had it been worse, had she been bruised, broken, bleeding, rushed to the hospital in that ambulance instead. I shook my head. The logistics were too confusing. I didn't know if Medicaid covered an ambulance ride, and I pictured a bill I couldn't afford for thousands of dollars. And I couldn't leave my car—that was almost family to us; it had the cleaning supplies in the back that provided our entire income. I'd have to pay to replace them if something happened to them, and I couldn't afford to. I couldn't leave without knowing what was going to happen next.

Mia hugged her bear, staring at the equipment in the ambulance. My mind flashed again with images of her eyes staring wildly at me while she breathed behind an oxygen mask, her hair caked with blood, her neck in a brace. She raised her arms for me to hold her again. I carried her back to our car, got the camera from my purse, and took several pictures while I waited for the police to decide our fate.

One of the cops approached me: the shortest one, bald, with a belly hanging over his belt. He asked me the same questions I'd already answered: why I'd stopped, how I'd stopped, how far I'd pulled over, and if I'd immediately put my emergency flashers on.

"Ma'am, we'll continue our investigation and report it to your insurance company," he said. "It's unknown if the male who hit you has insurance."

My knees momentarily felt like they were going to give out. Did I have uninsured-motorist coverage? I must have. I still had a loan out on my car. I think that meant I had full coverage instead of just liability. Right? I'd asked for that, right? I couldn't remember.

He pulled out another pad of paper and tore off a ticket, handing it over to me with my license, registration, and insurance card.

"Sir," I said, seeing the $70 amount on the ticket but not accepting it, trying to make sense of how I deserved this. I stared into his tiny blue eyes. "What will this mean for me financially?"

He looked at me, and then at Mia, who'd also turned her head to stare at him. "I don't know, ma'am," he said, annoyed, and then extended the ticket toward me, adding, "You can fight it in court." But I knew that meant I'd have to fight him. A police officer. This heartless man, placing a ticket in the hand of a sobbing mother who'd almost lost her child, who couldn't afford to replace the car, let alone pay the ticket.

I stared at the ticket for being illegally parked and looked up to see the tow truck approaching.

"Ma'am! Do you have anyone to pick you up?" the police officer asked. Judging from his tone, he must have asked more than once.

"I don't know," I said. Everyone I could think of calling was at work and miles away. The cop suggested I get a ride with the tow truck, but I again asked if that would cost money and he again said he didn't know. "Why doesn't anyone know how much things cost?" I said, crying again. He shrugged and walked away. The fireman had taken my cleaning supplies out of the back of my car, along with the car seat and Mia's bag with Hello Kitty on the front for weekends at her dad's.

We stood on the side of the road, watching our car get pulled up the ramp of the tow truck, the back tire sideways and dragging like a broken limb. At my feet in the grass was my tray of cleaning supplies, a bag of rags, and two broken mop handles. Mia still hung her arms around my neck. The scene started to clear. We were about to be left.

20

"I Don't Know How You Do It"

Why would you do that?" Jamie yelled into the phone, his tone getting higher, more urgent. "Why would you stop on a highway? How could you be so fucking stupid?" The exact words I'd been repeating in my head already. In his voice, even.

"Okay, I'll call later," I said before I hung up.

Mia started crying. She wanted to talk to him. She wanted him to come get her. I felt a familiar sinking in my stomach, fear that he might use this to get custody, that this might be the thing that won him the case he always threatened me with whenever I did something he didn't like. He wanted me to have to pay him child support. He wanted me to suffer.

Grandpa's light blue Oldsmobile crept through the traffic still backed up from the accident. A few cops waved him in. Even though he was shorter than the shortest cop, who'd handed me a ticket, Grandpa was all business when he got out of the car, nodding at the handful of first responders who remained. But when he walked up to us on the side of the road, his face was red, flushed. I thought for a moment he might be angry with me. "Are those things coming with us?" he asked, pointing to the pile of belongings awkwardly stacked on the shoulder of the highway. I nodded.

After I clipped Mia's car seat into place, we climbed into the huge car, and Grandpa said he needed to get gas. We pulled into a gas station and parked next to the pump. Grandpa looked at me for a second and then looked back at Mia. His eyes started to water.

"I don't have enough money," he said, his face reddening again.

"I'll pay," I said, reaching for the door handle.

"Maybe I'll go get us some coffee," he said. "You probably need some coffee? I just switched to green tea. Do you want some green tea?"

I wanted to joke about needing a few shots of whiskey but realized I'd be serious in my request. "Sure, Grandpa," I said, forcing some kind of grin. "Coffee would be great."

Grandpa cared for my grandma through most of their marriage as her schizophrenia progressed, and her death a year and a half earlier had left him with a lot of spare time in the most desperate, lonely way. They'd known each other since kindergarten. As husband and wife, she towered over him, especially with the inches her teased hair added, because he stood only slightly over five feet tall. When I was Mia's age and stayed with them, Grandpa never missed a chance to show me off to his friends, telling people about the tape recordings he had of me singing "Popeye the Sailor Man" and offering to play them.

He moved out of the house after Grandma died. It was the only house I'd known him to live in, besides the trailer they'd had, and it felt strange to know that it was gone. For a while after that, he rented a room from a woman in town. I remember visiting, seeing the knickknacks I'd grown up admiring and playing with, and thinking how strange it felt to see him there, barely able to afford a single room. He still worked as a real estate agent, but the recession had slowed business drastically, and it hadn't recovered. He started sleeping in the storage room at his office. My inability to help him brought a deep guilt for me, especially after he'd taken us in once during a fight with Travis. I wished so much I could somehow help.

Every time I saw him, he tried to give me some family heirloom or coloring book with my mother's name scrawled in the front. Sometimes I'd take a few to appease him and then leave them in my car to donate. I didn't have room for any of that stuff. Grandpa would still insist I take them, telling me their stories: "Your great-great-great-grandma sold her wedding ring to buy that sewing machine," he'd say. I couldn't keep any of those heirlooms or give them the space they deserved to live in. I didn't have room in my life to cherish them.

Travis returned my call while I pumped gas. He didn't want any details; he just wanted to know where to come pick us up. I'd almost forgotten that I'd left a message on his phone. I felt like he'd want to know what happened. Maybe I wanted him to know. His voice sounded rushed, and I heard a diesel engine in the background.

"What are you doing?" I asked. Mia stared at me through the window. I twitched my nose at her, trying to smile, and pressed my finger to the glass. She touched the glass with her finger from the other side.

"I'm hooking my parents' truck up to the trailer," he said, breathing heavily. I wondered if he thought he'd come pick up our smashed car.

"No, Travis," I said. "We're fine. Everything's taken care of." I hung up before he could tell I was lying. I was too vulnerable to see him. I knew, even with my whole body still trembling with shock, that if Travis came to rescue us, to help put everything back in order, I'd risk wanting to be with him again. I'd spent all this time trying to make it on my own. Despite having called him, I didn't want to go running back to his arms again.

On the way home, it started to pour rain. I asked Grandpa to stop at Walmart and to wait with Mia in the car while I went into the store. I hurried inside with my head down, avoiding eye contact. I imagined that anyone who looked in my direction recognized me as that girl with the daughter she'd almost killed on the shoulder of Highway 20. I wanted, more than usual, to scream in the middle of a Walmart, to the point of it being so near uncontrollable it scared me. I couldn't stop hearing the sound of the windows exploding. The sound repeated itself, so loud that I shut my eyes and clenched my jaw to keep silent.

"Where are the fucking mermaid dolls?" I realized I said out loud when a little girl and her mother looked at me. The dolls were sold out; the space where they had hung was empty. But beneath it was the upgraded version: a bigger doll, with more hair, and a button you pushed to hear her speak, for $19.99. I grabbed it. I would juggle the bills later. There was no way I wasn't going to retrieve my daughter's fucking doll that afternoon.

When we pulled up to the studio, rain continued to fall as Grandpa and I brought in my cleaning supplies and bags. A piece of glass fell from one of the bags onto the floor in our apartment, where it embedded into Mia's heel but somehow caused her so little pain, she didn't notice it at first. It was her only injury. Physically, anyway. And I could fix it.

Grandpa stood in the apartment, in the small open space by the door, looking around. He'd never visited us here. None of my family had. I wondered if he could tell I'd gotten rid of things that he'd handed down to me.

"You don't have a microwave," he said, his gaze fixed on the corner where the kitchen was.

I looked at the counters, bare except for a cutting board

and dish rack and too small for much else. "I don't have room for a microwave," I said.

"You could put it on top of the fridge," he said, pointing to where I'd put a plant. "I have one at the office that I don't use. I'll bring it over."

"Please, Grandpa," I said, reaching down to pick up Mia. "I just don't have room."

His eyes watered again. My phone started buzzing in my pocket. I recognized the long set of digits from my mom's international phone numbers.

"You called my mom?" I asked, unable to hide that I was annoyed.

"Of course I did," he said. "She should know her daughter and granddaughter were in an accident."

I felt my jaw clench. I knew that, now that Grandma was gone, Mom never missed a Sunday afternoon call to Grandpa. I knew she asked him if he'd seen us, or how we were doing, or what we were up to. In the moment, more than ever, I didn't feel like she'd earned the right to any information about our accident. I had needed her that summer, when Mia dealt with so much sickness and needed tubes in her ears. I had needed her many times since she'd moved to Europe. I had needed her and couldn't call to tell her. We could barely have a conversation anymore, our phone calls echoed with horrible reception while William sat close, listening to everything. I could almost hear him breathing. He'd chuckle whenever Mom made a joke. I couldn't handle it. I couldn't anymore. So I had stopped talking to her completely, again deciding it was less painful to have her out of my life than in it. It was easier not to want or expect anything at all from her. I was angry at her for leaving her life here. For staying away. I would never understand how she could. I didn't want to try.

Grandpa left, and I put Mia in the bath with bubbles and her new doll. Mom called again. I sat on the toilet next to the tub and saw my phone light up in my hand. I ignored it and watched Mia play with her new mermaid. Mia sat in the bath, her skin slick under bubbles, hair sticking to her cheeks. I wanted to crawl over to her, wrap her up in my arms, and place my ear on her chest to listen to her heart.

I wondered if Mom had ever felt this way about me. I wondered why she never leaned in close after she hugged me good night, to give me reassurance of her presence, that she loved me so, so much. I wanted to know, but not enough to ask. Sometimes I'd imagine asking her, demanding it over the phone, but I knew nothing would come of it. She was there; that was enough for her. Maybe that's all she ever felt she needed to be.

Mia stayed up late that night, not just from the stuffy nose and itchy, painful eyes but because I didn't want to put her to bed. The happy chirps of her voice kept me from falling into sobs. When she was watching me, I knew I needed to stay strong. We lay down in our twin bed, our heads on the same pillow, and faced each other. Then her eyes closed, her body twitched with sleep, and she let out a sigh, then rhythmic breaths. I watched her, listening.

Mia slept for only an hour before a coughing fit woke her up again. I had already given her all the medicine I could. Her barking cough turned into a sort of growl, angry to be awake and so tired at the same time. I tried shushing her, singing "Wagon Wheel," the song she'd loved lately, but nothing worked. Finally, from an almost primal place in my memory, I started to recite *Goodnight Moon*:

Goodnight room, goodnight moon.
Goodnight cow jumping over the moon.
Goodnight light, and the red balloon.
Goodnight chairs, goodnight bears.

Mia calmed immediately to listen and fell back to sleep. I stroked the space between her eyebrows with my finger, crying as silently as I could, in disbelief that she'd survived.

The following morning, I watched as Mia ate her oatmeal. I sat with a sort of fascination, still in awe of the miracle that she wasn't hurt, so much that she didn't seem real. I'd called Lonnie the day before to tell her what had happened and to request a day off to get things sorted, not knowing at the time how I'd do that. My body and mind were on autopilot. After breakfast, a man I'd been on a few dates with, Todd, was coming over to pick us up. Todd and I were supposed to go out that weekend, and somehow the night before I had remembered to cancel, unable to come up with any reason other than the truth. I didn't want to admit that I was in trouble, that even my own family wasn't able to help me out. Todd insisted I borrow a car he didn't drive anymore, and I flinched at the thought. I really didn't know what I thought of Todd, or if I liked him in a serious way or not. Some men, I'd discovered, had a bit of a hero complex when it came to dating me. They wanted to rush in and rescue the damsel in distress. I didn't like to play that role, but in this situation, I didn't have a choice. We absolutely had to have a car.

I described Todd to Mia as "my friend," explaining that he would take us to a spare car he said we could use for a while.

"Then I'll take you to your dad's," I explained, cleaning up the breakfast dishes. I took in a big breath and held it, the opposite of what I was supposed to do in moments like this, when my heart lurched and started to race. I would have to make the same journey as the day before, travel the same road, get back in a car with Mia. No matter how much I wanted to stay in bed, glued to Mia, I had to work. I had a house to clean the next day—one of my larger houses that took up most of my time on Thursdays. On top of that, classes started the following week, and I needed to organize my books and passwords for accessing the materials. And I supposed I had to celebrate my birthday in some way.

As Todd drove us down I-5 toward the borrowed car, Mia sat quietly in the back seat. Her car seat seemed fine, but I knew, since it had been in an accident, it needed to be thrown away once I could afford a new one. Every time I looked at it, it reminded me of how close I had come to losing my daughter.

Suddenly, Mia blurted out, "Ruby died, Mom." Ruby was the name she had given to our Subaru, because of her maroon color and because I'd called her a Suba-Ruby once after I'd proudly packed all my cleaning supplies in the back for the first time.

I turned to look at Mia and put my hand on her leg. She felt so fragile and small. I felt tears welling up in my eyes again. I'd found Ruby used but in immaculate condition, with only one hundred thousand miles on the odometer. Mia and I sometimes spent half our day in that car. Ruby had been over twenty years old, but it was one of the nicest vehicles I'd owned in several years. Our loss was great. Unimaginable. I couldn't think about it.

"Ruby died because of me, Mom," Mia said, looking out the window, her voice small. "Because Ariel went out the window."

"Oh, honey," I said, trying to turn my body to face her from the front seat. "No. It was an accident. It's not your fault. If anything, it was my fault."

"You're crying," Mia said, her face turning red, her lower lip pouting, tears starting to swell in her eyelids. "You just wanted to save my Ariel."

I couldn't look at her anymore, but I kept my hand on her leg. I wanted so much to cover my face with my hands, to allow my eyes and mouth to contort and submit into a mute sob. Instead, Todd and I glanced at each other, and I gave him a slight smile. I had to be okay. I had no choice.

Todd pulled off the freeway, down a few streets, and parked behind a two-door Honda Accord. It reminded me of the cars that boys drove in high school, a life-sized version of the toy race cars my little brother had played with. He checked the fluids, turning signals, brakes, and headlights with a knowledgeable efficiency that I found attractive. Todd did have a lot of qualities I admired—he worked construction while building his own cabin on a wooded property near Port Townsend—I wasn't sure why my heart wasn't there.

"I was about to sell it, so you can use it as long as you need," he said and then handed me a key.

"Thank you," I managed to get out, and hugged him. I hoped he knew how much he'd saved me from total despair and possible homelessness. But then, how could he? I hadn't told him how desperate my situation was. I'd wanted to appear somewhat as an equal to him, rather than, I don't know, who I was. Dating anyone felt like a joke in that way.

When I pulled out of the parking spot, my hands shook. My body felt jumpy, as though I'd had ten cups of coffee. *I shouldn't be driving*, I thought. *I'm not ready*. I thought for sure I'd get us in an accident again, yet I was the only one who could get us to where we needed to go.

At a stoplight, knowing the freeway entrance was coming up, I wished there was someone I could call to help or even talk to. But I couldn't think of anyone who'd be able to understand what I was going through, unless they knew what it was like to be a single mom, the lone parent obligated to make ends meet like I did.

When I talked to friends about my life, giving them even just a little peek into the window of the logistics, the stress, the constant juggling, I would hear the same thing again and again: "I don't know how you do it." When their husbands went out of town, or they worked late all the time, they'd say, "I don't know how you do it," shaking their heads, and I always tried not to react. I wanted to tell them those hours without your husband aren't even close to replicating what it was like to be a single parent, but I let them believe it did. Arguing with them would reveal too much about myself, and I was never out to get anyone's sympathy. Besides, they couldn't know unless they felt the weight of poverty themselves. The desperation of pushing through because it was the only option. They couldn't know how it felt to be me, the morning after the accident, about to drive a car down the same road where there was still glass from my car's shattered windows, going on with my life like everything was normal, because that was the only choice I had.

Though I'm sure my clients would have understood, the electric company wouldn't. I wanted nothing but to sit on the couch with my sick kid and refill her sippy cup of juice while we watched her *Curious George* DVD three times in a row. But I had to get back to work. And I had to drive. I wasn't sure which seemed more impossible.

It was never a matter of "how" I did things. I'm sure any parent would do the same. Single parenting isn't just being the only one to take care of your kid. It's not about being able to "tap out" for a break or tag team bath- and bedtime; those were the least of the difficulties I faced. I had a crushing amount of responsibility. I took out the trash. I brought in the groceries I had gone to the store to select and buy. I cooked. I cleaned. I changed out the toilet paper. I made the bed. I dusted. I checked the oil in the car. I drove Mia to the doctor, to her dad's house. I drove her to ballet class if I could find one that offered scholarships and then drove her back home again. I watched every twirl, every jump, and every trip down the slide. It was me who pushed her on the swing, put her to sleep at night, kissed her when she fell. When I sat down, I worried. With the stress gnawing at my stomach, worrying. I worried that my paycheck might not cover bills that month. I worried about Christmas, still four months away. I worried that Mia's cough might become a sinus infection that would keep her out of day care. I worried that Jamie's behavior was escalating, that we would get in a fight, that he would go back on his offer to pick her up at day care that week just to make it difficult for me. I worried that I would have to reschedule work or miss it altogether.

Every single parent teetering on poverty does this. We work, we love, we do. And the stress of it all, the exhaustion, leaves us hollowed. Scraped out. Ghosts of our former selves. That's how I felt for those few days after the accident, like I wasn't fully connected to the ground when I walked. I knew that at any moment, a breeze could come and blow me away.

21

The Clown House

I called it the Clown House. The wife had an affinity for Thomas Kinkade landscape paintings, which filled most of the walls on her main floor. But the long staircase leading to the upper level was lined with paintings of clowns. Sad clowns. Close-ups of clown faces with eyes that followed me around. She had clown figurines, too, but the paintings were the worst. They made me feel helpless. I'd stare in a mix of horror and disgust and curiosity—why would anyone want those on their wall? What if the electricity went out and the beam of a flashlight caught one of the faces? Didn't it scare the shit out of them?

Once a month, I cleaned the bottom floor, where two bedrooms and a bathroom were set up for their two adult sons. It seemed like the boys had never lived in those rooms, but most of the relics from their childhood were neatly arranged. I dusted the Bell Biv DeVoe cassettes, the yearbooks, the Mickey Mouse clock; fluffed the pillows; and sat the teddy bears upright afterward. But that day, the first day at work after the accident, I again went straight for the bathroom first.

Shutting myself in the tiny room with the toilet seemed a natural response to blaring emptiness pulling at me from every direction. Bathrooms were a good place to hide. I wanted to crouch, belly-down on the floor, fingers laced over the back of my head like a tornado drill, like everything was about to fall on top of me. After the accident, the Clown House, a massive, three-story home with views of the town I used to live in with Travis, seemed to amplify how out of control my life was. How unsure I was of our future. How, financially, we might not survive.

I sank to my knees in front of the toilet and took a breath in, counting to five while I let it out, before stopping to fold the toilet paper into a triangle on the bottom—one corner tucked under, then the other, until a neat point formed. My hand dropped down to my cleaning tray to pull out my yellow gloves. Bits of glass from the crash flew all over the floor.

The tears blinded me. The toilet closet, which moments ago had comforted me like an embrace, now seemed like a trash compactor. I reached for the door handle and bolted out, gasping for air. From my throat came the sound of a guttural yell before I broke into sobs. The day before, Jamie had glared at me on the ferry dock after he rushed to take Mia from me like he was some kind of superhero rescuing his daughter from the evil witch who'd put her in danger. Mia started crying, reaching for me. "No, my love," he'd said, "you need to come with me." Then the glare.

I sat in front of the shower, my forehead resting on my knees, running the fibers of the maroon rug through my fingertips. The sound of car windows exploding shook in my ears, an overwhelming tightness rising in my chest. *I'm on the clock,* I said to myself. *I'm having a nervous breakdown on the clock.*

There were pieces of glass in the fingers of the gloves. I shook them out and put the gloves on, but the tears kept blinding me, so I pulled them off and put my hands over my face in an effort to hide.

I reached for my phone and pressed the button to call Pam at home. "I can't stop crying," I said. "Pam, I don't know what to do. I can't stop crying." I gulped for air.

"Stephanie? Are you okay? Where are you?" Her voice sounded so concerned, so motherly, I let out more sobs.

"I'm, uh," I said, putting my hand on my mouth before any more embarrassing noises could escape. I couldn't think of the owner's name. "The big house with all the clown paintings."

"The Garrisons'?" she asked.

"Yeah," I said. That sounded right. "I'm doing the downstairs today, too." My words came like I'd been running. "There's glass in my supplies. Glass sprayed all over Mia. She could have died."

"Well," she said, then paused, like she was searching for words. "You had no way of knowing...they say people drift toward things they're looking at when they're driving...but you didn't park there thinking that would happen, right?"

I thought of the driver—who I assumed had been texting or lighting a cigarette or distracted in some way—instead, looking at me, standing in the median. Had I been the distraction that caused him to drift?

Pam knew my financial situation. She knew I needed these hours, that I couldn't afford not to work them, not to get paid for them. That morning, she listened to me tell her about having to drive—how my hands shook, how I had to pass the scene of the accident again, how I had tried not to look at the black tire marks and broken glass on the side of the road, but how I had seen them anyway. I had only one house to do that day. But I couldn't do it.

"Why don't you take today off?" she suggested gently after listening to me. "And tomorrow, too."

"I'll be able to work tomorrow," I argued. It was just the Farm House. It'd be a challenge. "I'll be fine." I tried to assure myself more than her. "Maybe if I take today to call the insurance company and make a plan, then I'll feel more in control of everything," I said, starting to believe it myself.

"Okay," she said, probably smiling. "Then I need you to get back to work. *You* need to get back to work. It's not going to do you any good to keep falling apart like this." She paused. I heard the TV in the background. "Trust your strength," she added. But it was hard for me to trust it was still there.

When I ended the call, I sighed, not realizing how much I'd needed some compassion. The day before, my dad had yelled at me over the phone because I'd posted about the accident on Facebook. He said anyone would be able to see the photo of my mangled car and use it against me.

"They'd have to be my friend to see it," I said, annoyed at his paranoia and hurt that it was the only thing he seemed to care about. "I need to be able to tell people, Dad."

"I don't think you should talk about it at all," he snapped. "Do you realize the insurance company might think it's your fault? Have you even thought about that?" But he didn't, or couldn't, understand how much I'd needed support right then, even if it was from comments someone left under a photo, even if they were thousands of miles away.

"Yeah, Dad," I said softly. "Yeah, I thought about it." I paused, listened to him take a drag off of a cigarette and exhale the smoke. I wished he'd invite me over; offer to order me a pizza. Anything other than a lecture. "I, uh. I gotta go, Dad." I noticed that he didn't say he loved me before saying goodbye. Then again, I didn't say it, either.

Instead of going home, I went to the junkyard to clean out my car. The beaded necklaces and stained-glass daisy still hung from the rearview mirror. I collected my coffee cup, made by a friend, which fit two shots of espresso perfectly. I pulled the "Alaska Girls Kick Ass" sticker off the back window. I took a dozen pictures of Ruby's mangled back end, now unrecognizable. The back corner had been pressed in, near the gas cap, which now bent forward, crinkled like discarded tinfoil.

I put my hand on the back hatch, where the window met the edge, on the corner, beyond where the wiper could reach. My eyes closed; my head dropped. I swore I felt her pain.

This tank of a car had kept my girl safe and now faced being sold for parts and flattened. "Thank you," I said to her.

By midafternoon, I sat on my couch, looking out at gray skies that seemed to hold the type of rain that came down by the bucketful. Tuesday had been hot and sunny, but the weather had returned to the usual cold dampness that came with fall in Washington. I tried to be thankful that we didn't have to stand out in the rain that day. I couldn't believe it had only been two days before.

I paced the square of open floor in my apartment, phone pressed to my ear, listening to scratchy classical music. A policeman called to notify me that the other driver had a minimum amount of insurance, so I called them right away. "Well, just send me the model number of the car seat, and we'll send you a check for that," the agent from the other insurance company said on the phone after several minutes. "I can get you paid for your missed work, too. Also, we'll get you a rental and move your car to another lot. We should have reimbursement for the repairs or the cost of the car by next—"

"Wait," I said. "So, it's not my fault? You're taking responsibility?"

"Yes," she said. "We are taking full responsibility for this accident. You were pulled over to the side of the road, you had your hazards on, and you were parked. You are not at fault for this accident."

Her voice was so full of sincerity. *It's not my fault. It's not my fault.* I even started to believe it.

Most of my life as a mother had been tiptoeing uneasily on a floor, both real and metaphorical, becoming hesitant to trust the surface at all. Every time I built back a foundation, walls, floor, or even a roof over our heads, I felt sure it would collapse again. My job was to survive the crash, dust myself off, and rebuild. So I made a decision to trust my gut; and when I went back to work, I told Pam that I could clean only one house a day. By the time I dropped Mia off at day care, drove to one house, and cleaned it, the prospect of driving to another and starting all over again was too much. I was done.

Back at the Clown House two weeks later, I lugged my supplies up the staircase, past the moving eyes to the master bathroom. The bathroom had double sinks, a stand-up shower the size of a formal dining room table, a jetted tub on a corner platform. The tub, again, stopped me. There was something about the idea of feeling cradled, or held. I sat inside with one knee up while I dialed an attorney. I still needed to figure out how to survive the financial ruin the accident had caused.

I told the lawyer everything about the incident and what the insurance company said they'd cover, but the amount they offered for my car would barely pay off the loan. I needed a car immediately. He gave me a few key phrases to use the next time I talked to the woman who'd been assigned to my case. When I called her a few hours later, my voice shook as I repeated the rehearsed lines.

"My daughter and I have been extremely affected by this accident," I said, trying not to sound like I was reading from notes. "She isn't sleeping well and startles easily at loud noises." I told her about our neighbor's car backfiring, how Mia now jumped, startling herself, sometimes to the point of running to me in tears. I mentioned my own stress level, how I was now unable to juggle and complete tasks that I'd previously been able to do with ease. "The emotional stress we've been under, feeling the constant tremors from this accident, along with my financial inability to afford a replacement vehicle, have put us under great amounts of hardship." I took a deep breath. "We need treatment for this. I need therapy, and possibly medication. Mia needs help, too. There's no way I can afford that on top of the expense of a new car." I paused to take another deep breath. "If your company is not willing to cover our costs from emotional trauma, I will seek legal counsel in order to be properly compensated." I had been tracing the words on a piece of paper as I spoke, but at the last line my fingers froze. I sat, trembling and waiting.

"I'll see what I can do and get back to you," she said. Within an hour, she called back with an offer that would pay off my loan and give me just over a thousand dollars to use toward a new car, in addition to lost wages. I tried to stay formal in thanking her, but I wish she could have seen my smile after I hung up the phone. I hadn't smiled like that in such a very long time.

I'd been watching online classified ads for days, but a good car for twelve hundred dollars was hard to find. Then, there she was. A little Honda Civic wagon. 1983. Light blue. Travis and Mia came with me to check her out. An older couple who owned a detail shop had put in a couple thousand dollars to get her fixed up for their nephew. They'd rebuilt the engine, replaced the brakes, and put new tires on her. The nephew decided he didn't want the car, so technically he was the one selling her. She purred. She had a manual transmission. She'd been owned by a couple who'd saved the original paperwork they'd signed when they bought her new off the lot. I offered $1,100. They took it. Mia and I named her Pearl, the shiniest thing to come out of a dark situation.

Pearl handled our daily commuting decently well, and the relief of having her made my stress level drop immensely. My schedule, thankfully, was still full, and a good distraction. If I had an open afternoon, I filled it with a private client. I posted about my cleaning services in local mom groups on Facebook instead of Craigslist, after I began receiving too many responses asking me to clean naked or in a sexy maid costume. The first time it happened, the man framed it as helping me out. As if cleaning wasn't degrading enough.

After paying for gas to drive to work, my take-home pay from Classic Clean was a little more than half of what I got paid an hour. After the canceled clean at the Weekend House, I tried to keep my commute to less than forty-five minutes and stopped accepting new clients that were reaching outside my radius. But Lonnie insisted I take a new one. "It'll be worth it," she said. "They're really nice." The new client had a large home, custom-built with detailed woodwork and river rock. I cleaned it only a few times and thought of it as the Loving House. To get there, I drove up a winding single-lane road through tall evergreens. On top of the hill, where the house was, I could see the farmland nestled in the valley below. The husband and wife were home when I cleaned. Photographs of their adult daughter and her children covered the fridge and shelves. The spare bedroom off the kitchen seemed constantly poised for their return.

The husband greeted me at the door, eager to help me carry in my supplies. A fluffy golden retriever wagged its tail and sniffed at my feet. I removed my shoes and smiled at the wife, who smiled back from the chair I rarely saw her leave. Lonnie, in telling me the history of the Loving House, said the husband had cared for his wife full-time through a long illness. I thought it was cancer or something else serious, maybe terminal. The TV was always on, blaring *Dr. Oz* or home improvement programs. But when the wife spoke, her husband rushed to turn down the volume. I had trouble understanding her; she spoke so quietly and with a slurred voice. Her husband would feed her lunch and then carry her to the hallway bathroom afterward.

They'd traveled together for much of their marriage, choosing to have a child later than most. Their living room shelves were lined with drums, wood carvings, stone statues of elephants, and mountaineering books. Whenever the husband spoke about their life, he would gently ask his wife if she could recall the happy memory. If she did, he smiled with such kindness and love that I ached a little for their life.

The first time I cleaned their house, I went over the expected hours it would take to clean. The kitchen and bathrooms hadn't been detail-cleaned in a long time, and it took extra time to scrub the surfaces. When I was finished, I put on my coat, and then I paused to wave goodbye to the woman in the chair. She motioned for me to come over and reached out to take my hand. With the other, she placed a ten-dollar bill.

"That's more than I take home in an hour," I said, surprised that I'd blurted out that information. "That's almost twice as much."

She smiled, and I turned to continue walking out the door, mumbling a thank-you. Before I got to the door, overcome with the moment, I turned and said, "Boy, am I gonna get Mia a Happy Meal tonight!" Both smiled, and we chuckled a little at that.

When I had gathered my things, the husband rushed over to insist I go out the garage instead since it had started to rain a little more heavily.

We loaded my tray of supplies, clean rags, and bag of rags to be washed that weekend in the back of my wagon, and he asked me to follow him back into the garage. "We don't get visitors much anymore," he said and handed me a treat to give the dog. Trying not to blush at being called a visitor, I commented on the motorcycle parked by the back wall. He smiled and told me his daughter had come to stay for a week over the summer so he could go on an annual motorcycle trip down the coast with some friends.

We both stood quietly, hearing the words unsaid. I wanted to ask about his wife, wanted to know what their life was like, how he remained happy and at peace through it all. Instead, I admitted to wanting a road trip myself. "Even a day off or two would be nice," I uncharacteristically mentioned. I never talked to my clients about the labor intensity cleaning their homes for low wages required.

"Oh, yeah?" he said with sincere interest. "Where were you thinking about going?"

"Missoula, Montana," I said, reaching down to pet the dog, thinking how Mia would love to have one just like it some-day. "I'm from Alaska. Seems like it's the next best place."

"It is," he said, smiling. "Beautiful area. Unbelievably open. It's true what they say about the sky being bigger there."

I smiled, letting the vision, the dream, rush through me. "Hopefully we get a chance to visit," I said.

He nodded at me, then told me to get going so I could pick up my little girl. As I backed my car down the driveway, I waved at him. Being in that house made me feel as though I'd witnessed love in its truest form. They had so much that it came spilling out of their open garage door.

That house was such an anomaly, I already sighed at the memory of it as I drove home. Most weekdays were filled with a mind-numbing loneliness. I was by myself constantly—driving, working, staying up at night to complete assignments for my classes. The exception was the two hours with Mia in the evenings for dinner, her bath, and bedtime stories. My advisor at Skagit Valley Community College had looked at me with wide eyes when I told him I was a single mom who worked full-time. "What you're trying to do here is pretty much impossible," he told me, referring to the course load I had signed up for on top of my other responsibilities. After our meeting, I walked out to the parking lot, sat in my car, and didn't start the engine for a long time.

But the homework wasn't hard, just annoying. I had to ful-fill core classes like math and science, classes higher-education institutions decided you needed to complete, to pay for, to receive a degree. Some of the credits for courses I'd taken throughout my twenties transferred over, but I still needed physical education and communication, both of which I did online, sitting at my computer, alone, in total and complete irony.

If I didn't get my assignments done during the week, I caught up on weekends when Mia went to Jamie's. I could work ahead on assignments. Each class blurred into the other. I took an anthropology course, and one about weather, all of the information vanishing from my mind immediately after the open-book test. It didn't make sense to spend so much time and money and energy on school. At the beginning, the end is such a long way away. And I didn't even know what the end would look like. I just knew that to get there I had to complete assignments about the names of different clouds. And, well, lie about my exercise routine.

On those long weekends without Mia and surrounded by homework, sitting at our round kitchen table, long periods of staring out the windows seemed inevitable. They each had a thin layer of moisture on them that I wiped off several times a day when we were home, feeling like the only difference between "outside" and "inside" was a few degrees and an old pane of glass.

With the misty weather, I'd entered a persistent battle with the black mold that made Mia and me sick. Mia seemed to have constant gobs of snot dripping from her nose. I coughed like I worked in a coal mine, sometimes until I threw up. Once, in a panic after I'd tried to diagnose myself from looking up symptoms online, I drove to Urgent Care. My glands were so swollen I couldn't move my head, and I thought I had meningitis. Two weeks later, I got a $200 bill for the few minutes I'd spent talking to a doctor. I called the hospital's billing department in a wave of rage, prepared to not pay the bill at all, not caring what it might do to my credit. By filling out several forms, I finally convinced them to lower my bill through a program they offered for low-income patients. All I had to do was call and ask. It always struck me that programs like that were never mentioned. Billing offices only said to call for payment options, not to lower your bill by 80 percent.

Weather that forces you indoors also forces you to take a long look at the space you call home. I thought of my clients who lived alone. I imagined them walking through empty rooms, the vacuum cleaner lines still visible in the carpet. I didn't want to end up living like them. My clients' lives, the homes they worked so hard to afford, were no longer my dream. Even though I had long since let that dream go, I still, in my most honest moments, while dusting rooms covered in pink, flowers, and dolls, admitted that I desperately wanted the same for my kid. I couldn't help but wonder if the families who lived in the houses I cleaned somehow lost one another in the rooms full of video games, computers, and televisions.

This studio apartment we lived in, despite all its downsides, was our home. I didn't need two-point-five baths and a garage. Anyway, I saw how hard it was to keep them clean. Despite our surroundings, I woke up in the morning encased in love. I was there. In that small room. I was present, witnessing Mia's dance routines and silly faces, fiercely loving every second. Our space was a home because we loved each other in it.

22

Still Life with Mia

As temperatures dropped, I lay in bed at night, staring at the ceiling, chewing on my lips in worry every time I heard the creak of the baseboard heaters coming on. Mia and I slept together for warmth in my narrow twin bed. I hung blankets and sheets on the windows to keep out the creeping cold. When frost persistently covered the ground and our windows, I closed the French doors to our sleeping area and we lived in the small room that was our living room and kitchen, and about the size of most of the guest bedrooms or offices I dusted. I folded out the love seat at night for us to sleep on. Mia jumped on it in excitement, again calling it a sleepover. It was a bigger space for us to sleep, but she still slept curled up against my back, an arm over my neck, with her breath warming the skin between my shoulder blades. In the mornings, when my alarm started buzzing and beeping in the darkness, I'd roll onto my back to stretch. Mia hugged my neck, then put a hand on my cheek.

One night after Christmas, winter rain turned to snowflakes the size of quarters, covering the ground, piling inches deep. Mia and I stayed up well past her bedtime, knowing we wouldn't be able to drive anywhere the next day, to watch the snow. Mia put on her snowsuit and, by the light of a street-lamp, made snow angels in the yard, while I measured the snow on Pearl's hood—fourteen inches. I hadn't seen a snow-storm like that since I lived in Alaska.

The next morning Pam called to tell me to stay home. She didn't want to risk me getting stuck on the road between clients' houses. Most everything shut down in the Northwest when it snowed only a few inches. Even the freeway below our apartment was silent, with a few parked cars, abandoned by their drivers, scattered along the shoulders.

Mia bundled up immediately, not complaining that her snow pants were still damp from the night before, asking when we could go outside. A former teacher of mine who lived in the neighborhood sent me a message on Facebook, asking if I needed a sled. He said he had a great one, with a rope and everything, that he'd leave for me on the porch. When I told Mia about it, she started jumping up and down, asking, "Now? Can we go now?" I hesitated. Every fiber in my body wanted a couch to sink into, endless mugs of tea, wool socks, and if I really let myself dream, a roaring fire with books to read and a dog curled up at my feet.

"It's a long way to walk," I told Mia, knowing it wouldn't matter. I could have told her we'd be walking all day, and her excitement wouldn't wane. It was quite a trek for a three-year-old to walk uphill for a mile in snow that came up to her thighs. I had to carry her on my back most of the way. Halfway to the porch where we'd find our new sled sitting on it like a trophy, I had to stop walking. I looked out behind us, over the entire city, draped in thick snow and silence.

Mia and I spent most of the morning outside, with me dragging her home through the neighborhood on the sled, where she lay on her stomach, eating handfuls of snow. I kept seeing signs of snowplows on the main streets and started to wonder if they'd get to ours. The house we lived in sat on the corner of an alley at its lowest point. Each way out was uphill. Pearl, being the teeny car she was, had wheels about the same size as the Red Rider wagon I sometimes pulled Mia around in. I didn't have snow tires, or even chains, and couldn't afford them anyway.

After the sun warmed the snow for most of the day, the temperatures dropped below freezing that night, not getting any warmer the next day. Our street was a thick sheet of ice. I watched my upstairs neighbors attempt to get their car up the alley and fail. Another day of work gone. Maybe I could skip a credit card payment that month or take money from the available credit, deposit it into my bank account, and make a payment with that. It was halfway through the month, so most of my bills were already paid, but my current paycheck wouldn't come for two more weeks when they'd all be due again. And with the weather, it would now be about $100 lower.

We spent most of those snow days in the living room and kitchen. In the bedroom area, it was so cold that we could see frost on the windows through the French doors, and Mia put on her coat before going to grab a toy. Our television got only local stations, so she played her favorite DVDs over and over again. The one about the Hello Kitty fairy-tale ballerina, with the high-pitched voices, made my head hurt. Eventually we turned it off and got out the watercolors instead.

Mia painted pictures while I nodded in approval or read stories to her. I didn't get time off with Mia very often— usually just every other weekend when she wasn't at her dad's. With the absence of money to spend, I had to get creative in keeping her jumpy body and active mind entertained. If it rained, we couldn't afford to go to the Children's Museum or even the McDonald's Playland so she could burn off energy. We didn't enjoy sunny days at the zoo or waterparks.

Sometimes just walking behind a two-parent family on a sidewalk could trigger feelings of shame from being alone. I zeroed in on them—dressed in clothes I could never afford, diaper bag carefully packed into an expensive jogging stroller. Those moms could say things that I never could: "Honey, could you take this?" or "Here, can you hold her for a second?" The child could go from one parent's arms to the other's. There were countless times I told Mia she had to walk, because my arms were tired and I couldn't hold her anymore.

During the first snow day, I tried to hush my inner voices of guilt and shame that wondered if Mia would have had a better life with someone else, if my decision to bring her into the world was the wrong one. I put my chin in my hand and watched her carefully paint another smiling face. We both wore sweatshirts and two pairs of socks. The air smelled like frost.

My heart ached for my daughter more than it usually did in those months as I watched her struggle through transitions between her dad's house and mine. The Sundays I drove the three-hour round trip to pick up Mia had become an afternoon of jaw-clenching stress and terror for us both. For most of the previous year, when I picked Mia up on those afternoons, she'd sleep most of the way home, exhausted from a weekend of her dad parading her around his friends to show what a good father he was. Other times she'd cry for Jamie, which tore and stabbed me with anger at the same time. I had never regretted my decision to stay in Washington as much as I did on those afternoons. Poverty was like a stagnant pond of mud that pulled at our feet and refused to let go.

On the recent Sunday before the storm, Mia screamed at me the whole way home, for the entire ninety-minute drive from the ferry terminal to our apartment. I could never know what had happened, what he'd said to her to make her so angry. That afternoon, she yelled in almost the same primal, animalistic voice she'd used after her surgery.

"I hate you!" she repeated, kicking her feet. "I want to kill you! I want you dead!" Her dad took advantage of every possible moment to manipulate her into thinking that I kept her from him, telling her how sad he was that she wasn't at his house. If he really wanted her to be with him more, he would have tried. He would have, at least, made sure she had her own room. But she didn't know that. He just liked Mia wanting that. He liked seeing her cry for him. When she was only a year old, she'd return to me inconsolable, and I'd hold her for hours, her body stiff with rage and agony, a mess of hot tears and screams until it wore her voice and energy down. It was all I could do to hold her in my arms, wishing safety for her more than anyone else.

The afternoon of the storm, stuck in our own snow globe, I was content to drink tea and coffee and watch my daughter hum songs to herself as she dipped her paintbrush into a new color. Mia was too young to verbalize her feelings of loss, confusion, sadness, longing, or anger, but knowing this didn't soften the afternoons when she would rage instead. My instinct was always to hold her, but she'd kick and scream even louder now. Sometimes I screamed back. I'm sure, through the thin walls of that apartment, my neighbors grew concerned. In those moments, I didn't know what to do. I had no resources, no parents to call, no parenting coach or therapist or even a group of moms I'd connected with. I'd asked my child to be resilient and cope through a life of being tossed around from one caregiver to the next, and she screamed from underneath that weight. How would a stay-at-home mom, whose child had tantrums for normal things, understand my daughter's anger?

Not that I hadn't tried to connect with people. That fall, Mia's day care had a parents' night or some kind of potluck, and I stuck around long enough to socialize. Most of the children Mia's age who attended preschool had parents, as in plural. They flocked around Grandma Judy, soaking up her jovial nature. Mia had been running in and out with a group of kids, leaving me to stand on my own, and I heard a couple of women next to me complaining about their husbands. I couldn't help but turn my head to look at them, and they couldn't help but notice I'd heard.

"It's so hard on your own!" one said to me, the one who'd been listening to her friend complain. I nodded, forcing the sides of my mouth up to resemble some kind of smile.

"So, Stephanie," the other woman said, "you're a single mom, right? My friend just went through a horrible divorce, and she's in such a tough spot. Do you know of any organizations that could help her?"

"Um, sure," I said, my eyes darting nervously. Three women stood around the table beside us, holding tiny plates of carrot sticks and bits of broccoli with ranch. All of them now looked at me. The token single mom. I mumbled out a few programs for food and childcare.

One of the moms, a short lady with brown, bobbed hair and a round face, sniffed and held her head high. "When Jack got laid off last winter," she said, "all three of us had to move into my parents' house. Remember that?" She nudged the woman next to her. "That tiny room with Jilly's little bed scrunched up against the wall? It was like we were homeless. We were homeless!" The friend she'd elbowed nodded, making a sad face. "But thank goodness we'd saved for emergencies."

Another mom nodded. They all turned back to me for a response. I looked down at Mia's long-forgotten plate of chips and a soggy hot dog I'd been holding for her. I hadn't contributed any food, so I chose not to eat any of it. I had absolutely no idea what to say. What would they say about the room Mia and I lived in? I couldn't provide her with a home, or food, and accepted handouts to help with the tiny space we occupied. The most frustrating part of being stuck in the system were the penalties it seemed I received for improving my life. On a couple of occasions, my income pushed me over the limit by a few dollars, I'd lose hundreds of dollars in benefits.

Due to my self-employment, I had to report my income every few months. Earning $50 extra could make my co-pay at day care go up by the same amount. Sometimes it meant losing my childcare grant altogether. There was no incentive or opportunity to save money. The system kept me locked down, scraping the bottom of the barrel, without a plan to climb out of it.

One of the moms in the group asked who it was, who got divorced, and they nestled into their comfort of gossip so I could slink away.

Maybe they did feel a little like me. Maybe their marriages left them feeling more alone than I knew. Maybe we all wanted something we had equally lost hope that we'd ever have.

I thought about Mia's rages, about almost losing her in the car accident, about wearing our coats in the house because we couldn't afford to turn up the heat. About entire weekends without Mia spent cleaning toilets and scrubbing floors.

That winter, I made another decision and wrote in my online journal with renewed purpose. The blog I'd kept up until that point had been about whatever struggles I'd been having, unsure where else to put it. Every once in a while, I wrote about a moment of beauty, of clarity, of marvel at the life Mia and I had. I decided to make the entire focus on just that, changing the theme of our life, and called it *Still Life with Mia*. I wanted to capture those moments, like the one I was in now, sitting at our table, me deep in thought as I watched her paint, to keep them fresh in my memory.

The online journal became a lifeline I'd been craving, an outlet for words and pictures, a way to cut through the stress and fear of my life and focus on what I loved most—my daughter and writing. I took a photograph of Mia's face engaged in wonder. Those seconds of time were the ones I found made me feel as if I'd been there for her even more than I was.

This wasn't the life I wanted for us, but it was the one we

had for now. *It won't always be this way.* I had to keep telling myself that, or the guilt for calling this room a home, telling my daughter that this was all there was, whether it was space or food, would consume me. I wanted so much for her to have a house with a fenced backyard and a cement patio or sidewalk for hopscotch. Mia said she wanted a sandbox and swings like they had at school whenever I played the "imagine our dream house" game with her. Visualizing where we'd end up, where we'd live, what we'd do, seemed to be just as important for her as it was for me.

This was the start of our journey. The beginning. Sitting at that table, I felt time pause for a moment, for as long as a stroke of her brush. For that moment, we were warm. We had each other, we had a home, and we knew the strongest, deepest kind of love. We spent so much time scrambling from one thing to the next, getting through it, getting to the end, and starting over again, that I would not forget to fully breathe in the minuscule moments of beauty and peace.

Pam called that afternoon, and I talked to her from where I sat at the kitchen table, staring out at the snow. "Are you able to get out?" she asked with a wince or thread of hope in her voice.

"I tried to move my car earlier," I said, standing to walk into our closed-off bedroom to look out the window. "It rolled out of its parking spot to the street and the tires spun in place from there." I shook my head, a former Alaskan in every sense of the word. "My neighbor had to come out and try to get it back in the spot I had it, but we couldn't." I scratched at the frost on the window. I had left Pearl parked where she was, her bumper barely out of the road. The cold spell wasn't supposed to let up for another day or two. Although most of the main roads were fine, several of my clients were tucked back in the woods or on hills. If I got stuck, I risked not being able to pick up Mia in time, and I didn't have anyone to call in a pinch.

I wondered for a minute if Pam would fire me for not being able to work. I'd never missed this much work before, and that history at least seemed to work in my advantage. But for a few seconds, I didn't care. I hated the job almost as much as I hated relying on it. I hated needing it. I hated having to be grateful for it. "I'll make it up," I said to Pam.

"I know you will, Steph," she said, and we hung up.

I scratched at the frost on the window some more. Mia had the television on again. My breath came out in little clouds. When I reached to pull a few of Mia's stuffed animals away from the window, little bits of their fake fur stuck, frozen, to the glass.

Dusk grew on the horizon outside. I decided to make Mia pancakes for dinner with a small spoonful of mint chocolate chip ice cream on them. For myself I chose a package of ramen with two hard-boiled eggs and the remaining frozen broccoli. Mia took a bath, and I wrote in the online journal under its new name and posted photos from our walk through the snow to get the sled. Mia's cheeks were bright red, her hair sticking out of her hat just long enough to curl around the sides as she carefully licked snow off the tip of her pink mitten. It had been so quiet. The only sound was our feet compacting the snow.

Along the rim of the bathtub, Mia lined up her herd of My Little Ponies, hand-me-down gifts from a friend. "I'm done with my bath, Mom," she called out to me, and I lifted her, still covered in bubbles, her skin rosy from the warm water, onto the towel I'd laid on the toilet lid. She was getting so heavy. So much time had passed since she was a tiny infant in my arms.

That evening, we slept on the pull-out sofa bed for the second week in a row. Mia jumped up and down, excited for another sleepover with me, another viewing of *Finding Nemo*.

She fell asleep halfway through the movie. I got up to turn down the heat. It would be three hours before I could start to doze off, and I found myself wishing for wine or even decaf coffee—something to keep me warm. Instead, I crawled back into bed next to Mia's warm body, feeling her breathe and twitch in her sleep. Finally, I drifted off as well.

PART THREE

23

Do Better

Em-i-lee-ah?" the nurse called out. I roused Mia by moving my shoulder out from under her head.

"Here," I said, standing and reaching down to pick my daughter up to hold in my arms. "She goes by Mia."

The woman neither acknowledged what I said nor that I opted to carry my three-year-old. She just told us to come with her. After a brief pause to stand Mia on a scale, we sat in another chair to wait.

"What seems to be the problem here?" the nurse asked, her attention on the file she held instead of looking at me.

"My daughter has had a bad cough at night for the last week," I began, trying to remember how long she'd been suffering, how many times I'd sent her to day care when she should have stayed home. "I think it might be a sinus infection or allergies, maybe? Her eyes get really red sometimes, and she complains of her ear hurting a lot."

The nurse, a larger, gruff-looking woman, continued to somewhat ignore me, but now she had a look of pity for Mia, who sat in my lap. "Oh, sweetie, your ear hurts?" she said in a baby voice.

Mia nodded, too worn out to be shy or argue. She let the woman take her temperature and clip a plastic thing on her finger to check her pulse and oxygen levels. Then we sat there to wait. I leaned my head back to rest on the wall, closing my eyes, and tried not to think about the work I was missing. It was the Plant House again, whose owner became so annoyed over my having to reschedule that Lonnie said she all but threatened to cancel her service. Mia coughed her guttural bark again. She was too young for cough syrup, and it wasn't like I could afford it anyway. Mia woke up twice a night, crying out in a howling sort of way with her hand grasping the side of her head, and coughed in her sleep.

The pediatrician who opened the door wasn't our usual one, since I'd called that morning for a same-day appointment. This woman was smaller, boyish, and had her black hair bobbed like Mia did. "Okay." She looked at the chart, squinting. "Mia." *So the nurse heard me after all,* I thought, while Mia lifted her head at the sound of her name.

"Why don't you have her sit up here," she said, patting the papered seat on the examination table. She looked at Mia's face while I talked, then in her eyes. "What are your living conditions like?" she asked. I frowned at the question, fighting off an urge to feel incredibly hurt and offended. She could have said "How are things at home?" or "Is there something that could be making her sick?" or "Are there any pets in the home?" or anything but asking what our living conditions were like. Like we lived in a ... then I thought of what we lived in, and my shoulders fell.

"We live in a studio apartment," I said softly, admitting some kind of secret, part of me afraid she'd call child protective services if I indulged what our living conditions were actually like. "There's a lot of black mold that keeps showing up on the windowsills. I think it's coming from the basement. There's this shaft that comes up into our bedroom, and you can look down it and see the dirt floor." The doctor had stopped examining Mia and stood with her hands clasped in front of her. She had the tiniest watch with a black band. "It has a lot of windows." I looked down at the floor. "I have a hard time keeping it warm and dry in there."

"Your landlord is required by law to do what he can to get rid of the mold," she said, looking in Mia's ear. "That one's infected," she mumbled, shaking her head, almost like it was my fault.

"He cleaned the carpets," I said, suddenly remembering. "And painted before we moved in. I don't think he'd do anything else."

"Then you need to move."

"I can't," I said, putting my hand on Mia's leg. "I can't afford anything else."

"Well," she said, nodding at Mia, "she needs you to do better."

I didn't know what else to say. I nodded.

I looked at Mia's hands where they rested in her lap, fingers laced together. They still had that chubbiness to them, dimples instead of knuckles. I felt my failures as a parent every time I opened the door to our apartment, but it was nothing like the burning shame I felt in that moment.

As I carried Mia out to the car, I needed the weight of her head on my shoulder and the tickle of her hair under my nose. The pediatrician had given us a prescription for another round of antibiotics and a referral back to the specialist who'd put Mia's ear tubes in almost a year before.

When we saw the specialist a few days later, they put us in a room with a long, padded brown table. After sitting there for several minutes, the specialist rushed in, again barely acknowledging us, and said, "Why don't you put her on the table there." I stood up, still holding Mia, who'd been sitting in my lap, and sat her on the table again. "No, lay her down," he said, turning his back to us to rustle through boxes of instruments. "I need her head under the light."

Mia's eyes went wide as I said, "It's okay, Mia, he's just going to look at your ear." It was hard to be sincere as the specialist rummaged around, calling in a nurse for help, before turning abruptly to me, forcing out a sigh. He sat next to the table on a rolling stool, quickly sticking an instrument in Mia's ear. My daughter, who hadn't been able to sleep without doses of ibuprofen and gingerly placed her hand over her ear when she went outside, opened her mouth in a silent cry of pain. The specialist worked quickly, first examining her ear, then cutting a hard piece of cotton to the size of Mia's ear canal, which he placed in there, adding a few drops of liquid.

"There," he said. "You'll need to put antibiotic ear drops in there like I just did."

"She's already on antibiotics," I injected.

"Do you want your daughter to get better or not?"

I didn't know how to reply. "When I gave her those ear drops before, she got dizzy and fell over. I had to hold her down to get them in."

"You're the mom," he said. He was standing by the door, looking down on me as I sat with Mia in my lap. "You need to do whatever it takes." Then he opened the door, exited, and closed it behind him so fast I felt a breeze. His words, like the pediatrician's, burned into me: I wasn't giving Mia what she needed.

Spring in the Skagit Valley is called Tulip Season. It begins with fields of yellow daffodils, purple irises, and the occasional crocus. As the weeks go by, tulips of every color bloom, carpet the ground. The locals like to say there are more tulips in the Skagit Valley than Holland. Tens of thousands of tourists descend on the area, clogging up back roads and freeway exit ramps, cramming the restaurants and parks. But although the tulip fields, with their stripes of red, purple, white, and orange, are stunning, I have never much cared for the flower.

Tulip season is a digging out from the long winter, but it also means rain, dampness, and mold. By April, the dehumidifiers in the Plant House were constantly set to high, and another air filter appeared in the bedroom. I wiped tiny spiderlike growths of black mold from her windowsills, knowing I'd have to do the same at home.

Mia coughed at night, relentlessly. Some evenings, when we walked into the apartment, her eyes turned bright red and filled with goopy deposits. It seemed obvious that it was the house—that the home I'd chosen, with the vent that pulled in air from the hundred-year-old moldy basement, was making us sick.

Besides always being sick, my own symptoms didn't bother me too much as long as I could afford over-the-counter allergy medication. I'd been tested for sensitivities to allergens a year earlier, when my income was still low enough to qualify for Medicaid. The test revealed that I reacted to dogs, cats, some type of grass and tree, dust mites, and molds. "Indoor allergens," the doctor had said. I'd just started working for Jenny, and my chest cold hadn't let up for weeks. They'd given me inhalers and saltwater nasal sprays. Moving out of Travis's trailer—which had black mold in the walls and feral cats living beneath it—had done me a lot of good, but I still had allergy symptoms from the hours spent cleaning up dust mites, cat dander, dog hair, and mold spores in houses across the valley.

The Cat Lady's House gave me burning eyes, a runny nose, and a cough that lasted until I could change my clothes and shower. First thing in the morning, I cleaned the master bathroom. The bedroom was pink-carpeted and contained two litter boxes and three scratching posts. While I moved the litter boxes and vacuumed where they'd been, four cats stared at me from plastic carriers lined up on the bed. My presence was an inconvenience to them, and it meant they were trapped in boxes for the day. They growled if I came too close.

The days I cleaned her house, I doubled up on my dosage of over-the-counter allergy medication. But when I ran out, it felt like I'd snorted cayenne pepper. On those days, I cracked the windows, desperate for some relief. But I never told Lonnie or Pam.

When I did my taxes through TurboTax that spring, I nearly fell out of my chair. With the Earned Income Tax Credit and Child Tax Credit, I'd get a refund of nearly $4,000. "That's more than I make in three months," I mumbled out loud, into the darkness of our apartment. It didn't seem possible to get that amount. I anxiously waited for the IRS to accept my forms, feeling like I'd gotten away with something. In a notebook, I listed things I could do with the money—get a tune-up, oil change, and CV joints for the Honda; pay off the credit card debt; finally buy kitchen sponges and dish soap, toothbrushes, shampoo and conditioner, bubble bath, vitamins, and allergy medications. Or we could maybe go on a road trip.

Like many, most of what I knew about Missoula I had read in Norman Maclean's *A River Runs Through It*. People who visit Missoula in search of places to fly fish can attest to the pull of that particular novel, or the movie made from the book. But for me, it was the way John Steinbeck wrote about Montana in *Travels with Charley* that convinced me to leave Alaska and begin heading toward Big Sky Country. I chose Missoula not because of Maclean, but for David James Duncan, author of *The River Why*, who, at a reading in Seattle, admitted to living and sometimes teaching at the university there. What compelled me to dream about waking up one summer day to drive east for nine hours was, plainly, a hunch. A hunch that had grown into a constant hum. One I'd had for more than half a decade.

Missoula's wages are low and housing costs are high. That much I knew from conversations I'd had with people who used to live there but couldn't afford to anymore. Jobs aren't easy to come by, and they don't pay well in a small college town with nearly seventy thousand people. Parents of college kids rent apartments for them, driving up rent costs in sought-after parts of town, where even a one-bedroom basement apartment goes for at least eight hundred bucks. When I thought about whether or not to relocate, this conundrum remained at the forefront of my mind. But when I spoke to people who lived in Missoula, they deeply loved their town. Those who had moved there said that while they had given up competitive salaries or high wages, it was worth it because they got to live in Missoula.

I wanted to know why Steinbeck wrote so lovingly of the place. Why Maclean claimed the world increased rapidly in bastards the farther one got from Missoula, Montana. People spoke of this place like a sensational flavor of ice cream they'd had on vacation once, one that they'd never been able to find again and weren't sure if they'd dreamed of or not.

The night the tax refund money hit my account, we went out to eat at Red Robin. I let Mia get a chocolate milkshake. We went to the store and filled the cart with food we normally couldn't afford: avocados, tomatoes, frozen berries for pancakes. I bought a bottle of wine. Over the next week, I bought a frame and a full-sized mattress and a heated pad so I didn't have to heat the whole room at night. I found insulating curtains and cheap rods on clearance. I bought Mia a kid-sized trampoline for her to jump on instead of the couch and bed. I bought myself something I'd been wanting for several years— a titanium, tension-set diamond ring for $200. I was tired of waiting for a man to come into my life who would buy one for me. It was more money than I'd spent on something unnecessary in years. As hard a decision as it was, I needed to make a commitment to myself. To trust in my innate strength. I could do this, all of this, just fine on my own. The ring that slid down over the middle finger on my left hand served as a constant reminder of that.

With money, even temporarily, life felt almost carefree. I filled my gas tank without subtracting the total from the amount remaining in my account. At the store, I didn't go through a process of mental math—the date, what bills had been paid, what bills were due, how much money I had, how much I'd pay, or what credit cards had available balances—before deciding if I could afford to buy paper towels. I slept—without extra clothes on to keep warm, without a knot in my stomach, without too much worry. But Mia still tossed and turned, coughed and sneezed, waking up complaining of pain in her throat and ears. And while I could temporarily afford to take time off to take her to the doctor, I couldn't keep the sinus and ear infections from consuming her.

Late at night, when I needed a break from homework, I scrolled through the classified ads. I gazed longingly at photos of houses, two-bedroom apartments, all completely out of my price range. My income barely covered my rent at the studio, roughly half of what the other places would cost. Even though I had a little extra income now, it wasn't sustaining. It was a cushion to catch us in case we fell. And, if I'd learned anything, when you're teetering on the brink of making it, you always lose your balance and fall. I shook my head and clicked away from the ads, back to my homework. Even dreaming seemed like something I couldn't afford.

For days, I heard the pediatrician's voice in my head. "She needs you to do better." How could I do better? It didn't seem possible to try any harder than I already was while dealing with hoops placed in front of me to jump through, which sometimes held me, trapped in place.

That week, I'd submitted a copy of a handwritten paystub from Classic Clean to renew our childcare grant, and a woman from the DHHS office called me, demanding I submit a real one. When I kept trying to explain that it was my boss's handwriting, and an official paystub, she threatened to pull my grant approval and deny my assistance immediately. I started sobbing. She told me to go to the local office to get it sorted out the next day.

People lined up outside the Department of Health and Human Services office long before it opened in the morning. Not knowing this, the first day I arrived about thirty minutes after the doors were unlocked. Every chair in the waiting room was full. I grabbed a number and stood leaning against a wall, watching the interactions between mothers and children; between caseworkers and clients who didn't understand why they were there, why they were denied, why they had to come back with more paperwork.

A chair opened, but I let an older woman, wearing a long skirt, holding the hand of a small, meek child, take it instead. I glanced at my watch. An hour had passed. When I looked at it again, another had gone by. I started to get nervous about my number being called before I needed to go get Mia from day care. She would have been bouncing all around me here. Not like the children who surrounded me, sitting quietly, whispering to ask if they could go to the bathroom. Most stereotypes of people living in poverty weren't seen here. In the lines on their faces, I could see the frustration, the urgency to get out of there so they could go to the store and buy food, go back to work. They, like me, had been completely drained of hope, staring at the floor, waiting, sincerely needing what they asked for. We needed help. We were there for help so that we could survive.

When my number glowed in the black box, I rushed toward the window, fearing they would call the next number if I didn't get there fast enough. I placed my purple folder on the counter, pulled out all the copies of the checks I'd received from clients and the handwritten paystub. The woman picked up a couple papers while she listened, then examined the paystub.

"You need your boss to print out an official one," she said and stared at me. I blinked. Her expression didn't change.

I told her I had been there all morning, that my boss's office was forty minutes away. I couldn't spend another day here, waiting.

"If you want to keep your childcare grant, that's what you need to do," she said. I'd been dismissed. It was almost one o'clock.

Lonnie shook her head as she printed out a paystub for me. This paystub was for a pay period that was weeks ago. All my self-employment income came from checks handwritten by my clients. I had no idea how this situation could possibly make sense. But the next day, I waited outside for the office to open, then waited for hours to present my income for the past three months, a written schedule of my current work hours, and letters from several of my clients formally saying I worked in their home at the time I said I did.

Without food stamps, we would have frequented food banks or free meals at churches. Without childcare assistance, I wouldn't have been able to work. The people lucky enough to remain outside the system, or on the outskirts of it, didn't see how difficult those resources were to obtain. They didn't see how desperately we needed them, despite the hoops they made us jump through.

When I cleaned Henry's house that Friday, he noticed I seemed down. I still had about a quarter of my tax refund left. It was sitting there for the time being, until my car broke down or Mia was sick, or a client canceled, or all the above. Though I still put myself to sleep imagining Missoula—what it would be like to walk across the bridge over the Clark Fork River, or lie in a field looking up at that big sky—it seemed impossible to consider making a trip now.

"I don't think I can afford to visit Montana," I said to Henry after he asked what was wrong. He waved in the air like my words smelled bad. For a year now, he'd heard me mention Missoula, but only in an "oh-I'd-like-to-visit-there-someday" kind of way. My face must have looked so mournful that he saw the weight of that statement. So much so that he got up from his desk, walked over to the shelf, and started looking through travel books and maps. Then he handed me a book about Glacier National Park and a large folded map of Montana.

He spread out the map across his desk and pointed to places I needed to go. He refused to believe that the trip to Missoula was an impossible option. While I appreciated the gesture, encouragement, and support, my smile wasn't sincere. A huge part of me was scared. Not of the journey—though I did fear my car breaking down—but of falling in love with Missoula and then having to return to the Skagit Valley, to the mold in my studio apartment above the freeway. It would be like saying goodbye to a better life, one that I would not get to have.

In wanting that life, in wanting to get ahead, my job at Classic Clean stopped making sense. Over a third of my wages went to gas. After bringing this to Pam's attention, she did offer a small travel allowance, but it was a quarter of what I spent just to get from one job to the next. Plus, the anonymity started to wear me down. Between working alone and taking online classes, my life was one of solitude. I craved human interaction, even if it was a situation where I'd been hired by someone to work. I needed my job to have purpose, meaning, or at least feel like I'd helped someone.

24

The Bay House

One afternoon, I walked into the Financial Aid Office at Skagit Valley Community College and said I wanted to take out the maximum amount of student loans. This hadn't been an easy decision, and I started shaking as I waited for the person behind the counter to help me. Taking out these loans meant I'd turn down work, available work, and go into debt instead. But my exhaustion had reached a level of impossibility. There wasn't any other way to explain this rash decision. Mia seemed constantly sick, and I spent only three hours a day with her. My back hurt during the day and would stiffen while I slept, the pain waking me up at four a.m. Loan money meant I could focus on finding private clients and landscaping, instead of working for Classic Clean. It meant spending more time with Mia.

It also meant the opportunity to volunteer at the Domestic Violence and Sexual Assault Services as a receptionist. I thought of it like an internship that my loans paid me for. Volunteering would pay in experience, diversity on my résumé, and letters of recommendation. My classes at the community college were preparing me for a paralegal degree. The only jobs I allowed myself to dream about were the practical ones that could earn me health insurance and retirement funds.

"Your Honor, the father is a full-time worker," Jamie's

lawyer had said three years earlier, before revealing that I was then homeless and unemployed. Standing in front of that judge, hearing Jamie obtain respect and admiration for working and for living in the stable housing he'd kicked us out of, had been demoralizing. The experience planted a deep-rooted fear in me. Even though I wanted to move to a better living situation, it would be the ninth time Mia and I had moved since she'd been born.

In most of our dwellings, she didn't have her own room. While judges were rumored to say, "I don't care if the child sleeps on a concrete floor! They will have overnight visitation with their father," mothers fighting for sole custody—especially ones who'd escaped abuse—had to provide a sort of life that was simply impossible to obtain. In court, Jamie's lawyer described me as a mentally unstable person, unable to care for her own child full-time. I had to fight for the ability to mother my nursing infant, the infant Jamie had screamed at me to abort. I had been ground to a pulp by that judge. Like I had been in the wrong for leaving a man who threatened me. I knew there were countless women out there in the same situation as I had been.

Maybe I could go to law school and become a civil rights attorney. I could help people who'd been in the same violent situation as I had been with Jamie, and I could advocate for them. But there was another voice nagging at me, a louder voice that refused to be ignored. Part of me demanded that I become a writer. But I soothed the insistent voice by telling myself this was just for now, while Mia was still little—and then I'd be a writer. This promise to myself felt like throwing buckets of water on the only fire that was left in me, the only part that dared to dream.

On one late-night search for a better place to live, I found a two-bedroom apartment built over a garage. The front door faced the mountains and the ocean. It was way out of my price range. The ad explained that the owners lived in the main house with their three little girls, three dogs, and a cat who stayed mainly in the garage on the constant hunt for mice. Instead of closing the browser window and feeling that familiar ache for another life, I emailed them and asked if they'd be willing to trade rent for cleaning and landscaping services.

The following afternoon, I pulled into their long driveway, past a large property that had been cleared of all but the largest trees to reveal the view of the bay and hills beyond. Their driveway curved to the left and became almost engulfed in large trees and lined with blackberry bushes. The house was in a neighboring town, farther from where most of my cleaning clients lived. I knew that living there would mean I wouldn't be able to work for Classic Clean anymore. Maybe, I thought, as I maneuvered down the driveway, if I found a better place to live, one that was also farther away, it would make sense for me to quit.

When I could finally see the house, I nearly closed my eyes at the beauty of the scene in front of me. The sun was just beginning to set behind the mountains, and the entire sky had turned a deep pink. I parked in front of the goat pen, between the apartment and a house with windows lining the front.

A toddler waddled around the cement pad in front of the garage on a wooden bicycle. A tall, lanky man wearing a frayed gray hoodie and jeans watched me get out of my car. I knew from emailing his wife, Alice, that his name was Kurt. We shook hands, and I introduced myself and explained that my daughter was at her dad's. He rubbed his hand through messy brown hair in an attempt to make it lay flat. "Follow me," he said, catching the toddler and picking her up. "I'll show you around."

As we walked, I felt an intense pull toward this property, one that, if I believed in those things, was like the universe pushing me in the direction I was supposed to go, as if this had been decided for me and all I had to do was follow along. I followed Kurt to the side of the garage and stood next to a garden bigger than our entire studio apartment. He motioned to raspberry and blueberry bushes and then to a large patch of grass next to it.

"Part of the renter's deal with us is that they mow this," he said, crossing his arms. "Our last renters kind of had a problem with that." I watched his daughter toddle toward the grass, imagining Mia with her.

"In addition to the barter?" I asked.

"Barter?" he repeated, looking at the sky, like that sounded familiar but he wasn't sure why.

I nodded and said, "I emailed Alice, and she said it might be possible for me to trade part of my rent working in your yard and cleaning your house?"

His face changed a few times from confusion to possibly recalling her saying something like that to nodding in agreement at the idea. Though he probably wasn't, he seemed stoned, like most of my Fairbanks friends were at any given hour of the day. My kind of person, I thought. I liked him immediately.

He looked down and smiled at me. "Just wait until you see up there." He nodded to the apartment above the garage.

Kurt walked ahead of me up the stairs, carrying the toddler on his hip. He and Alice and their growing family had lived in the apartment above the garage while they built their house, he explained. When we rounded the first bend in the stairs, I stopped following. Kurt turned and smiled at the awe on my face.

The last of the sun's rays had painted everything a reddish orange. At that moment, I couldn't recall seeing a more beautiful sunset.

"Is it like this every night?" I asked, my voice just a whisper.

Kurt laughed. "Well, when the sun is actually out," he said. He was making a joke, because in Northwest Washington there were entire winters, nearly half the year, with less than a dozen days of sunshine. "Good thing it's almost summer."

The apartment had two bedrooms that were separated by a bathroom with a tub. There was a cabinet under the sink and shelves for towels. The kitchen had a propane stovetop, a dishwasher, a full-sized fridge, and a window that looked out onto the backyard where the family kept chickens.

All the floors were wood. In the front room and kitchen were two skylights, and there was one in the bathroom. Glass French doors opened to the covered porch. Insulated windows lined the western wall of the living room.

"Cable's included," Kurt said, and nodded to the wire coming out of the wall. I looked at him and blinked. "If that's important to you," he continued. "I'm a bit of a football fanatic."

"I haven't had cable for most of my adult life," I said. I wanted to laugh hysterically. I wanted to pinch myself.

"It's really small," he said, opening the closet in the bedroom, "so I added a lot of closet space. Those cabinets on the wall above this are totally open and huge. I think Alice put bedding up there or something."

"Wow," I said. "That's amazing."

"Well," he said, "I wouldn't call it that."

"No, really," I said. "My closet right now is a glorified broom closet. Our whole place is half the size of this whole apartment."

"Huh," he said, to fill an awkward moment. Then he seemed to remember something, and walked toward the kitchen. "You can have the eggs when we go out of town," he said, pointing down to the chicken coop. "I mean, if you move in here." I smiled and asked where they were going. "Oh," he said, snapping his fingers, like he'd forgotten to tell me, "we go to Missoula for a few weeks every summer with some friends. It's a great place to raise a family. Have you been?"

My breath caught in my chest. I didn't know how to answer, how to tell him that I'd pined for that town for the past six years, that my only regret in life was not leaving for college as planned, not telling Jamie that I was pregnant, and having the baby by myself. I had a sudden urge to tell Kurt all of this, but I bit my lip.

"I haven't," I said, shaking my head, trying to remain calm. "But I'd like to."

I followed Kurt inside the main house to meet Alice, who was busy at the stove preparing dinner. The oldest two girls played on the floor with an entire bin of Littlest Pet Shop toys. I had never seen so many all at once and thought about how Mia carried around a single frog from the series. I could imagine her playing on the floor with the girls, just as I imagined laughing with Alice and drinking wine together at the table. Maybe I wasn't just finding a new place to live, but new friends as well.

Alice called over to the girls to get cleaned up for dinner. "Would you like to join us?" she asked, gazing at me. She stood a few inches shorter than me, barely as tall as Kurt's chest. Her brown hair was pulled back into a tight ponytail, revealing ears that stuck out a bit. She looked like she'd been one of those cute girls in high school—someone I would have envied.

"Sure," I said, smiling, trying not to let happy tears brim over my eyes. "I'm happy to meet you." Though I sincerely was, Alice intimidated me a little. Without even knowing her, I assumed she was like the mothers at Mia's day care who limited screen time, scheduled craft projects, limited sugary snacks, and served appropriate servings of fruit and vegetables at every meal. A mother with the privilege, time, and energy to mother well and who might judge me for not doing the same.

Alice put my plate on the table, opposite the two older daughters, who dutifully ate their carrot sticks first. Kurt offered me a beer, and I accepted. It was the same generic kind from Costco that Travis used to get, and the taste brought me right back to his house. When they asked me what I did for work, I said that I cleaned houses, but I wanted to be a writer. Kurt said he'd read a bit of my blog, which confused me for a second, but then I remembered that my email signature contained a link to it.

"I don't know how you do it on your own," he said, staring at me for a second too long. The look in his eyes made me squirm, and I sensed awe in his voice. From the corner of my eye, I saw Alice furrow her eyebrows and look down at her plate.

That evening, it felt like my feet weren't touching the ground. Alice and Kurt said they had an inflatable pool and that the girls played outside most of the day in the summer. Alice worked full-time at a bank, but Kurt, a teacher, had the season off. He said Mia would be welcome to go down to the beach with them or play in their yard. They even had a fire pit where they roasted marshmallows.

By the time I got home, Alice had already emailed me to officially ask if I wanted to move in. I emailed back an enthusiastic yes. She immediately responded, saying I could start moving my stuff in anytime. Over dinner, we'd discussed the barter arrangement, which would make my cash rent a full fifty dollars cheaper than my rent at the studio.

It was mid-March. I had two weeks to move to avoid paying rent on two places. My financial aid award letter had arrived a few days before. It felt like things were falling into place—so much that I started to grow suspicious. Maybe it was too good for us. Maybe we didn't deserve something that good.

25

The Hardest Worker

When I told Pam I was moving, she understood what it meant. She didn't fire me. I didn't quit. We both just sort of agreed that I wouldn't be able to work there anymore. She and Lonnie told me separately they were sad to see me go. I was their main employee, the one they could count on. That year, I'd received the highest total amount of Christmas bonuses they'd ever seen. One of my clients had recently called Pam to tell her I was irreplaceable.

I knew I was one of the hard workers, like Henry had said, but I also knew I could be replaced. I had to provide for my kid. The pull to live in a better environment was too strong, even though it meant turning down work. Staying in the studio meant that Mia would continue to suffer from illnesses she'd already had surgery for. Taking on debt and losing a job seemed an enormous risk, but I also had grown to understand something else: it would be extremely difficult to see a different future if all I could think about was making it through to the next paycheck.

As a poor person, I was not accustomed to looking past the month, week, or sometimes hour. I compartmentalized my life the same way I cleaned every room of every house—left to right, top to bottom. Whether on paper or in my mind, the problems I had to deal with first—the car repair, the court date, the empty cupboards—went at the top, on the left. The next pressing issue went next to it, on the right. I'd focus on one problem at a time, working left to right, top to bottom.

That shortsightedness kept me from getting overwhelmed, but it also kept me from dreaming. "Plan for five years from now" never made it to that top corner. Saving for retirement or Mia's college education never made it on my radar. I had to keep an underlying faith that things would eventually get better. That life wouldn't always be a struggle. My mom, the first in our family to go to college, had built her whole life on breaking that cycle. A master's degree allowed her to pursue her dreams, even at the cost of losing a relationship with me. But she had grown up in a run-down house, while I had grown up in the suburbs—a privilege that perhaps created my confidence that things would get better. I wondered about the people who waited in lines next to me for benefits who didn't have such a past to look back on. Did they share any piece of this confidence? When a person is too deep in systemic poverty, there is no upward trajectory. Life is struggle and nothing else. But for me, many of my decisions came from an assumption that things would, eventually, start to improve.

There wasn't any fanfare in quitting my job. Most of my clients wouldn't know I'd left, that I had been replaced by a new person. Maybe they would vacuum or position the throw pillows differently. Maybe the clients would come home to find the shampoo bottles arranged in a new way, but most of them probably wouldn't notice the change at all. When I thought about a new maid taking over my jobs, I wondered again what it would be like to know a stranger had been in your house, wiping every surface, emptying the bathroom garbage of your bloody pads. Would you not feel exposed in some way? After a couple of years, my clients trusted our invisible relationship. Now there would be another invisible human being magically making lines in the carpet.

youngest daughter was born. Since then, between the full-time job and the girls, she hadn't been able to keep up on the house or yard, and I wasn't sure what Kurt did to help.

I would keep track of my landscaping hours and submit them, like a timecard, to Alice in an email. It seemed like a fantastic deal for both of us, but Alice still seemed hesitant, judging by the small pile of legal documents she planned to have notarized. She swore it was to protect both of us in case anything happened, but it still seemed odd. I'd done lots of trades by then, and most people seemed more trusting.

Kurt admitted he'd read more of my blog, commenting on what a good writer I was. I blushed and thanked him. It had been a rough couple of years since I started writing online. Hardly any of that I wanted to talk about in person, but having it published for anyone to read caused me to assume they already knew everything so I didn't have to explain myself. Kurt called it inspirational. I smiled, but winced at the word. People had said that about me before. How can barely surviving be an inspiration, I started to ask.

"If you can handle life with a three-year-old by yourself, in a tiny space, with so little, then I can, too," one commenter had written.

The blog was an outlet for the beauty of life, but also for my frustrations. Life had still been so relentless in throwing one obstacle at me before I'd been able to fully clear the last. I couldn't get ahead.

My lived experience seemed vastly different than that of my peers—not even just the moms at the day care. Many times, I ducked out of possible interactions or potential chances at making friends with people I actually liked because I felt like I'd only be a drain. I'd suck people of the resources they had available for friends without being able to give anything back. Maybe I could take their kid for an afternoon for a trade, but it stressed me out not to be able to provide snacks or food. A hungry kid coming to my house on a weekend afternoon

Pam encouraged me to become licensed and insured, since I would rely purely on my self-employment income. But the suggestion conveyed a permanence and the beginning of a lifelong career. I'd need a company name, she said, something that seemed official. Pam had started out that way. But as much as I appreciated her advice, I didn't want this to be my start. I wanted it to be a means to an end, and that end was a degree. A ticket to never having to scrub anyone's toilet but my own.

I didn't tell the woman in the Cat Lady's House it was my final day, but I did hug Beth at Lori's House. I'd miss her coffee and conversation.

When I left the Chef's House, I smiled and waved and then flipped it off. I'm pretty sure the owner never aimed when he peed. I snuck out of the Cigarette Lady's House the same way I'd been sneaking a look at her things. I'd miss her cashmere hoodie with sleeves long enough to cover my hands and pet my cheeks when I put it on. I'd miss trying to piece together her life, trying to figure out if she was happy or sad, eating lettuce and fat-free dressing while smoking cigarettes at the kitchen counter, watching the small television that hung from the top cabinet. I left the Porn House literally giggling with glee before gazing at the Sad House, realizing I hadn't been there in a month. I wondered how long he'd go on suffering. How long he'd have to wait for his life to end.

Before I left Henry's house, we spent a long time talking. It was hard to tell him I couldn't afford to continue working for the company he'd used to keep his house clean for so many years. He held up his hands and shrugged a little, then started to suggest that maybe I could help with landscaping, before remembering he already had a crew of men outside mowing his grass and trimming the bushes. I had the urge to comfort him, suggesting he could be a reference for my résumé. This made him straighten again, and then he began rattling off all the qualities he'd be happy to tell anyone who asked.

"You're a hard worker," he said, lightly stamping his foot and making a fist in declaration. "One of the hardest workers I've ever seen."

"I really needed to hear that," I said softly, and smiled at him. I wanted to explain how difficult the decision had been, how uncertain my future was. All I had were a handful of my own clients and student loans to float us through until fall. I wanted to tell him I was scared. It was an odd moment, yearning for comfort from a stranger, but Henry seemed almost like a father figure to me.

The woman who lived in the Farm House happened to be there on my last day. I'd grown to like her. She had called the office once to tell them how much she loved the way I cleaned her master bathroom, and I had to admit that I felt proud of it, too—even though the glass shower was a bitch to get spotless. I always brought my tweezers with me to her house to pluck the stray hairs from my eyebrows in her light-up magnifying mirror. On my way out, she helped me load my cleaning tray, then asked me to look through a box of things in her SUV intended to go to Goodwill. I took a non-stick KitchenAid pan that would be perfect for cooking Mia's pancakes. Before I got in my car, she looked like she might hug me, but then she reached out to shake my hand. Even though we had a relationship of trust, there was still a divide. She was still a homeowner. I was still a maid.

Our new home had a washer and dryer downstairs in the garage. I could wash Mia's stuffed animals whenever her cough started to get bad. There was forced-air heat, and air filters and wooden floors, and I doubted mold would ever consider creeping in.

My landlord for the studio wasn't pleased when I gave him fifteen days' notice instead of thirty. He said he'd keep my deposit, subtracting whatever amount he lost in not having a tenant to pay rent the next month.

"I've done a lot of updates," I wrote in an email. "This place looks a hundred times better than it did when I moved in." I added photos of the new curtains in the living spaces and shelves and towel holders in the bathroom, adding that I'd leave it completely detail cleaned. And while he found a new renter by the time I moved out, he still kept part of my deposit.

I started making trips to the new apartment when I could, packing my car with as many books, clothes, towels, and plants as possible. Kurt and Alice invited us over for dinner one night so we could introduce the girls. They ran together in the yard, the huge black dog, Beau, barking occasionally while the two older dogs watched with indifference. At almost four years old, Mia fit right in with the older girls, who were two and four years older than her. Kurt and Alice seemed excited and a little relieved at Mia's sweet and playful personality.

After dinner, Alice pulled out several legal documents for the rental agreement, walk-through, and something she'd drafted for the work-trade on rent. Landscaping hours worked out to be about five per week spent pulling weeds from their naturally landscaped areas. And every other Thursday from nine-thirty to two-thirty, I would clean the house. I hoped it would be enough time. Their house was huge, but she said it took the regular cleaning company only two or three hours to finish it.

"How many cleaners did they have?" I asked, already knowing the answer would be more than one.

"I'm not sure," she said, looking at Kurt.

"Probably two or three," Kurt said.

"It'll probably take me six or even more in the beginning," I said, watching their eyes widen. "It'll get faster once I get to know your house. I work straight through, though. I'm probably a little slower than three people working all at once."

They seemed to understand, or at least they pretended to. I knew Alice had done all the housework herself before her

meant ten dollars of groceries, sometimes more. And they always seemed to want huge glasses of milk. I couldn't afford that.

The apartment over the garage made me feel like I had made it to the other side. I felt like I'd accomplished something by finding better living conditions, even if it meant losing my steady income. I'd gained a couple of new clients that week. My childcare assistance was approved to cover a volunteer position at the Domestic Violence and Sexual Assault office. I'd somehow found a place in the system that allowed me a tiny bit of time and space to get ahead.

But I couldn't shake the feeling that everything seemed a little too dreamy. One afternoon while I did homework, Mia and the girls drew chalk rainbows on the cement outside the garage, their laughter coming in through the open window. The sun was out, and everything felt perfectly in place.

When Alice called her older girls in for lunch, they whined, asking if Mia could come, too. The girls clambered up to my porch, Mia between them, breathless, all asking at once. When I smiled and said yes, they cheered. I watched them run back down the stairs, all of them giggling, and across the yard to the main house. Then I sat back down at my desk. The fact that Mia was off playing somewhere safe, instead of watching the same cartoon over and over, alleviated the guilt I usually felt at keeping her cooped up while I worked. The days of living in a one-room moldy studio apartment felt far away.

26

The Hoarder House

When I arrived for the first clean at what I would call the Hoarder House, the wife opened the door only a few inches. I saw her eyes go from alarm to hesitancy and back again.

"Hi," I said, smiling. "I'm here to clean your house? Rachel from the Facebook group connected us?"

She nodded, looked down, and opened the door enough to reveal her large, pregnant belly and a small boy clinging to her leg. I stood on the small concrete square of their front porch. From inside the house, a bird chirped. More children peered out at me from a large window to my right. When I looked at the woman again, she glanced nervously inside.

"This is my little secret," she said before opening the door enough to let me in.

I stepped in and wobbled. The door's path created a clear spot in the floor, the only clear spot in the entire room. My first thought was to not react. In our initial conversation, she'd mentioned needing help clearing out garbage and catching up on laundry. But this was much more than I had anticipated. Clothes, dishes, papers, backpacks, shoes, books. Everything had been left to collect hair and dust on the floor.

The family had stopped making payments on their house. She told me this while we stood in that one bare spot in the front room. I listened as attentively as I could, trying not to feel overwhelmed by the state of the house. She talked quickly and sounded exasperated. They had a rental to move into—the husband, wife, five kids, and soon, a newborn baby.

"We can't really afford to have you help me," she said, looking down at her hands on her belly. "But I'm losing my mind. The new house will be a fresh start. I don't want to move all this."

I nodded in response and looked around. Every available surface in the kitchen and dining room contained piles of dirty dishes. The corners in the living room had heaps of what looked like books and school papers, mixed with clothes, toys, and more dishes. On one wall, the shelves had fallen from a bookcase and books were strewn across the floor where they fell.

She mentioned they couldn't pay their bills. She mentioned food stamps. I felt horrible charging her anything, but I couldn't work for free. Though she hadn't asked me to come down on my hourly rate, I insisted she pay me half of what I normally charged.

"And how about five bucks for each garbage bag full of laundry?" I suggested, looking for a place to set down my things. "I can bring them back to my place and do it there." She didn't answer immediately. Her free hand, the one that wasn't stroking the top of the toddler's head, moved up to wipe her cheeks. It paused under her nose for a second, and she nodded. She closed her eyes tight, trying not to cry. "I'll get started in the kitchen," I said.

While I began pulling supplies out of my bucket, the boy who'd been hiding behind her leg came over to help. "He's not verbal," the woman said. "He hasn't spoken any words yet." I smiled at him, taking my yellow dish gloves from the little hands he held out toward me.

That first day, I spent four hours doing dishes, my fingers turning to prunes through the dish gloves. When the hot water ran out, I started cleaning the surfaces. Clean dishes, set out to dry on towels, covered the table, the stovetop, and counters I'd cleaned. How had she cooked for seven people in this tiny room with that little boy clinging to her? I couldn't tell what they ate. Much of the boxed and canned food in the cupboards was expired, some by as much as ten years. A peek in the fridge revealed shelves dripping with old produce.

A closet in the hallway housed a washer and dryer. Beside a small path leading to the garage, which had been converted to a master bedroom, clothes piled on the floor several inches deep. I started to bag some to bring home with me, stopping a few times to catch my breath. It must have been dust mites. They always made me cough like I was having an asthma attack, and I gasped between coughing fits. When I went for the final handful to fill the second bag, I revealed the floor underneath. And a large spider, and mouse droppings, and I swear what looked like snakeskin. Biting back a scream, I nodded and called it a day.

As I left, the woman thanked me. Tears brimmed in her eyes, and she apologized for the state of the house. "Don't apologize," I said, my arms loaded with cleaning supplies and bags of clothing. "I'll be back at the same time tomorrow."

Many of my private clients said my presence in their house gave them the motivation to do some cleaning themselves. Those were the ones who had me come once or twice. My regular clients—the biweekly, weekly, or monthly cleans— knew the drill: leave me alone so I can do my job. I didn't overbid a house to give myself more time. If I was finished with more time that visit, I stayed and did a little more. With the private clients, my reputation was on the line. I'd be the one they'd hopefully rave to their friends about. If they needed someone to hang out with them and chat and listen to their current struggles while we cleared out a huge mess, I could do that, too.

On day two at the Hoarder House, we cleaned the youngest daughter's bedroom. We bagged up twelve kitchen-sized trash bags, lugged them outside, and put them with the rest to go to the dump. Under the miscellaneous papers, Popsicle stick creations, mounds of forgotten food, deflated balloons, various twigs and rocks, and clothing too torn or small to wear, we found a little girl's room. I found a few figurines from a dollhouse, and I placed them carefully in the doll-sized living room. We put books and bins of My Little Ponies back onto a shelf, painted purple and pink. We put clothes in the dresser, shoes on the shoe rack. I hung a red dress with a matching coat in the closet. I found a pair of black shiny Mary Janes.

It felt good to clean that room. I thought about the times when Mia was at her dad's and I went through the clutter in her room. She hated throwing anything away, and I only convinced her to give away toys by bringing her with me to donate them to a women's shelter or consignment store where she'd get credit. But all the little Happy Meal toys, the drawings, the broken crayons, had to be thrown out. After hours of purging and organizing, Mia would come home, walk in her perfectly clean and organized space, and smile like everything was new again. I hoped the same for that little girl not much older than mine.

I bagged up more laundry before leaving, having returned the two other bags that had been cleaned and folded. At home that night, Mia helped me fold the shirts, socks, and dresses. She held up a skirt to her waist and commented how pretty it was. I watched her twirl around with it.

"Can I have it?" she asked, and I shook my head no. I explained they were another family's clothes. "Why are you washing them?"

"Because I'm helping them, Mia," I said. "That's my job. To help people."

Only then, when I heard myself say it, did I believe it was true. I thought back to the woman who'd thanked me for cleaning her house and put a wad of cash in my hands, holding them in hers for a second, then telling me I better get going before her husband got home. A couple of my land-scaping clients called me their best-kept secret.

I still carried around a day planner, scribbling clients' names in various boxes, memorizing the schedule as best I could for when someone called to ask if I was available at a certain time or day. I didn't have to wear a uniform or go to meetings with my boss or have my cleaning supply tray inspected. I didn't have to stop by an office, miles out of my way, to get bottles refilled with cleaning agents. Five-toilet days still slayed me, but I somehow felt a little better about cleaning them.

After each four-hour session, the Hoarder House looked more like a regular home. I righted the shelves in the living room, swept up all the birdseed, and found dozens of DVDs under the couch. Though I tried to hide it, I felt thankful that she never asked me to clean the bathroom. I'm not sure how long things stayed clean. I'd tidy up the kitchen one af-ternoon only to see pots and dishes with dried red sauce on them all over the counters and stove the next. I hoped it made her family happy. I hoped it made her feel more peace before her baby was born. Mostly I was glad to be done.

The building of the domestic violence nonprofit, where I vol-unteered, was tucked away in a nondescript office park by the railroad tracks in Mount Vernon. I wasn't just a hopeful vol-unteer receptionist, I was a client. The back room where I met with my domestic violence advocate had high windows near the ceiling that let in just enough sun to keep alive a scat-tering of houseplants. Christy, my advocate, had moved from Missoula in the past year. She talked about missing it a lot, especially after I told her the town had been wooing me for several years.

"Well, why don't you visit?" Christy said.

I was talking about the brochures from the University of Montana, the ones that showed up in my mailbox every few months like a persistent ex-boyfriend who wanted me back, the postcards and booklets about the creative writing program with bearded, smiling men in Carhartts fly fishing.

Christy nodded her head and smiled. She set down my application for a scholarship, which I'd asked her to help me with, and looked at me.

"You should go visit and see what you think," she said. She always sounded calm and peaceful. "My kids loved it there. Missoula's a wonderful place to raise a family."

"Why put myself through that?" I asked, almost in a huff. "I mean, what if I really like it? It would just make me feel bad." I picked at the mud on my pants, dirty from weeding a client's yard that morning.

"Why couldn't you move there?" Christy challenged, leaning back in her chair.

"He wouldn't let me," I said.

"Mia's dad?"

"Yes, Jamie," I said, crossing my arms. At our first meeting, I'd recited my script—the one I repeated again and again to therapists or anyone who asked about my history. It began in the homeless shelter, covered the no-contact orders, court case, and panic attacks. That Jamie lived three hours away and Mia saw him every other weekend. Today I added that I wondered if Mia wanted to live with him.

Christy's voice dropped a little. "Whether or not you move to Missoula is not his decision to make."

"But I'd still have to ask for permission to move."

"It's not asking for permission. You give notice of relocation, and he has a chance to object," she said, making it sound so simple. "If he does, you both present your case, and a judge has the final word." She looked down at my application again. I stayed quiet, letting her words wash through my mind. "It's really rare that they won't allow mothers to move," she added.

"Especially if they can prove they'll have better opportunities for education."

I set my jaw and stared at the floor. Just thinking about going to court again gave me heart palpitations.

"Don't think of it as asking for permission," she said. "It's giving notice."

"Yeah," I said, turning my attention to the fibers in the chair cushion.

"So, explain to me how this works?" she said, picking up the application packet.

Another advocate, the one in Port Townsend who had helped me when we were homeless, introduced me to a scholarship for survivors that she called "The Sunshine Ladies," but I hadn't qualified for it at the time. If it hadn't been for that name, I never would have remembered it. Even though it was formally called the Women's Independence Scholarship Program, an Internet search of "Sunshine Ladies" brought me to the right place.

A scholarship specifically for survivors of domestic violence wasn't without an overwhelming amount of paperwork and a long list of qualifications. I hadn't qualified for one major reason when I considered it before—recipients must be out of the abusive relationship for at least one year. But I also needed a sponsor, preferably through a domestic violence program, to handle the money for me. WISP would send the organization the scholarship funds, who then worked with me on the best way to spend them. I suppose this was a way to have some idea of where the scholarship funds went, but the process sounded daunting.

"Ask for five thousand dollars," Christy suggested as we made our way through the paperwork. "The worst that can happen is you get less."

"I wonder if I could reach people with my writing," I said, more to myself than to her.

She nodded and smiled in encouragement. "The Univer-

sity of Montana has a wonderful creative writing department!" she exclaimed, turning to pull up the homepage. "I
think it's one of the top in the nation?"

"I know," I said. "That was my plan, before I was pregnant."
I tried not to sound too disappointed. But that was before I
had a kid to care for. Before I'd needed a steady income and
health insurance. Before I had not only my future but a child's
future to think about. "An art degree just isn't practical," I
said, and Christy nearly laughed, but she saw that I had tears
in my eyes.

I didn't want to hear her encourage me otherwise. Just like I
didn't want to hear her encourage me to visit Missoula. Those
dreams seemed too big to pursue. The yearning for it felt similar to the times I sat at our kitchen table to watch Mia eat,
drinking coffee instead of feeding myself. My hunger for Missoula was too big, and it was too painful to even dream.

"Imagine how much Mia would appreciate seeing you try,"
Christy said in a voice thick with encouragement.

Missoula did not let up. It came up in conversations with
anyone I felt even an ounce of kismet with. It had been doing
that for years, but now I started paying attention. I allowed
myself to feel its nudges and pulls.

Unfortunately, other things had a way of not letting up, too,
of not getting better, of continuing their relentless ways when
I ached for a break. My new landlord, Alice, proved to be
my most difficult client. For weeks, I spent dozens of hours
in her house, trying to clean in a way that wouldn't bring
complaints. She'd walk me through the kitchen, pointing out
places I'd missed. I used her rags and cleaning supplies but upset her when I left the used rags in her washing machine. "You
need to wash those," she'd said, after calling me on my phone,
asking me to come over, so she could point at them in person.
"That's just creating more work for me." I wanted to tell her
how inappropriate and weird this would be under normal circumstances for a client to do this. Instead, I gathered the rags

from the machine, carried them over to the garage to wash, dry, and fold before leaving them in a neat pile on her porch.

Alice also started accusing me of lying about the amount of time I'd spent weeding. These things had never happened to me. I'd never received complaints. Not since the Trailer next to the Barefoot Bandit House.

One afternoon, Alice called, again, wanting to talk to me at her house. I knew by then what was coming. She said I wasn't upholding my side of the contract for the barter, that I was failing to clean well enough, that she was canceling the contract.

I nodded, turned, and walked away from her. Back in my apartment, I looked around. It seemed impossible that the rent had just doubled. I stared out the window at the bay in a stunned silence. The inside of my chest seemed to pull into itself and tighten.

"Hey, are you doing okay?" Kurt asked me later that afternoon as we stood outside at the play structure in their yard. "Alice said you looked like you were going to cry after she talked to you."

"I just got some bad news," I said, looking down at the ground.

He nodded. "Yeah," he said, pushing the toddler on the swing. "I get that. Alice's been stressed because she's getting laid off."

My ears started ringing in a sound like television static. I understood now why she'd fired me. It wasn't my incompetence. She'd fired me because she couldn't afford the barter anymore, or wanted to do it herself to save money, and tore me down in the process. Alice drove up with the older girls then, who ran to join Mia. I watched them all run to get their bikes, giggling and squealing. I thought about all the legal documents. If I tried to fight to keep the barter, it would possibly result in a legal battle that I couldn't afford. I'd lose what remained of a friendly relationship that my daughter needed in order to play with her friends. There was no way I could afford to fight.

"I can't afford my apartment without the scholarship," I said to Christy at our next appointment, after explaining what had happened.

"You'll get it," she said, like they'd already told her I would and she was keeping it a secret from me. The application packet had grown to almost fifty pages. I was still waiting for a few more reference letters. "Have you thought any more about Missoula?"

I had. Quite a bit. Jamie's behavior had been escalating, which always made me fearful for Mia's well-being. She spent a week at his house while I finished up classes for spring quarter, and she had returned a couple of pounds lighter. I'd taken her to the doctor for a sinus infection before she'd gone and had to take her back in because she'd gotten worse. Two pounds off her small frame was a lot to lose. She was wetting her pants again, and I couldn't figure out why. She hadn't done that in months.

Jamie now lived on his small sailboat, and when Mia visited, she stayed there with him. Neither Mia nor Jamie knew how to swim. I feared Mia falling off the boat or dock without a life vest in the middle of the night. I feared what sort of kid I'd get back after she spent time with him. Whenever I called, I heard several male voices in the background. When I asked, she didn't know any of their names or where her dad was, just that she was on the boat. Picking her up started to feel like some sort of rescue operation.

I told Christy about this—about my landlord, about the pull of Missoula. School would be busy in the fall, but I had only two summer classes. I still took out a maximum amount of loans to cover my almost doubled living expenses. Mia went to day care while I worked and volunteered whenever I could.

After Alice fired me, I spent two days looking for resources, knowing I wouldn't have enough to pay bills in June, before my student loans came through for the summer semester. I found an odd grant at school to help pay for part of June's rent—a "homemaker" grant, specifically for women with children to help with housing costs. Even the twenty-dollar gas vouchers from the department that gave out utility grants helped.

I held my breath each time I checked the mail. Day after day, there were bills and advertisements, but nothing from the scholarship committee. The month seemed to creep by ominously. If I didn't get the scholarship, we'd have to move out of the apartment. But if I did, we'd have more than enough money to stay. To take my mind off the scholarship, I took Mia to beaches and parks. We spent a lot of time with Kurt and the older girls, wandering off to the bay where they'd roll around in mud. When Mia was at her dad's, I hid in my apartment, reading or doing homework with the doors open to the summer sun.

One weekend, I pulled *The Alchemist* off my shelf to read. The short book took two whole days to get through, since almost every page had a line that I'd underline, read again, and had to stare out the window to think about for a while. My mom had given me the book after I'd moved back to Washington from Alaska. She explained the theme was about the main character's journey to find his destiny, only to discover it had been at home all along. I'd grimaced at this. Sure, Northwest Washington felt magical when the sun shone, and there are parts of Highway 20 that wind through Deception Pass where I knew the trees like old friends. But the feeling of home stopped there. I didn't feel like I belonged there. I wasn't sure I ever had.

The Alchemist's theme, this Personal Legend, pulled at me. I'd wanted to be a writer for nearly twenty-five years.

"I think I'm ready to visit," I announced to Christy at our next appointment.

On the way home from day care pickup, Mia and I sang along with Paul Simon's "Diamonds on the Soles of Her Shoes." I smiled whenever she said "empty as a pumpkin" to the lyrics "empty as a pocket." The album had played regularly in the car for a few weeks—as we drove to and from day care, as we set out for our weekend adventures. Smiling and singing along to the same song might as well have been eating the same ice cream sundae.

I turned the car onto our road, and Mia started asking if she could play with the girls. "Hang on a second," I said, slowing at the mailbox. I'd been trying to not check as much. It was too much of a disappointment to see it empty.

"Mia!" I said from the mailbox. I held up a large envelope from WISP, Inc. One of those flat-rate pocket envelopes for documents. I opened it and looked at the letter.

Inside the envelope was sunshine confetti that peppered my floor at home. They'd accepted me for the scholarship program! Mia scooped it up with her fingers. WISP had not only granted me $2,000 for the fall, but they'd given me $1,000 for the summer. We not only didn't have to move again, I'd have enough extra to take a vacation between summer and fall quarters. I could visit Missoula.

A line from *The Alchemist* flashed through my mind like ticker tape: *When you want something, all the universe conspires in helping you to achieve it.* With the scholarship money, I'd have the means to save my wages, get my car fixed, and drive over two mountain passes to see a city many of my favorite writers wrote love stories about.

27

We're Home

Somewhere around Spokane, driving east on Interstate 90, the road opened, flat, with nothing ahead, behind, or beside me. The grass, brown and burnt from the sun, twitched from the wind, fighting to stay alive. Farmers wheeled large metal sprinklers across their land in efforts to keep it green for their cattle. On the two-lane divided freeway, a girl in a green Subaru passed me on the left. I could see that she had boxes, laundry baskets, and garbage bags packed in the back seat and wagon of her car. In contrast, I had a couple of old army backpacks full of new tank tops along with my few pairs of shorts.

We both had our whole lives ahead of us, that girl in the Subaru and me. Maybe she was moving to Missoula for college like I would have, if I hadn't torn up those applications so long ago, but that was where our similarities probably ended. I imagined her as myself, nearly five years before, singing along to whatever played on her stereo. I thought she should have been me.

I brushed the thoughts away and pressed down on the gas pedal, chasing her, chasing my ghost self. Driving to Missoula wasn't just me pursuing my dreams; it was finding a place for us to call home.

When I arrived, alone in the dark, Missoula's downtown

strip still seemed to pulse with the remains of the hot summer day. When I got out of my car to stand on the curb, looking up and down the street, two girls in their early twenties passed me, nodded, and smiled. One sang. The other played a ukulele. Both had flowing skirts and sandals. They reminded me of girls I'd met at parties in Fairbanks. Hippie types who hadn't a clue about makeup, knew how to start a fire, and weren't afraid to get their hands dirty in the garden. I'd missed these people. My people.

On my first morning, I wandered, the early sun already prickling my skin. The grass felt dry and inviting to sit in, so unlike the wetness of Washington. Near campus I read a book in the shade of a huge maple tree. Lying on my back, I stared at the sun through the waving leaves. I stayed like that for most of the day, gazing up at the surrounding hills and mountains, noticing the river flowing under a footbridge. That evening, I discovered a park in the heart of downtown. Food vendors lined the edges of a canopied square. People milled about in the grass or on park benches. A band played on a stage. I couldn't remember the last time I had felt so happy, the last time I relaxed and let music fill my chest. I wandered the park with a dizzy smile, then noticed that, oddly, everyone else was smiling, too.

After years of living in the absence of friendliness, after the toxicity with my family, losing my friends, the unstable housing and black mold, my invisibility as a maid, I was starved for kindness. I was hungry for people to notice me, to start conversations with me, to accept me. I was hungry in a way I'd never been in my entire life. Missoula brought that out. Suddenly I wanted a community. I wanted friends. And it seemed okay to want that, because, walking around, judging from appearances, I was surrounded by the possibility of those things. Most locals smiled at me from under hats showing the state of Montana's outline or its 406 area code. One morning at a small café for breakfast, every table filled, I counted sixteen pairs of Chaco sandals, including my own. I saw women with body hair, and most people had tattoos. Men carried babies in cloth backpacks and slings. I ran into old friends from Fairbanks. I'd never been so immediately embraced by a place. And it had only been a day.

Without knowing it, I had chosen one of the best weekends of the summer to visit. As I explored, the River City Roots Festival transformed the town. Main Street shut down. Vendors sold tie-dye shirts, pottery, art, and wooden bears carved with chainsaws. A small sea of people in camping chairs settled next to a stage to listen to music for most of the day. Food trucks lined the side streets, and a beer hut sat in the middle of it all. Missoula loves a good party.

And so it went. I spent each day of my trip exploring the town. I climbed up mountains. I traversed trails, listening to the guttural sound of deer in the thickets. I walked along streams and bloodied my toes on jagged rocks. For a few minutes on the side of a mountain deep in a valley beyond town, sweaty and dehydrated, I couldn't find the trail I'd been walking on. I was hungry, thirsty, yet full of excitement that I was lost, however momentarily, in the wilds of Montana.

I had fallen in love with Montana. Like Steinbeck. Like Duncan.

"I'm moving to Missoula," I said in a text to Jamie. "I have to. This place is amazing." I waited for him to reply, my heart pounding, but he didn't. I wondered what he'd do to manipulate Mia into not wanting to go. I wondered if he'd threaten to take me to court or possibly try to take her. These were the anxieties that'd kept me from even attempting this trip. But I was no longer asking him; I was telling. As cheesy as it seemed, I thought, somehow, my love for Missoula and wanting a better life for Mia would carry us through. It would get us there.

Jamie let Mia call me the next day. It was midmorning, and the phone rang as I sat on a grassy hill by the Clark Fork

River. Behind me, a carousel spun in slow circles next to a wooden play structure teeming with children. I'd been reading a book, jotting down thoughts in a journal.

"Hi, Mom," Mia said. I could hear Jamie's voice in the background, then her grandma's. They were urging her to speak. Finally, she blurted out, "I don't want to move to Montana."

"Oh, baby," I said, attempting to form my words like a hug. I imagined the scene, Mia standing in the living room of her grandmother's house, and Jamie holding the phone to her ear, his face, eyebrows raised, expecting her to repeat the line they'd practiced. "Mia, I'm so sorry you're going through this," I said, and then Jamie took the phone from her.

His voice was between a growl and a whisper. "I'm going to tell her you're moving her away from me so she'll never see me again," he said to me. "I hope you realize that. That you're so selfish you don't care if she never sees me again. She'll see. She'll hate you for it."

I tried to picture Mia's big, dark eyes watching him as he spoke. I knew how he looked when he was angry, how white drops of spit gathered on his lips in front of his crooked teeth.

"I want to talk to Mia again," I said, cutting him off.

When Mia came back to the phone, her voice sounded happy. "Did you get pink cowboy boots for me?" she asked, her chirpy self again.

I smiled. "Yes," I said. "Just like I promised." I told her about the store with an entire aisle of pink boots and that I'd found a pair for her, along with a stuffed horse. "And a metal lunch box with a cowboy on it!"

When we talked again a day or two later, she sounded dazed. She wasn't sure where her dad was, even though I'd called his phone. I could hear older male voices laughing in the background, but Mia said she didn't know who they were. I regretted not bringing her with me, but if I had, I'm not sure we would have returned. I imagined us finding a floor to crash on and filling out the relocation paperwork at the local courthouse. I imagined us spending the end of summer napping in the grass, exploring the mountains and rivers.

But I had a few more days of my first vacation in five years, and I tried to make the best of it. That Saturday, I walked through the local farmers' market. There were so many kids Mia's age, many wearing disheveled tutus and with nests of hair. I could have been walking with her, in a tank top, my tattoos visible, she in her pink plastic high heels and fairy dress. We would have blended in with everyone. No one would have given us a sideways glance like they did back in Washington. Mia would have played with the pack of children climbing up the fish statue. This could be our home. These people could be our family. I was sure of it.

On the drive home, I sank into the quiet of the car and the sounds of the road. Each mile that I got closer to Washington, I felt an ache in my heart, like I was going in the wrong direction. For five hundred miles, the journey of the last five years played like a movie in my head. I saw Mia toddling toward me in the homeless shelter. I felt the stress and desperation to provide a good home for her. All the driving we'd done. The car crash. Those cold nights on our pull-out love seat in the studio. Maybe *The Alchemist* had been right. Maybe if I took the first step toward my own dreams, the Universe would open and guide the way. Maybe, to find a true home, I needed to open my heart to love a home. I had stopped believing that home was a fancy house on a hill. Home was a place that embraced us, a community, a knowing.

Months later, just a few days after Christmas, with Mia in the back seat, I drove the rolling hills toward Missoula again. "Can you see the lights?" I asked, turning down the radio, pointing out the twinkling stars of the valley. I glanced in the rearview mirror, saw Mia shake her head from the car seat.

"Where are we?" she asked, staring at the snowy hills rolling past the window.

I took a deep breath. "We're home," I said.

After years of constant movement, Mia and I slowly settled. Her dad disappeared for the first several months we were there. He didn't answer his phone, didn't show up for the video chats we'd painstakingly fought over to schedule in the new parenting plan, and I didn't know how to explain why.

Mia began running from me: at home, in the grocery store, on the sidewalk, and into the street. I carried her, kicking and screaming, stooping to pick up her pink rubber boots when they fell off during a tantrum. I knew it was a natural response to change, to losing her dad, to being uprooted and replanted in a place where winter had kept us inside since we arrived. Her behavior was bigger than anything I'd experienced, and I didn't know how to handle it. It started to feel too dangerous, too tumultuous and exhausting to take her anywhere. One morning, I had to complete two errands: the post office and the store to get tampons. Mia refused, for two hours, to get dressed or put on her shoes, kicking and screaming and fighting so hard I might as well have been trying to hold her under water. The panic attack hit me straight and fierce, left me crawling on the floor, gasping, while Mia walked happily to her room to play with toys, content in winning another battle.

Things, as they usually do, have a way of clicking into place. I found work cleaning a large office building, plus a couple of clients who wanted me to clean their homes. One weekend, I picked up a magazine in the office's waiting room called *Mamalode* and submitted a short piece. They published it in print, and I couldn't stop staring at my name.

The same magazine had an advertisement for a movement-based preschool at a local gymnastics center. After meeting with the owners, they agreed to let me clean the facility in exchange for tuition. One of their employees moved in with us, paying a small amount of rent with the caveat that they'd be there while I went to work before dawn, before Mia was awake.

On a late spring day in Missoula after our move, Mia made an announcement: "Mom, we should go hiking," she said, after looking at the blue sky through the window. I sat at the kitchen table of our downtown apartment, waiting for her to finish her breakfast. My eyes fluttered in exhaustion. I savored the weekends when I could sleep in and spend extra time sipping coffee before going through my notes from school.

Because of that, I hesitated to go. I was too tired to fight Mia, and though she hadn't been running from me as much since starting preschool, my level of trust remained very low. But she looked so eagerly at me, and I saw more excitement in her eyes than I had since we got here. It was the first hot, sunny weekend, and it reminded me of the magic I'd felt when I first came in August. I stood up from the table and started packing protein bars and water bottles in a backpack. "Let's go," I said. I'd never seen her put her shoes on so fast.

The University of Montana sits at the bottom of a mountain—officially called Sentinel, but called "The M" by the locals, for the visible switchback trail snaking up to a large, white capital letter "M," made from concrete. For months, I'd stared at it while walking to class, watching the tiny dots of people climb up the hill. I envied them, but I always seemed to have an excuse for not attempting it myself.

We drove to the parking lot at the base of the mountain. Several people stood at the stairs leading to the trail. They all wore proper running or walking shoes, drinking from their water bottles, and looked ready to hike the trail up the side of the mountain.

"Okay," I said, smoothing out my cargo shorts and second-guessing my decision to wear sandals. "How far should we go?"

"All the way to the M," Mia said. Like it was nothing. Like it wasn't a goal I'd set for myself the first time I visited. Like walking to the M didn't mean climbing halfway up a five-thousand-foot mountain.

When we started out on the trail, I figured we'd make it halfway to the M before Mia would wear out, that I'd end up carrying her piggyback to the car. But she skipped around each switchback, past hikers sitting on benches to take in the view.

I watched her in disbelief, my near five-year-old daughter running up the path in her skirt and Spider-Man shoes, the arms of a stuffed giraffe snapped around her neck. She ran so fast that she passed other hikers, and then waited for me to catch up. In contrast, I huffed, dripping sweat. This was easily the hardest walk I'd done in years. I called ahead for Mia to stop, nervous she'd get to the M and slip down the slab of its surface, or just keep going over the edge. The trail and the mountain were too steep for me to see the path above. At times, I'd see Mia leaning over the edge of the trail, her little hands in fists of determination. Mine were doing the same.

When we got to the end of the trail, we sat on the top of the M, taking in the view for a few minutes before Mia stood up and announced we should keep walking. I followed her, stunned that she wanted to keep going. She seemed perfectly content to march to the top, occasionally squatting to look at ants or inside gopher holes. I urged her to drink water, to eat a blueberry Clif Bar. And we kept going up the trail.

There are several options for getting to the top of Sentinel, but we took the route that loops around the side. Even though the hike is less steep than the other trails, the climb to the very top from the backside is still intense. I had to rest every ten steps or so. Mia paused a few times with me. Maybe it was the endorphins, or the heat of the sun, but I felt fizzy with happiness. I could tell those final steps were a struggle for Mia's little legs. She could see how tired I was.

At the summit, she raised her hands over her head and laughed. I snapped pictures of her there, dancing at the top, so far above town. Our home. We sat on the edge, the mountain sloping down below us, looking over Missoula. From where we sat, the buildings looked like tiny dollhouses and the cars like shining dots. I sat there, making a mental map of the town in my head—Missoula felt so big to me, had occupied so much space in my head and heart, that it seemed strange to see it from above in its entirety.

Immediately below us was the campus where I went to school and the auditorium where, in two years, Mia would watch me walk across a stage to accept my diploma for a bachelor's degree in English and creative writing. From the mountain, I could see the lawn and the trees I'd lain beneath the summer I'd visited, where I'd dreamed of being a student. I could see our apartment, the parks where we played, the downtown where Mia and I braved slippery winter sidewalks. And I saw the river running like a lazy snake through it all.

Mia walked the whole way back to the car. In the setting sun, the light cast dark orange against her skin. She looked confidently back at me a few times. "We made it," she seemed to be saying with her eyes. Not just up the mountain but to a better life.

I guess they're in and of the same.

Acknowledgments

This book was raised by single moms. I love that I can say that. Because single moms are fierce and brave and resilient and courageous and strong in how they live and especially how they love. I am forever grateful to the single moms who were my book doulas; who loved this book from its beginnings:

Debbie Weingarten, the very beacon of friendship, who read so many horrible drafts of this thing (and its proposal!) and immediately answered countless frantic and celebratory texts. Kelly Sundberg, whose calm voice talked me through moments of completely freaking out so poignantly it became my inner narrative. Becky Margolis, best neighbor, listener, and fancy dinner date ever, who has blessed Mia in being her "other mom." Andrea Guevara, whose ability to see the heart and pure essence of people astounds me. And finally, to Krishan Trotman, my incredible editor at Hachette. This book surely would have been a rambling jumble of "and then this happened" without your careful, thoughtful, and gloriously intensive edits. Thank you for putting so much of your soul into this book. It couldn't have had a better person to guide it into the world.

To Jeff Kleinman, the end-all, be-all of dream agents. You have no idea how much I have relished all of your emails and texts full of exclamation points.

To my teachers: Mr. Birdsall, my fourth-grade teacher at Scenic Park Elementary in Anchorage, Alaska, for bringing out the writer in me. Debra Magpie Earling, for saying my "Confessions of the Housekeeper" essay would be a book with such conviction that it became my own prophesy to fulfill. Thank you for bringing out the storyteller in me. Also to Barbara Ehrenreich, Marisol Bello, Lisa Drew, Collin Smith, Judy Blunt, David Gates, Sherwin Bitsui, Katie Kane, Walter Kirn, Robert Stubblefield, Erin Saldin, Chris Dombrowski, Elke Govertsen, for patiently ushering and guiding my written words into coherence with utmost encouragement and empowerment. Thank you.

To my daughters, who are the reason for everything: Coraline, your smart smiles and soft snuggles got me through many long days of writing and editing. Mia, my sweet girl, Emilia Story. Thank you for making me a mom. Thank you for living this journey with me. Thank you for believing in me. Thank you, especially, for always, always humbling me in your ability to be exactly who you are and no one else. My whole chest swells with how much affection and adoration I have for the both of you, and I love you more and more every day.

To my readers and supporters over the last several years. To the Binders. To those in the broken system of government assistance and who live their days in the crushing hopelessness of poverty. To those who were raised by single moms, and the ones raising children on their own. Thank you for continuously reminding me of the importance, the vitality, of sharing this story. Thank you for holding this book in your hands. Thank you for joining me on this journey.

Thank you all for walking beside me.